DISTRICT INSPECTOR JOHN A. KEARNEY

- THE R.I.C. MAN WHO BEFRIENDED
SIR ROGER CASEMENT

DONAL J. O'SULLIVAN

TRAFFORD PUBLISHING

© Copyright 2005 Donal J. O' Sullivan.
All rights reserved. No part of this publication may be reproduced, stored in a retrieval system, or transmitted, in any form or by any means, electronic, mechanical, photocopying, recording, or otherwise, without the written prior permission of the author.

Note for Librarians: a cataloguing record for this book that includes Dewey Decimal Classification and US Library of Congress numbers is available from the Library and Archives of Canada. The complete cataloguing record can be obtained from their online database at:
www.collectionscanada.ca/amicus/index-e.html
ISBN 1-4120-6403-1
Printed in Victoria, BC, Canada

Printed on paper with minimum 30% recycled fibre. Trafford's print shop runs on "green energy" from solar, wind and other environmentally-friendly power sources.

TRAFFORD

Offices in Canada, USA, Ireland and UK
This book was published *on-demand* in cooperation with Trafford Publishing. On-demand publishing is a unique process and service of making a book available for retail sale to the public taking advantage of on-demand manufacturing and Internet marketing. On-demand publishing includes promotions, retail sales, manufacturing, order fulfilment, accounting and collecting royalties on behalf of the author.

Book sales for North America and international:
Trafford Publishing, 6E–2333 Government St.,
Victoria, BC v8t 4p4 CANADA
phone 250 383 6864 (toll-free 1 888 232 4444)
fax 250 383 6804; email to orders@trafford.com
Book sales in Europe:
Trafford Publishing (uk) Limited, 9 Park End Street, 2nd Floor
Oxford, UK ox1 1hh UNITED KINGDOM
phone 44 (0)1865 722 113 (local rate 0845 230 9601)
facsimile 44 (0)1865 722 868; info.uk@trafford.com
trafford.com/05-1314

10 9 8 7 6 5 4 3 2

CONTENTS

1 JOHN A. KEARNEY - THE EARLY YEARS. 5

2 TRANSFER OF JOHN A. KEARNEY TO TRALEE. 29

3 SIR ROGER CASEMENT 41

4 AUSTIN STACK AND THE RISE OF THE
VOLUNTEERS IN KERRY. 65

5 THE EVENTS OF GOOD FRIDAY AND
EASTER SATURDAY, 1916 97

6 A CATALOGUE OF DISASTERS IN CO.KERRY
DURING HOLY WEEK, 1916 123

7 PROMOTION TO DISTRICT INSPECTOR
AND TRANSFER TO BOYLE 133

8 ORGANISATION OF A NEW POLICE FORCE
– THE 'CIVIC GUARD'. .147

9 STACK'S CAMPAIGN AGAINST
KEARNEY AND THE 'CIVIC GUARD' 157

10 THE 'KILDARE MUTINY' 181

11 THE DEPARTURE OF
JOHN A. KEARNEY TO LONDON 193

APPENDIX A 215

APPENDIX B 217

BIBLIOGRAPHY. 219

1

JOHN A. KEARNEY - THE EARLY YEARS

EARLY CHILDHOOD AND DEATH OF HIS MOTHER.

John Andrew Kearney was born on February 16th 1871 at Moyvoughley, a small village, located between Moate and Ballymore, Co. Westmeath.

At the time of John's birth, his father, Thomas Kearney was a constable in the Royal Irish Constabulary stationed in the village. Thomas had joined the Irish Constabulary - later to become the Royal Irish Constabulary in 1867 - on May 8th 1862. He was then aged twenty-three years. He came from a family who had been farming for several generations at Walsh Island, County Offaly. He underwent his recruit training at the Constabulary Depot in the Phoenix Park. In his early service he had served at Moate in the same county but like so many other members of the force he served in several stations during his service. After Moyvoughley, he was allocated as an Acting Sergeant to Littleton, Co Westmeath in 1874; to Ballinagore in 1875; to Castletowngeoghan in 1876 and in January 1882 he was transferred to Rochfort Bridge - all in Co. Westmeath. He was sergeant - in - charge of the latter stations.

Thomas Kearney had one brother, William, and a sister Mary Anne Kearney. They both emigrated to the U.S.A. early in their lives.

John A. Kearney's mother, whose maiden name was Anne Moran, was employed as a teacher at Moyvoughley national school when she met Thomas Kearney and they got married in 1869. She was a native of nearby Littleton where her father had served in the RIC. She continued to teach until 1874 when she resigned to move with her husband to Littleton where he had been appointed as Acting Sergeant. She was the youngest of six children. Her father - Justin Moran - was a member of the Irish Constabulary. He was a native of Cuoloo, Merlough, Co Galway. He joined the force on April 7th 1837 and after undergoing training at Ballinrobe Depot in Co Mayo, he was allocated to Dysart station in Co Westmeath. On July 8th 1844 he was transferred to Moyvore [also in Co Westmeath]. He later moved on transfer to Littleton in the same county where he was sergeant - in - charge. He died while still serving there in 1861. It was a rare co - incidence that John A. Kearney's father should have served at the same location in later years.

Justin [also known as Martin] Moran, recorded many details about his service, experience and duties performed while in the Irish Constabulary - with details of the Great Famine period during which he served.

One of Justin's sons - Michael also joined the RIC and served mostly in County Roscommon and in East Galway. He married a lady from Roscommon and on his retirement he came to Moyvoughley and purchased the former RIC station there. He lived there with his family until his death in 1922. One of his [Michael's] sons, Patrick who was born on March 4th 1888, also joined the Royal Irish Constabulary and served in Belfast City. He was on duty there during the famous Belfast riots and was on duty there for the launch of the 'Titanic' in 1912. On June 15th 1915, he was discharged from the RIC at his own request to join the 'Irish Guards Regiment' in the British army. He was seriously injured in action and was unable to re-join the RIC. He died in July 1968 aged 80 years. With seventeen other young men from the Moyvoughley area, who joined the British forces and fought in the First World War [some of whom lost their lives in action]. his name is commemorated on a nice memorial wall plaque on the front wall of the old school [now a community hall] in the village.

John A. Kearney was the only boy in his family and he had two sisters. His sister Mary Anne who was born in 1873 died in 1875. His second sister - Margaret - was born in 1876 at Castletowngeoghegan.

In January 1877, the second great tragedy to befall the Kearney family occurred when John's mother died. She was only 30 years of age and her death was apparently due to some complications arising from the birth of Margaret, some time before. John was only six years and his little sister was only nine months. The family was devastated.

Despite John's young age at the time, he never forgot the terrible grief, which he experienced on seeing his mother's coffin leaving their house and the funeral to Balrath cemetery - situated between Castletowngeoghegan and Ballinagore. During his life he also vividly remembered his mother's grave being made, just beside that of his little sister who had died two years previously.

He also remembered the relatives, on his father and mother's sides of the family, who came to her funeral and shared their grief with them. Mrs Kearney's brother Patrick, was at that time the principal teacher at Castledaly National School near Moate, his wife was also a teacher at the same school. Mrs Kearney was regarded as a brilliant teacher, highly intelligent, with a good knowledge of the Irish language. She was also a loving and affectionate mother. The tragedy was a serious blow to John but it probably helped to give him strength and courage in his later life, when he personally had to cope with more than his fair share of family tragedies.

Thomas Kearney then employed an elderly housekeeper named Madge Moloney from Ballinagore, to look after the household duties and his two children. However, she was too advanced in years and not being able to cope, left after some time. The Kearney children looked upon her as a mother and they were heartbroken when she left. It was like losing their mother all over again.

Another housekeeper, Anne Gasberry, was then employed to look after the Kearney family. In later years, John described her role and influence as follows:

"She too was motherly, kind and affectionate and we children returned her love.

She was deeply religious and altho' her teaching wasn't always strictly orthodox, still it had an effect in moulding our characters. My father being absent on long tours of duty, she was more in 'touch' with us than he. Anyway, he did, in the circumstances, the best he could do for us - and he was kind and affectionate".

Mrs Gasberry remained as a housekeeper with the Kearney family until John and his sister had grown up and were capable of looking after themselves. She gave extraordinary service to the family while she was with them, and John always remembered her with affection.

The absence of John's father on long tours of duty was very understandable as this was during the terrible Land War in Ireland, which made huge demands on the Royal Irish Constabulary at the time.

In January 1882, Thomas Kearney was transferred as a sergeant from Castletown –geoghegan to Rochfort Bridge. Considering the circumstances of the Kearney family at the time, this transfer would appear to be a rather strange decision by the RIC authorities. Perhaps Sergeant Kearney had sought it himself, to improve the quality of his living accommodation, the opportunity for a better education for his children or for some other good reason.

At Rochfort Bridge, John at first attended the local national school and later the Convent schools. He regarded the nuns as being splendid teachers. On the appointment of a new teacher at the local national school, he returned to it and made excellent progress under the new teacher, whose name was Mr Hunt from County Sligo. John's sister attended the Convent

Schools and received a very good education.

On completing his primary education, John's thoughts turned to the important issue of doing something worthwhile in life. The Kearneys were a staunch Roman Catholic family and strong Christian beliefs were a core value.

SERVICE IN THE IRISH CHRISTIAN BROTHERS.

In 1887, a friend of John's named Pat Reynolds, whose father was also a member of the RIC joined the Irish Christian Brothers. This was a great teaching order with schools and colleges all over Ireland, in the U.S.A., Canada, Australia and elsewhere. The opportunities presented by the Order appealed to John A. Kearney, and he was very impressed by the letters that he regularly received from his friend Pat Reynolds. He discussed the idea of joining the Order with his father, who did not oppose it.

On March 19th, 1888, after going through the usual preliminaries, he joined the Order as a Novice, in the company of another local boy named Joe Noonan, who was then only 15 years of age. They entered the Novitiate of the Order at Marino in Dublin, but, on the same day, his friend Joe was transferred to the Junior Novitiate of the Order at Baldoyle, Co Dublin. In later years, the same Joe Noonan, went on to become the 'Superior General' of the Irish Christian Brothers.

John's religious title in the Irish Christian Brothers was 'Brother Andrew'. After leaving the Order he used the name 'Andrew' as his second name.

He remained on at the Marino Novitiate, where there were between forty and fifty other youths in the same age group. It was a big change from the dull life of Rochfort Bridge. What struck him most of all was the religious fervour of everybody in the Novitiate and the strict silence which was observed outside of recreation hours - not for fear of censure from the 'Masters', but as a religious duty.

He loved the daily routine at the College and became deeply involved in all aspects of the training programme. Every subject was thoroughly taught and explained. He had to work harder than most of the other Novices, who had the benefit of attending their local Christian Brothers' schools in the towns from which they came. He kept at his studies and eventually fared as well as everybody else. He developed a particular liking and aptitude for physical training, which was taught by a retired British Army Sergeant Major. The Novices played cricket during the summer months and Gaelic football in the winter.

The usual daily routine at Marino started with a wake-up call at 5 a.m. This was followed from 5.30 a. m. to 7 a. m. by the entire community assembling in the oratory for meditation. After meditation, they attended Mass at 7 a.m. in the Convent church. Breakfast was served at 8 a. m., while one member of the community read passages from some religious book. Following breakfast, everybody prepared for school. Silence was strictly observed, except on feast days when the director suspended the vows. Following night prayers, everybody was in bed by 10 p. m.

After a year at Marino he moved on to the Christian Brothers Training College at Portlaoise to continue with his teaching studies. He spent some time there before moving to Tipperary town. In Tipperary he took charge of the junior school. He was very conscious of the fact that the Christian Brothers had been founded to provide education for the children of the poor and relied on voluntary donations for their existence. Parents who sent children to their schools made regular donations if they could afford it. The Order was outside the scope of Government grants because it refused to divorce religious instruction from secular instruction. The Order also refused to remove religious emblems from its classrooms.

John got on well in Tipperary and had fifty pupils in his class. He had the assistance of two monitors [trainee teachers]. He introduced physical training to his pupils and then to the school which had about 500 pupils. The pupils, parents and the members of his community very much appreciated this. He was very lucky in being able to obtain the services of a military gym sergeant from the Manchester Regiment, then based in the Tipperary town military barracks. The sergeant was an excellent gymnast and physical training instructor.

Each year the Christian Brothers rented a house at the sea-side for one month of the summer and John spent those holidays at Dungarvan and Clonee in County Waterford and at Crosshaven, in County Cork. With the other brothers in the community, he looked forward to these holidays as they broke the monotony of the year. He enjoyed them. While enjoying all aspects of his teaching profession and leading a very active life in the community, he began to have doubts as to whether he had a real vocation for a life time of service in the Christian Brothers. He was successfully passing all his annual examinations. In addition to the ordinary subjects he acquired a good knowledge of mathematics, algebra and the classics. He learned some French and Gaelic as well.

On entering the Novitiate, the Novices received their religious habits and each year at Christmas time, they renewed their religious vows of poverty, chastity, obedience and perseverance for a further year. They were not finally professed or 'fully fledged' Brothers until they had spent about ten years in the Order. John renewed his vows each year until 1891 when he appears to have got restless and discontented in Tipperary and began to have doubts about his future. It may have something to do with the fact that most of the Brothers in the monastery with him were elderly men and perhaps he had little in common with them. Other Brothers with whom he maintained contact at other locations seemed to have happier times, where they were based.

LEAVING THE CHRISTIAN BROTHERS.

During 1892, he really had serious doubts about his vocation and he wrote to his father that he was contemplating leaving the Order. His father left the decision to him, as he felt that John was not happy in the Christian Brothers and that he did not have a vocation. At Christmas of that year he did not renew his annual vows and left the Order. His father travelled by train to Limerick Junction railway station near Tipperary town, to meet him, and they both went to stay with relatives named Delaneys at Walsh Island, Co Offaly, over that Christmas. This was a good decision on the part of John's father, as it spared John the ordeal of facing back to his home village over the Christmas period. After a few weeks he returned to Rochfort Bridge where he received a hearty welcome from all his old school friends.

His sister Margaret and Ann Gasberry, the housekeeper, were both delighted to see him. He had been continuously absent from his home for five years. It must have gratified him to have received such a welcome, as youths who left home to join the priesthood or religious orders invariably found it very difficult to return to their homes and face their friends, if they failed to pursue the religious career on which they had embarked.

He had of course benefited considerably in relation to his educational achievements from his time in the Irish Christian Brothers. He had received an exceptionally high standard of education and had developed a love for research, writing, history and the classics, which would stand him in good stead for the rest of his life. Considering the happy and contented time, which he spent in the Order, it must have been a difficult decision for him to make, but he had the courage to leave, when he began to doubt if he had a real vocation for the 'calling' as a Christian Brother. His old friend Pat Reynolds who had been based at Lismore, Co Waterford, had also left the Order and emigrated to the U.S.A where he died in New York a short while afterwards.

John's father had retired on pension from the RIC in June 1892. John did not want to be a burden on his father's small income and immediately started looking around for employment. He applied for a position with the Department of Customs and Excise but did not succeed in getting a placing. Like so many sons of policemen before and since, he turned his attention to joining the RIC. As happens in many professions, it has always been acknowledged that 'policing runs in families'; which makes it very much a hereditary occupation. This was very relevant in John A. Kearney's situation and at the earliest opportunity he submitted an application to join the RIC like his father and maternal grandfather did before him.

JOINING THE ROYAL IRISH CONSTABULARY.

Worthwhile job opportunities for young men at the time were particularly scarce and many young men had to accept employment for which they were over-qualified but they had to get on with their lives. Up to 1918, it was always claimed that, in Ireland, every parent wanted to have a son or sons in the RIC and that they looked forward to their daughters meeting and getting married to members of the force. The only other wish they may have held for their sons, was that they would become priests. This was a fair indication of the high esteem in which the force was held by the Irish people, and the rank and file members of the force were unquestionably 'the cream of Irish manhood' - coming from the best of Irish families and being of excellent physique, character, etc.

Ireland has a unique distinction in the history of policing. It is acknowledged world wide as being the cradle of modern policing. A *Baronial Constabulary* force was established in Ireland in 1787 and while it had many shortcomings, it was a police force of a type. In 1786, Dublin got a police force to police the city and a year later a similar force was established in

Belfast.

Robert Peel became Chief Secretary in Ireland and was faced with serious outrages in different parts of the country. In 1814 he introduced the *Peace Preservation Force*, [54 Geo. 3, c.13] which was a uniformed force and which was mobile This enabled it to travel to any part of the country, where serious disturbances were taking place and to restore law and order. Each section was under the control of a full-time Superintendent Magistrate. The first detachment was sent to quell outrages in the Barony of Middlethird in County Tipperary. The units of the force operated as a type of 'flying squad' or 'task force' and had a good measure of success.

In 1822, Peel successfully pushed through the *Constabulary Act of 1822* [6 George 4, c 103.] against huge opposition from the local Magistrates who wielded considerable power at the time. This was an organised police force with training for recruits, uniforms for all the members, a proper rank structure and pay. The force was known as the *County Constabulary Police* and it had a strength of 313 chief constables and 5,008 rank-and-file members. It was organised on a county basis and was under the control of an Inspector General who was in charge of each province. It had a training Depot in each of the provinces - Ballinasloe for Connaught; Ballincollig for Munster; Philipstown [now Daingean] for Leinster and at Armagh for Ulster. The force was dispersed in small units - usually consisting of one Sergeant and four constables - in towns and villages throughout the country.

The *County Constabulary Force* was the first organised police force in the British Empire or in the world. The main drawback, which became apparent with the force as time went on, was that it lacked central control, resulting in each province having a different set of standards and priorities, depending on the view of each Inspector General as to how his province should be policed. The Force provided a very good service to the Irish people, firmly establishing the concept of policing for the first time.

Ireland was very fortunate in having another Chief Secretary in Ireland who had vision and courage in the 1830s. He was Thomas Drummond . He saw a need to reform the existing Constabulary Force and bring it under central control. In 1836, he pioneered and successfully had an Act passed through the British Parliament [6 William 4, c. 13], that amended the provisions of the 1822 Act, relating to the policing of Ireland. This Act established the *Irish Constabulary*, which had different command structures and brought the force under the direct control of one Inspector General, based in Dublin. It established a standardisation of rules and regulations and a new Code was introduced for all officers and men. It had a uniform system of management and in a short time became very efficient. Like its predecessor of 1822, the Irish Constabulary Force was also armed.

A new Constabulary Depot was constructed in the Phoenix Park and was completed in 1842. All recruits were trained there. A Cadet system was introduced shortly afterwards and they also received their training at the Depot. A mounted police section and a reserve force was also maintained at the Depot. The first Inspector General with responsibility for the entire force was Colonel Shaw Kennedy. He had the assistance of two Deputy Inspector Generals. The Headquarters of the Constabulary was set up in a complete wing of the Lower Castle Yard at Dublin Castle.

The Irish Constabulary played a major humanitarian role in dealing with the Great Famine of 1845 - '48. It successfully put down the Young Ireland Rebellion of 1848 and it had major success in quelling the Fenian Insurrection of 1867. In acknowledgement of the Constabulary's success in putting down the Fenian Rebellion, Queen Victoria bestowed the Royal title on the force. At a most impressive ceremony at the Phoenix Park Depot on September 6th 1867, the Lord Lieutenant - the Marquis of Abercorn - decorated nine officers and men for gallantry. In the course of his address he said:

"I am now authorised to inform you that, as proof of Her Majesty's satisfaction of the gallant conduct of the Irish Constabulary and of her confidence in their loyalty and devotion, she has been graciously pleased to command that the Force shall be henceforth called 'The Royal Irish Constabulary' and that they shall be entitled to have the harp and crown as badges of the Force".

The Royal Irish Constabulary progressed to being a most successful police force. It went through a very difficult period during the Land War of the 1880s until the law and order situation settled down once more. The Force policed the whole of Ireland, with the exception of the Dublin Metropolitan Police Force, which remained in existence until 1925, when it was amalgamated with the Garda Siochana. The Irish Constabulary replaced the old police force in Belfast in the 1860s. From the 1890s the RIC enjoyed the support and confidence of the Irish people and this remained so until after the executions which followed the 1916 Rising and the growth of the Sinn Fein movement in Ireland. During that period from 1890 until 1916, the RIC went about their duties unarmed and were not under threat. It would have been regarded as the 'golden era' of the force. This was the era when John A. Kearney decided to join.

The minimum height requirement for joining the Force was five feet nine inches with a minimum chest measurement of thirty - six inches and he had no problem in meeting these requirements. A candidate also had to be of good character, honest and of sober habits.

When he applied for membership of the RIC he underwent a medical examination by a naval doctor at Mullingar, Co Westmeath, who pronounced him as being medically fit. He was five feet and ten inches in height. He then underwent a written examination consisting of reading, writing, arithmetic, English and dictation that he had no problem passing. At that particular time there were many candidates for the force and the normal waiting time to be enlisted was about two years. John A. Kearney was called within six months of making his application, which was probably due to his exceptionally high educational standard and the fact that he produced a number of educational certificates when making application. In the official RIC Personnel Register his previous occupation is designated as 'Teacher'. He would have been considered by the RIC as being ideal recruiting material with education and intelligence above average. Farmer's sons who had only a primary school education made up the majority of the rank-and-file members. He was allocated Warrant Registration Number 55958.

TRAINING AS AN RIC RECRUIT AT THE DEPOT.

He travelled to the Depot at the Phoenix Park on July 15th 1893 and after a very detailed medical examination by the Surgeon to the Force, he was admitted as a recruit. He quickly settled in to the training programme at the Depot but admitted that he did not find it easy at first. The summer of 1893 was very hot. Three hours strenuous drill each day wasn't easy and this was followed by three hours of classroom instruction in Police Duties. Getting up at bugle call at 6 a.m. was no great problem for him but this was followed by one hour's drill from 7 a.m. to 8 a.m. before breakfast.

When he got into the Depot routine, he began to enjoy it. He held the drill instructors in high regard and from his previous experience in life, he concluded that the police duty school was conducted very efficiently.

He also found that the Police Duties taught there on Acts of Parliament and the Common Law whetted his appetite for more research and more knowledge. He graduated to the Musketry section at the Depot, which was known as the First Squad. Duties in that section included, maintaining sentry and guard duties at the Depot over a 24 hour period, with about five fully armed [rifle, sword and ammunition] sentries covering two hour periods alternately.

He developed a liking for every aspect of the recruit-training programme, and he regarded his time there as the most enjoyable time of his life. He made several friends amongst his peers and had no problems getting on with his teachers or superiors.

ALLOCATION TO COUNTY LIMERICK.

On successfully completing his six months training course, he was assigned to the County Inspector for Limerick and was first allocated to Rathkeale, [Co Limerick]. In August 1896 he went on transfer to Ballinacurra station and exactly one year later he was transferred to Corbally, which was adjacent to Limerick City. The sergeant - in - charge at the latter station was Sergeant William Beckett, [Regd. No. 46733]. He was an Ulster Presbyterian and John A. Kearney claimed that he was one of the most upright and honourable individuals with whom he had served in the RIC. His exceptional qualities and integrity made a life - long impression on John A. Kearney and he was delighted to have met him at the early stage of his career. He served with one other member in the force who also had qualities similar to Sergeant Beckett and that was District Inspector Britten, whom he later met in Tralee.

John A. Kearney was obviously very highly regarded as a police constable by his superiors because on June 1st 1899 he was appointed as Acting Sergeant and was assigned to William Street station in Limerick - which was the City and County Headquarters for Limerick.

PROMOTION TO RANK OF SERGEANT.

On October 1st 1901 he was promoted to the rank of Sergeant and assigned to Ballygar station in County Galway. He was then only thirty years of age and was making excellent progress in his career. Fifteen to seventeen years' service as a constable was the normal pre-requisite before a member was promoted to Sergeant.

While stationed at Ballygar, he had responsibility for the investigation of a murder, which took place there. Murders were a rare occurrence at the time and this particular one happened within a family circle. The investigation was very well handled under Sergeant Kearney, and three people from the same family were convicted of manslaughter. A young woman was sentenced to six years Penal Servitude, her mother was sentenced to twelve months imprisonment with hard labour, and her father was sentenced to six months imprisonment for the crime.

Sergeant Kearney married Bridget Wallace, aged 23 years, on 24th June 1902. She was a native of Glin, Co Limerick. The couple had two daughters, Ethna and Eileen and a son - Dermott - who was born on June 10th 1906. The quality of the barrack accommodation at Ballygar was not good and in August 1906 he moved on transfer from Ballygar to Ahascragh, [Co Galway]. The married accommodation here was much better for the Kearney family. He was the sergeant in charge of the station.

THE TRAGIC DEATH OF MRS BRIDGET KEARNEY.

A major tragedy struck the family on July 4th 1907 when Mrs Bridget Kearney died after a short illness from peritonitis. She was only twenty-eight years of age. She was interred at the burial place of her family at Kilfergus, Glin, Co Limerick. Sergeant Kearney was left in a very difficult domestic situation, with two little girls aged four and three years and a one year-old baby boy. This was a particularly strenuous time for him with his extra domestic responsibilities along with his responsibility in running an RIC station. He was devastated by her death and described it as *"an awful time"*. He coped quite well with the tragedy that had befallen him. His sister and his late wife's sister rallied to his support and remained with him for some time following the bereavement. After some weeks his sister took the three children to her home at Glasson, near Athlone, Co Westmeath, where she then resided with her [and John's] retired father.

The fact that he had to cope as a child with the death of his own mother may have helped him in getting over this huge crisis in his life.

PROBLEMS WITH 'CATTLE DRIVES'.

The year 1907, was a particularly busy year for the RIC at Ahascragh. It arose from a dispute between landlords and tenants over the 'eleven months grazing system'. This dispute went on in many parts of Ireland at the time, but it was particularly serious in some parts of Co. Galway. It was so serious at the time, that it necessitated the transfer of young RIC men from Counties Antrim and Tyrone on a temporary basis to augment the station-party at Ahascragh. The dispute arose from a system, which existed, whereby landlords rented out land for grazing for a period of eleven months. The small farmers who rented out this land had to remove the animals as soon as the eleven months expired. They had no guarantee that they would have the grazing in the following year and this created a lot of unease and a lot of uncertainty for them. The landlords held the whip hand and many of them treated their existing tenants badly by letting the lands to somebody else in the following year. When the lands were re-let to a stranger, the farmers in several parts of the country retaliated against the landlords by organising 'cattle drives'.

The 'cattle drives' took place at night, when a number of the affected farmers and their sons assembled and drove cattle belonging to the landlord or the new grazing tenant off the land and drove them for a considerable distance away from the land. This resulted in the owners of the animals having to spend much time searching for them and then having the problem of driving the exhausted cattle back to the grazing lands again - or to other grazing lands. 'Cattle driving' was regarded as a very serious crime and the problem kept the police very busy in trying to prevent it or in arresting suspects for the crime and bringing them before the Petty Sessions. The RIC had instructions to arrest all persons caught in the act of committing the crime and to have them brought before a Resident Magistrate to be dealt with in accordance with the law. The ironic aspect of the problem was that much of the land in question had been seized from small farmers who couldn't pay rent to the landlords during the Great Famine or in the years that followed.

Another motive for the 'cattle drives' was that the local farmers wanted to have these big estates divided between them, so that they could have permanent farms of their own.

There were several hundred acres of grazing in the Clonbrock Demesne in Ahascragh sub-district and the cattle drives were a regular nightly occurrence there. They created a lot of turmoil. Fortunately there was no loss of life and no serious injury as a result. John A. Kearney stated that occasionally there was some good humour attached to them.

The RIC at Ahascragh received information that a major 'cattle drive' had been arranged for the Clonbrock Demesne in the sub-district at midnight. About forty members of the force were employed to deal with the matter. They were under the command of the County Inspector, Mr T. D. Smith, who some time later became the Inspector General of the Royal Irish Constabulary. They were moving across country in the darkness to arrest those taking part, when the County Inspector tripped and fell over a newly made cock of hay in a meadow. This gave rise to a lot of merriment amongst the RIC personnel, but the County Inspector wasn't too pleased. It was approaching midnight when in the distance they saw a lot of small lights in an old ring-fort. On getting closer they found about fifty men assembled there and they were lighting their pipes before participating in the 'cattle drive'. Fifty prisoners were taken and it strained the resources of the RIC to keep them in custody. The prisoners were taken before a Magistrate in Ballinasloe and they were bound over to keep the peace and discharged. When this episode was over, John A. Kearney discovered that a number of men who had escaped arrest had carried out the cattle drive as arranged and drove the cattle to a field belonging to their owner near Moylough, Co Galway. In this case, Kearney conceded that:

"It was a success from the people's point of view".

Eventually the 'eleven months grazing' system was broken. Disputed estates were taken over by the Government and divided amongst tenants. New houses and farm buildings were built and new roads were made to access them. The Clonbrock and other estates, which had caused so many problems for the police, were later divided up amongst local smallholders.

JOHN A. KEARNEY RE - MARRIES.

On October 15th 1908, John A. Kearney married Miss Mary Catherine Manning of Ahascragh. She had emigrated to the United States as a teenager but had returned on holidays to visit her family when they both met. She was a daughter of retired RIC Sergeant Matthew Manning who was affectionately known amongst his colleagues in the Force as 'Big Matthew'. He had joined the Irish Constabulary on 25th March 1862 and his Registered Warrant number was 27557. He had served at several locations throughout the country including Counties Fermanagh, Kerry, Roscommon and Cork City. By co-incidence, John's own father had joined the force in May 1862 and had Warrant Number 27667. Both had been in training together at the Phoenix Park for some months. On January 1st 1868, both were temporarily transferred to Cork City, when 150 men, all over six feet in height, were transferred there as an auxiliary force to deal with some political trouble.

Mary Catherine was born at Lyreacrompane RIC station located in the Stack's Mountain area of North Kerry, where her father was stationed at that time. About two weeks after her birth, the family moved to Cloghane, in the Dingle Peninsula in West Kerry, to where her father had been transferred to take charge of the RIC station there. She had a brother Thomas Manning who served in the Medical Corps during World War One. He then joined the Royal Irish Constabulary but died prematurely at the Rotunda Hospital in Dublin as a result of a ruptured appendix. Michael, another one of her brothers was also a constable in the RIC. Mary Catherine's family - like her husband's - had a long association with the RIC as her paternal grandfather was also a member of the force.

Following his marriage to Mary Catherine, Sergeant Kearney was transferred to Ballymahon, Co Longford, in January 1909, in accordance with the strict RIC Regulations which prohibited a member from serving either in his own or his wife's native county. He was very pleased with this transfer as his father and sister lived in Glasson at the time and this was only eight miles from his new station. He obtained a suitable house in Ballymahon and he and Mary Catherine settled down to married life there, with the three children from his first marriage. His father and sister were also delighted that they were so close at hand. His family had earlier connections with Ballymahon as one of his uncles - Patrick Moran - had been school principal there for many years and following the death of his maternal grandfather at Littleton station, his grandmother and mother had come to live at Ballymahon for a while.

PROMOTION TO HEAD CONSTABLE.

In the latter part of 1909 and early 1910, he studied for the competitive examination for Head Constable and was successful. On October 19th 1910 at the relatively young age of 39 years he was promoted to the rank of Head Constable. Considering the slow progress of promotion through the ranks in the RIC, this was a remarkable achievement.

The rank of Head Constable was that of a non-commissioned officer - comparable in most respects to the rank of Inspector in the majority of police forces at the present time. The Head Constable played a key operational and administrative role in the force and he was the main 'link' between the lower ranks of constable and sergeant and the higher ranks of District Inspector and County Inspector. Their immediate superiors were the District Inspectors and they relied very much on the support, advice and basic common sense of their Head constables when the occasion demanded.

Only a very small number of Head Constables had been promoted to District Inspector in the RIC. The vast majority of the D. I. s were recruited through the Cadet system and their average age when joining was twenty to twenty-two years. When assigned to Districts they lacked the practical experience of policing, even though they were well-versed in theoretical knowledge. Like many other professions, the greatest asset that any policeman could have is a wide practical experience in the operational field. Head Constables had this quality which made their service invaluable to subordinates and superiors alike. They were with respect - and with some affection - referred to by their subordinates as *'The Head'*.

In one of the few books written about the RIC, titled "In the Royal Irish Constabulary", the author, District Inspector George Garrow Green, describes a consultation which he had with his Head Constable, while making plans to police an expected faction fight at a local fair in County Kerry:-

"My Head Constable, that grand vizier to an Irish police officer, endeavoured to re-assure me, saying 'as soon as you arrive there Sir, report yourself to a Magistrates act under his orders and throw the responsibility on

to him. They're rale [sic] devils to fight over there. The last time, Constable Cox lost an eye from a blow of a stone and another constable had his leg mostly cut off with a scythe".

A SENTIMENTAL JOURNEY.

Before leaving Ballymahon and taking up his new assignment as a Head Constable he made a very sentimental journey by way of a long cycle trip to the village of Moyvoughley where he was born. He visited the Catholic Church at Ballymore where he had been baptised. It was the first time he had visited it since his Baptism there. He also visited his uncle, Michael Moran, a former member of the RIC who resided in the old RIC barracks at Moyvoughley. Some people whom he met, remembered him as a young child in the village. He was only a few years old when he left it, but could remember some incidents, which occurred there in his childhood. Everybody whom he met, knew his mother very well as she had been a popular teacher in the village for some years before her marriage. It was a truly sentimental journey for him.

For more than a century his relatives have retained ownership of the old RIC barracks in Moyvoughley. When it closed for police use, Michael Moran, uncle of John A. Kearney purchased it as a dwelling house. He was a former member of the RIC and he had a son, Patrick, who also joined the force and served in Belfast in the early 1900s.

Michael Moran also had a daughter named Kate who married a local man named Kerrigan. Their grandson, Gerry Kerrigan, his wife Mary Ann and their children continue to live in the former barracks. The building is exceptionally well maintained by the Kerrigan family and is most attractive. The character of the building has been maintained and the original front door fitted to the porch of the building is still in use. The small building in the back yard, which was used as the outdoor toilet, is still intact. The backyard and other outbuildings are also intact.

A rare shrub growing at the front of the building for over 100 years, is reputed to have been brought by a member of the RIC from India, and planted there.

Directly across the road from the old RIC station is the two-storey disused school, where John A. Kearney's late mother taught when she married his father. Time has stood still in the centre of Moyvoughley village for over 100 years.

TRANSFER TO KILLORGLIN.

The newly promoted Head Constable Kearney was assigned to take charge of Killorglin RIC District in County Kerry in November, 1910. With his wife and family, he took up residence there in the accommodation provided in a section of the RIC station. Killorglin was a District Headquarters station, but it did not have a District Inspector. H/Constable Kearney had complete charge of the District. The other stations in the District were Boolteens, Glenbeigh, Glencar, Milltown, and Beaufort. There were also two Protection posts - at Brenlea and Bunglasha.

Having spent all his life, up to that time, at inland locations, where the country was very flat, he found a big change of scenery when he arrived at his new destination. Much of his district consisted of mountainous areas - including the famous McGillycuddy Reeks whose highest point is Carrantuohill, the highest peak in Ireland. He was fascinated by the beautiful scenery, particularly, by the 'Gap of Dunloe', where a temporary police station opened for business during the summer season. The Atlantic Ocean surrounded much of his territory. He was very conscious and appreciative of the fact that it was one of the most beautiful locations in Ireland.

In addition to the change of landscape he also discovered that there was a wide difference between the culture of the Kerry people and those of the Irish midlands. He illustrates this when quoting from an experience, which he had:-

"The people in manner were quite the opposite to those of the midlands. Just to give an incident, I was on patrol in Ballymahon one beautiful summer's day some miles outside the little town on the Westmeath border, when I saw a countryman coming along the road with his coat under his arm. 'Isn't it a fine day', I said. The man stopped and looked at me, 'well begob' he said 'you are the first man whom I met who spoke to me in the last three days'. He then explained that he lost some cattle at the fair at Clara in King's County and he was looking for them thro' Westmeath. 'They are a queer lot of people in Westmeath, not one would speak to me when I'd ask about the cattle'. The answer would be 'I know nothing about them or in many cases, a shake of the head only'.

"Now in Kerry, in a similar incident, the owner would be asked his name;

where he lived; the colour and description of the missing cattle; everything in connection with himself and his family etc. And all this in the most friendly manner."

On the other hand, he found that many crimes like discharging firearms into houses - as happened frequently in County Kerry - never happened in the midlands.

The Protection post at Bunglasha was in existence when H/Constable Kearney came to the Killorglin District. It was eleven miles distant from the station and was located high up in the McGillycuddy Reeks in the 'Windy Gap'. On a clear day it was visible from the police station.

Brenlea Protection Post was established during his term there to protect a caretaker on an evicted farm, formerly owned by a man whose name was Doyle. The latter suspected that a neighbour of his named Murphy - who was also his brother-in-law - was trying to take over his [Doyle's] farm from the landlord. Murphy reported to the RIC in Killorglin that shots were fired into his house with the obvious intent of murdering him. With a party of police, Kearney cycled out to Murphy's house and found a number of holes in the wall over Murphy's bed. Revolver bullets fired through the window had obviously made the holes.

The police carried out Investigations and Doyle was arrested and returned for trial. At the Cork Assizes, he was convicted for the crime and sentenced to seven years Penal Servitude. On the completion of the trial, Judge O'Brien, paid a very high compliment to H/Constable Kearney and to the RIC at Killorglin for the intelligence with which the case had been investigated.

THE 'CASTLEMAINE CONSPIRACY' CASE.

In March 1912, Kearney became involved in one of the strangest and most reported investigations and trials of the period, which became generally known as 'The Castlemaine Conspiracy'. As his children had scarlet fever at the time, he was off duty as a medical precaution when the crime took place. When the report of the incident was made, he got permission at once from the County Inspector to resume duty and take charge of the investigations.

The matter came to light on March 25th, 1912, when a report was made to the sergeant-in-charge of Milltown RIC station, to the effect that three men were shot and wounded when returning to Tralee from Castlemaine Fair. It happened at a point where three RIC Districts - Tralee, Killarney and Killorglin - met. Two men - a father and son - named McDonnell, who were well - known butchers in Tralee and another man from Tralee, to whom they had given a lift, were fired at and seriously wounded in broad daylight as they returned along the mountain road from Castlemaine towards Tralee.

Neither the police nor the injured men could assign any motive for the attack. Kearney went directly to the scene of the attack. Sergeant Whiston and Constable Clarke from Milltown station were at the scene when he arrived. Also there was Sergeant John McGuinness, a mounted policeman who was in charge of police transport at Tralee station.

The shooting was a very daring outrage and Kearney concluded that "the perpetrators were no ordinary local peasants".

On examining the scene it was found that one of the criminals had worn boots having rows of 'shamrock studs' - some of which were missing. Footprints leading from the scene were found by Sergeant Whiston and Constable Clarke. They traced the footprints through fields for over 1,000 yards. The culprits had avoided all gaps between fields - with one exception. There was a very good quality footprint at the latter gap but it was covered with water. Sergeant Whiston succeeded in draining away the water and taking good casts of the foot print.

Sometime before the shooting incident took place, District Inspector Cheesman of Killarney station had informed Head Constable Kearney about some serious crimes, which had taken place in the Killarney District. In one case, cattle had been driven over a mountain precipice and killed. The suspect for the Killarney outrages was a former British soldier named Ryan. In one instance police were protecting the caretaker of an evicted farm, at a fair. In the crowded fair, the police briefly became separated from the caretaker. As the latter became isolated from his escort, a revolver shot rang out. The caretaker was struck by the bullet and badly wounded. While Ryan was suspected of this crime, he was not brought to justice - nor was anybody else. Kearney compiled a profile of Ryan and his background. He learned that Ryan was a highly intelligent and well - educated individual. He had enlisted in the *'Connaught Rangers'* Regiment as a young man. He was one of only thirteen members of that Regiment who crossed the Tajella River at the Battle of Calenco in 1899. He had been recommended for a Victoria Cross.

Further enquiries revealed that Ryan, who was aged about forty years at this time, was employed as a farm labourer in the Farranfore police sub-district. Sergeant Thomas O'Rourke of Farranfore station established that a farmer named Bob Daly employed Ryan, a few miles outside Farranfore village.

Head Constable Kearney accompanied by Sergeant O'Rourke and a party of RIC men surrounded Bob Daly's house in the early hours of the morning. It was known that Ryan was a dangerous man and very quick with his revolver. The entire party was fully armed to deal with any armed resistance.

Kearney took it on himself to enter Daly's house with his revolver drawn. Having knocked at the door, Daly enquired from within as to who was there and Kearney told him that it was the police. When Daly admitted Kearney, the latter asked *"where is Ryan"?* Daly looked up towards the overhead loft and nodded to Kearney. A step-ladder gave access to the loft from the kitchen and Kearney rushed up the ladder with revolver drawn. There he found Ryan and another man named Clifford in bed.

"Are you Ryan?" Kearney asked the man whom he believed to be Ryan.

"Yes. What do you want of me?" Ryan asked in a surly tone.

Kearney ordered him to get up and get dressed, while he watched him closely and kept him covered with his revolver. When Ryan was dressed, Kearney told him that he was arresting him for attempted murder on March 25th and he also arrested Clifford.

When the prisoners and their escort arrived at Farranfore police station, the police removed Ryan's boots and found that they corresponded with the footprints, which had been found at the scene of the crime.

Investigations carried out by the police in the days that followed, established a motive for the shooting. It arose from a dispute about a farm of land, between a Father Foley who was a Parish Priest in Scotland and his family. Fr Foley had purchased the farm, which originally had belonged to his grandfather, and he placed two brothers and a sister of his on the farm, to run it for him. The brothers had refused to pay any rent to Fr Foley for the farm and wanted to hold on to it for themselves. Fr Foley had them evicted from the holding.

A caretaker with an escort of police was put in charge of the farm. It was located at Knockanish, a few miles from Tralee, Co Kerry. Some time afterwards, an attempt was made to blow up the farmhouse with a bomb.

Nobody was brought to justice for this crime.

The disputed farm was 'boycotted' - as happened in most cases of evictions. No person would make purchases of animals, crops or produce from these farms. In January 1912, at a market in Tralee, the McDonnells [who were victims of the shooting on March 25th] purchased turnips, which had been grown on the disputed farm. The McDonnells were warned about the purchase of the turnips by one of the young Foley brothers. McDonnell senior, told Foley to *'Go to Hell'*. H.C. Kearney and those investigating the shooting concluded that this was the motive behind the attempted murder.

The McDonnells were in hospital for many months. They were badly wounded by pellets all over their heads and shoulders. The man to whom they had given the lift was also badly injured. He was in hospital for a lengthy period and lost an eye as a result of the shooting.

Eventually all three were able to attend Court and give evidence. Ryan had been returned for trial to the Cork Winter Assizes in 1912. Clifford was discharged.

Ryan was found guilty of attempted murder and was sentenced to ten years Penal Servitude. The Attorney General personally prosecuted the case against Ryan who was defended by a very able young barrister named Maurice Healy.

Following Ryan's trial, Constable Clarke of Milltown procured further evidence relating to the case. It transpired that Bob Daly's wife was a sister of Fr. Foley - the P.P. in Scotland. Bob Daly, his wife's younger brother [Foley], Clifford and Ryan were heard conspiring and making arrangements to commit the crime. Daly, Foley and Clifford were subsequently arrested by Kearney and charged with conspiracy.

The three men were returned for trial to the Cork Winter Assizes of 1913. They were convicted of the conspiracy. Daly was sentenced to six years Penal Servitude, Foley was sentenced to five years Penal Servitude and Clifford was sentenced to 12 months imprisonment. On his release from prison, Clifford returned home and a few days later he was found drowned within a few yards of the spot where the conspirators had met and planned their conspiracy.

The *'Royal Irish Constabulary Magazine'* of May 1913, carried the following feature on the case –

"A case of abnormal interest and vital importance, is to be tried elsewhere than in Kerry at the next Assizes, as a change of venue has been obtained in connection with it. It relates to a charge of conspiracy to murder, which has been preferred against three men from the Castlemaine direction. It originated in the development of the case of attempting to murder three men, for which P.J. Ryan was sentenced to ten years penal servitude at the Cork Winter Assizes.

"Both cases have been worked up in a masterly manner, for which there has been no parallel in Kerry, during a period stretching back over twenty years. The evidence was collected particle by particle, and, like a piece of mosaic work, put together with so much ingenuity and skill as to make the picture of the crime perfect and complete. Head Constable Kearney of Tralee, was a prominent figure in the manipulation of these cases, and the legal acumen and detective capacity displayed in their development do immense credit to the artificer. The Head Constable has distinguished himself in other cases since his advent to Kerry, notably in a case near Killorglin, where the accused was sentenced to seven years penal servitude for firing into a dwelling-house. The Head Constable was highly complimented by the Judge on the occasion. He is adept in the art of criminal investigation and procedure, and, given an average share of good luck, he is certainly destined to adorn, in the near future, a more exalted sphere, than the one he now moves in."

The 'Castlemaine Conspiracy' case received widespread publicity at the time and it was exceptionally well investigated by Head Constable Kearney and his investigation team. The Attorney General said that it was the best worked case in Ireland since the Phoenix Park Murders of Lord Frederick Cavendish and Thomas Henry Burke who were murdered by the Invincibles on May 6th 1882. The Attorney General was so impressed with Kearney's efficiency that he had an interview with the Inspector General of the RIC and made representations to him, to have Kearney promoted to the rank of District Inspector. The Inspector General told him that it could not be done as Kearney was too junior in rank.

2

TRANSFER OF JOHN A. KEARNEY TO TRALEE

FIRST IMPRESSIONS OF HIS SUPERIORS IN TRALEE.

In August 1912, Head Constable Kearney was transferred to Tralee station. Tralee, was a District headquarters station and the County RIC headquarters for Co Kerry. It was a far more important station and carried much more status than Killorglin where he had been stationed as a Head Constable prior to that. Tralee was the biggest town and the administrative centre for County Kerry, with a population of about 15,000 within its urban area. It had several local industries and there was a lively import/export trade from its port. It differed to Killorglin in that it had excellent agricultural land and prosperous farmers in its hinterland. It was a busy station and a challenging position for Kearney who was taking charge of it.

There was official accommodation for the Head Constable and his family located on the first floor of the station and while it was comfortable, it was rather limited in size. On his transfer to Tralee, his wife and children moved with him and the family took up residence in the official quarters. The children attended the local schools in Tralee and were very happy. They remained in this accommodation until August 1916 and two more children - Mona and Thomas - were born there.

The County Inspector in Tralee at the time was obviously the product of an earlier generation of 'gentlemen' and Kearney's description of him is most interesting.

"The County Inspector there was Mr Black Law. Mr Law was on the verge of retirement. In his young days he must have been a man of much common-sense which he still retained and a large amount of dignity which reminded one of the early Victorian school of gentlemen. To see him dressed in his morning suit, black swallow tailed coat, fancy waist - coat, white shirt, winged collar and black tie, one was much struck with the dignity of the dress etc. and of the immaculate appearance of the man who wore it. But, alas, on looking back on his figure, one is struck with the uselessness of it. For a man who had much work to do, it must have been uncomfortable in the final degree. It must have been something in the nature of the

gorgeous uniform of that time worn by the Hussars, Lancers or Dragoons and the full-dress uniform of the Infantry. It was all for show and not for work".

The District Inspector in Tralee at the time was Mr Frederick Britten, an Englishman who held a B.A. degree from Oxford University and on whom Kearney recorded his assessment and opinion.

"On the other hand, Mr Britten, the District Inspector was much more of a democrat. If he had a dress suit he must have hidden it away in the attic as no one ever saw him encased in it.

"He was a man of sterling character - much more so than any other officer I met in the service. I personally never met his equal. One thing about him was that he wouldn't tell an untruth or have one under a wrong impression by the sophistry of words. This equally applied to official documents, correspondence etc. As a matter of fact, I believe he would die first before he 'would throw dust in the eyes' of those above him.

"All this left a strong and deep impression on me. He was a Church of England man. It was men like him made England great - a true Christian if ever I met one.

"It didn't mean that he hadn't faults and prejudices. He had. But all paled into in-significance in his sterling honesty of character.

"I have referred to Sergeant William Beckett under whom I served in my young days. He was a Presbyterian. He, too, had a strong effect on my character.

"Strange it was that Mr Britten, D.I., an Englishman and Church of England and Sergeant William Beckett, a Presbyterian and an Irishman had so impressed me - a Roman Catholic - by the noble points in their characters, that I tried to pass on to others, the traits of goodness displayed by those two men. No greater tribute can be paid by one man to another than this".

Mr Edward M. P. Wynne, was the Resident Magistrate in Tralee at the time. He presided over the Petty Sessions in Tralee and in adjoining towns and villages. Kearney was glad to renew acquaintance with him and later recorded his pleasure and reasons for doing so and the esteem in which he held him:

"Mr E.M.P. Wynne, Resident Magistrate, stationed in Tralee, was also a man to be admired. He had been a District Inspector in the R.I.C. and he

was a Company Officer when I was a recruit in the Depot. He was educated at Eton. He was one of the most charming men I ever met. Often when sentencing a culprit, either man or woman, he would do so in such a way, with such reluctance, and with so much respect, which no doubt about it, he felt, that the culprit smiled and thanked him.

"Mr Wynne had a wonderfully kind heart and I believe that he loved the people of Kerry for their many good points of character which he saw and admired. And Kerry people have many".

Kearney would have had contact with Mr Wynne almost on a weekly basis as he prosecuted court cases on behalf of the constables and sergeants under his command, at the weekly Petty Sessions in Tralee. Through this contact and experience he witnessed at first-hand how the Resident Magistrate adjudicated in the many cases which came before him.

Mr Wynne, was still serving as a Resident Magistrate in Tralee for some years after Kearney had left and he continued to serve as an R.M. in the area through the War of Independence until May 1920 when he - through no fault of his - became involved in a serious incident which caused him to leave Tralee.

On May 18th 1920, he was being driven by his driver named Daniel Breen on a horse drawn sidecar to preside at the Petty Sessions in Causeway in North Kerry. When, a few miles from Causeway village, they were held up by a group of armed men who shouted at Wynne and his driver to put their hands up. The driver jumped off the sidecar to take hold of the horse, which had become frightened when the shooting started. Wynne remained on the sidecar and drew his revolver and took aim at the gunman closest to him. In all, he fired five shots from his revolver and the first man he fired at, fell injured face downwards on the road. On seeing their comrade fall, two of the gunmen jumped over the roadside fence into a field and the others stopped firing. Wynne allegedly called them cowards and told them to 'come on' but they did not. The driver re-mounted the sidecar and they drove off towards their Causeway destination. Wynne looked back as they drove away and saw the comrades of the injured man coming to his assistance.

He continued on to Causeway and conducted the Petty Sessions there, which lasted for about an hour and a half. He returned to Tralee by motorcar rather than by his sidecar.

At Tralee Petty Sessions on the following week he spoke about the occurrence:

"I could have been attacked and easily shot at any time within the past few years, as I walked about quite alone. Therefore I am sure that this attack on me was not planned or approved by any responsible organisation. I trusted the Kerry people, and always found them kindly and courteous. During my time here, I have tried to be just and lenient where possible, and most sincerely regret what has occurred".

He had obviously hoped and believed that the I.R.A. had not been involved, but it had, as one of its members - Michael Nolan - was the man fatally shot by Wynne. He realised that he was then an automatic target for the I.R.A., he decided to resign and moved quickly to England. The I.R.A burned his furniture while it was awaiting transport at the local railway station, they also burned down his Tralee home after he had vacated it. He had been on the bench for almost twenty years in County Kerry and was held in high regard by everybody with whom he came in contact. The attempt on his life was a sad end to his stay in Kerry, but by the standards of the time, he was very lucky in escaping death or serious injury, as a number of Resident Magistrates were shot and killed by the I.R.A. in Ireland during that period.

Head Constable Kearney became well established in Tralee within a short time of his arrival. He had an excellent relationship with his subordinates and superiors and there was never any doubt about his ability or efficiency. Outside of the force, he created a favourable impression amongst all those with whom he came in contact. In the enforcement of the law he always managed to *'temper justice with mercy'*.

His level of intelligence was very much above average and he was a very 'well - read' individual. He read two newspapers every day – one English and one Irish. He was very much au-fait with world affairs and local happenings. He had a special interest in affairs of the British Empire throughout the world and in its Government and personalities.

POLICEMEN WHO WORKED CLOSELY WITH KEARNEY IN TRALEE.

While Kearney got on very well with all those who served with him, he was closer to three members of his station-party than to others. One of those was Sergeant Thomas O'Rourke, who was closely involved with him in the investigation of the Castlemaine Conspiracy case and who arrived on transfer at Tralee around 1914 from Farranfore station. He had served at Fenit, and Ardfert stations prior to that. He was a native of Stradussy, Kiltyclogher, Co Leitrim. His official designation at Tralee was that of 'Crimes Sergeant' and his duties would have involved the monitoring and supervision of subversive elements in the area. He had a passionate love for the Gaelic language. During the War of Independence he became very friendly with Tim Kennedy the I.R.A. Intelligence Officer for North Kerry.

Mr T. Ryle Dwyer, recounts the development of this friendship in his book *"Tans, Terror and Troubles"* as follows:

"Tim Kennedy was appointed director of intelligence for Number 1 Brigade, covering the northern half of the county. He reported directly to Michael Collins, with whom he had already become quite friendly since first meeting him during a holiday in Ballybunion in 1913. At that time, Collins had been with his mentor Sam Maguire.

"Kennedy shared a passion for the Irish language with the R.I.C's Special Crimes Sergeant, Thomas O'Rourke. He was the man in the barracks dealing with political crimes and political intelligence. As a result of their friendship, O'Rourke indicated how R.I.C intelligence was gathered, by explaining how they kept a watch on all national organisations, placed their own representatives within the I.R.B. and had their own civilian sources of information from members of the Masonic Lodges".

Having described how Kennedy managed to get copies of the coded telegrams destined for the RIC, through the local post office, T. Ryle Dwyer continues -

"Of course the coded telegrams were of no use without a means of breaking the codes, and Kennedy developed his friendship with Sergeant O'Rourke, who realised that his friend was probably involved in intelligence work. He told Kennedy that he was anxious to channel information to the Republican leadership. 'I hadn't much experience of intelligence at the time and I was scared to have much to do with the R.I.C', Kennedy explained. He therefore consulted Michael Collins, who advised him to seize the opportunity to ask O'Rourke to furnish a copy of the R.I.C code.

"I asked him for the key', Kennedy added, 'and he delivered it to myself. I sent it to Mick Collins and henceforth I was able to supply it to headquarters every month and after each change where the R.I.C. suspected that we had got it. Mick [Michael Collins] told me afterwards that it was the first

time he was able to procure the key regularly and it laid the foundation of the elaborate scheme of intelligence in the post offices".

Sergeant O'Rourke was involved in numerous house searches and arrests of Volunteers and Republicans and he gave evidence at several of their trials. He was a very active policeman. He retired from the RIC in 1920 and through Tim Kennedy's influence he obtained a vacant prison warder's house for himself and his family in the grounds of the County Gaol at Ballymullen, Tralee. He died in October 1933. His son Michael O'Rourke was a well-known school - teacher in Tralee for many years and he was President of the Kerry County Board of the Gaelic Athletic Association for several years prior to his death in a traffic accident in 1996.

Another policeman closely associated with Kearney was Constable Georgie Neazer.

He was a native of Ballycahane, Pallaskenry, Co Limerick. He was assigned to Tralee in 1912. While serving as a constable there he was assigned to political duties in 1914. He was very active in the supervision and monitoring of the Irish Volunteers and their activities and later the I.R.A. He had been successful in the investigation of a number of high-profile crimes - including attacks on the police - in the North Kerry area. He was promoted to Sergeant rank in 1917. He was involved in the investigation of an attempted murder by shooting of Michael O'Brien, who was a land steward on an estate at Rattoo, North Kerry. A suspect named James Slattery was arrested and even though O'Brien positively identified Slattery as being the man responsible, the jury failed to convict him. O'Brien had to have full-time protection following the trial.

Sergeant Neazer and Constable Garret Doyle, were on protection duty with O'Brien while he was attending a fair at Rathkeale, Co Limerick on March 23rd 1918. The three men were having a meal at the Hibernian Hotel in Rathkeale when a group of five local I.R.A. men under the command of their Commandant entered the dining - room and shot Sergeant Neazer dead. Constable Doyle was seriously injured but recovered. The I.R.A. took their revolvers and ironically no attempt was made to shoot O'Brien who was the man receiving full-time protection from the RIC. Sergeant Neazer was forty-three years of age and had nineteen years service in the RIC. He was married with three children.

Kearney also had a close friendship with Sergeant John McGuinness, who was in charge of the mounted police at Tralee station. They first met in the course of the 'Castlemaine Conspiracy' investigations in 1912.

Kearney had a very high regard for McGuinness' ability and integrity and they maintained regular contact with each other during their retirement, until McGuinness died in London in 1944.

RECRUITING IN TRALEE FOR THE FIRST WORLD WAR.

From the commencement of the 1914 -'18 War, Kearney kept up-to-date with its progress on a daily basis. When the War broke out, it did not come as a surprise to him. He kept in close touch with recruiting for the British forces at local level and later recorded the following observations made by him, about that period:-

"Then when matters were reaching a crisis in the matter of Home Rule, the world was startled by the outbreak of the First World War. From 1906, I saw it coming and many others saw the shadow long before that year. Nevertheless it caused consternation. However, on second thoughts the British were never finally beaten and never knew when they were beaten, and anyway never gave in. The Irish as a nation were as a whole optimistic as to the final result and this held good during those awful four years.

"The RIC in every District had the mobilisation posters under lock and key and on the word being given the Proclamations calling up the Reserve were posted throughout the country.

"Ballymullen Barracks in Tralee was the Depot of that famous Regiment - The Royal Munster Fusiliers - and Reserves and recruits began to roll in. And within a week, the First Battalion of a thousand strong were ready to proceed overseas.

"The Battalion entrained at 6 a.m from Tralee for England and within a week the Battalion was in the front line at Mons. I was present at Tralee railway station when they left and as a matter of fact I marched with them from Ballymullen Barracks.

"Mr Britten, District Inspector was there also. He came back and joined me and said that an English officer of the unit just told him 'That the Battalion was one of the best fighting units in the British Army'.

"I well believe him' I answered.

"The men were well set-up, sturdy and strong and certainly carried them-

selves well as soldiers.

"The Colonel in Command was of French descent, born in British India - a tea-planters son. He stood about six feet two inches in height and was of massive build.

"Their Brigade was attacked near Mons and the 'Munsters' were moved over a canal. From early morning, the Battalion was practically surrounded, but it fought on during the day and really held up a Division of the German Army. Numbers told eventually - the Colonel was twice wounded but continued to fight on. Almost every officer was killed or wounded and the few left surrendered. The Colonel was killed - a brave man.

"Ninety escaped over the canal and Lord French told me some years afterwards, that he kept the ninety men as his body - guard. But eventually he had to remove them as they were often drunk.

"Recruits rolled in, in large numbers to join the Royal Munster Fusiliers.

"In 1915, the Irish Guards Band made a recruiting tour throughout Ireland and came to Tralee. The Band wore full dress uniform - red tunic, busby, etc. Lieutenant - The Honourable Tommy Vesey [who was afterwards Lieutenant Colonel in Command of the Irish Guards] - was the officer in command. Lieutenant Michael O'Leary V.C. was also with the party. He had won the V.C. for a remarkable feat of bravery a short time before, in France, when an attack was being made by the Irish Guards on an enemy position.

"The Band played in Denny Street. Then a recruiting meeting was held. The Sinn Fein Volunteers moved along the street in twos and threes, but made no effort to stop or interfere. Twenty-five recruits - all over six feet - enlisted. And to my surprise, all the eligible R.I.C men in my command volunteered. This was the beginning of recruiting for the Irish Guards throughout the RIC. Thus was formed the Second Battalion of the Irish Guards.

"Curiously enough a few of the Sinn Fein Volunteers also enlisted in the Munsters and other Irish Regiments".

Kearney was particularly interested in the welfare of the RIC men who joined the forces and was always anxious to hear stories about their exploits - especially those relating to acts of bravery on their part. His pride in them was self evident, judging by the following record made by him, of various incidents, which happened where they were involved:-

"News of my men who joined the Irish Guards and other Irish Regiments used to reach us from time to time. We sent them parcels containing 'comforts' etc.

"There was a party in Knockanish protection post [located about four miles from Tralee], consisting of one sergeant and four constables whose duty it was to protect the caretaker of the evicted farm, and all of them volunteered for the army. The old caretaker - Mickeen Sullivan – aged about forty years also volunteered.

"The sergeant [Banahan] subsequently received a Commission in the Connaught Rangers while the others joined the Irish Guards and the caretaker enlisted with the 'Munsters'.

"I met Banahan some years later in Boyle. He reached the rank of captain. His Unit was in the Sixteenth Division. One morning the unit was in action – the unit was practically wiped out – Banahan was badly wounded in the legs with shrapnel.

"He with a number of other wounded, were being conveyed on ambulances to the base when he heard a shout of derision from the wounded Connaught Rangers who were in his ambulance. They were passing through the Munster Fusilier lines at the time. Banahan on looking out saw what was to him the blackest cook that he had ever laid eyes on, at his work cooking breakfast. The jeers and disparaging remarks of the wounded Connaughts who were able to use their voices reached the 'black cook' who looked up with a grin and a wave of his hand at the ambulance. Banahan saw him and recognised the cook as Mickeen Sullivan the caretaker from Knockanish.

"Many of the R.I.C. men who enlisted received from time to time, decorations for bravery. One of those was Humphrey Bray, who came from near Birr, in County Offaly. He was my clerk in Killorglin and as the saying goes 'he wouldn't knock a cat off a stool', meaning of course that he was a mild-tempered man. But from my observation I knew him to be cool and level - headed in danger and very determined - just the type of man you'd like to have beside you in the last ditch.

"He was recommended for the V.C. when as a Sergeant in command of a platoon of the Irish Guards, he passed through a Company of Grenadiers who were trying for twenty-four hours to take a pill - box. Sergeant Bray and his men passed through the Grenadiers who were lying partly entrenched on the ground. Bray's platoon approached the pill - box under fire and called on the Germans to surrender. They did. He was awarded the D.C.M.

"Another of my men named Fox from County Tipperary was also awarded the D.C.M. One afternoon in 1922, I was listening in Hyde Park to the soap - box spouters when I felt a tip on my shoulder. On looking around I came face to face with Fox. . Well, it was a grand surprise for both of us as Fox had enlisted in the Irish Guards in 1915 and I hadn't seen him since.

"He told me many a yarn of the Irish Guards in the War. One in particular, which took my fancy, was a tale of the Battle of Loos. The Guards were making an attack on the famous Loos Wood. They were held by machine gun and shrapnel fire and they lay prone on the ground in line.

"After a time, Fox felt somebody pulling at his boot. He looked back and saw Bray. 'Isn't this nice clod-pegging', said Bray quite coolly to Fox. Many casualties were occurring every moment to the right and left of them. In Ireland during the turf or peat gathering, youngsters often have a battle with bits of turf or clods. So, Bray in his own dry way compared the Battle of Loos and what they were going through to a battle of clods in an Irish bog. Fox told me that he enjoyed the joke.

"Captain Deanne, a Tipperary man, of the Royal Irish Regiment, now a District Inspector at Ballymote, [Co Sligo] called to see me in Boyle. He said that the bravest action he had seen during the War was that of a Sergeant Thomas Moloney of his platoon. An attack by them failed and a number of wounded soldiers of the Royal Irish Regiment lay in "no - man's land ". Sergeant Moloney went over the top and brought in one wounded man. He went over the second time and did the same - and again on the third, fourth and fifth time. Just as he mounted the trench for the sixth time he was just riddled by machine-gun fire and dropped back into the trench.

"By the way' said Deane, I have a brother of Sergeant Moloney in my District. Both brothers served in the R.I.C. Sergeant Moloney had joined up from Tralee.

"Sergeant Moloney was with me in Tralee as a young constable. He was of splendid physique and a native of County Clare.

"I well remember when he and others were leaving. We gave a 'do' the night before to these grand fellows. Two of the others - Casey was killed in action and Mahony was taken prisoner of war. Both belonged to the same Regiment.".

During the years 1913 - 1915, police work in the Tralee area was very much of a routine nature. The only diversion, was the activity of the Irish [Sinn Fein] Volunteers, which required monitoring and attention. The RIC had this situation very much in hand in that they knew all the individuals involved and they were familiar with their movements and activities. The attitude of the Irish Volunteers hardened towards the RIC, they became more aggressive and insolent in their attitude towards the force.

THE MONTHLY CONFIDENTIAL REPORTS OF THE RIC.

Long before this time - and as far back as the late 1840s - the District Inspector of each District submitted a 'Monthly Confidential Report' to his County Inspector in respect of his District, outlining the strengths and activities of all subversive, suspect and nationalist organisations; agrarian crime; crimes committed with firearms; illegal drilling; details of threatening notices sent and cattle-driving, etc. The reports from the District Inspectors were collated by the County Inspector who forwarded a report in respect of his county to Dublin Castle from where it was ultimately sent to the Under Secretary of State. These reports were very comprehensive and most reliable. Through them, the British authorities were kept up to date on the state of law - and – order throughout the country.

Early in 1916 it became evident to the RIC and the Dublin Metropolitan Police that an Insurrection was being planned and they later learned that it had been arranged for Easter Sunday 1916. As nothing happened on that day and being aware of Eoin MacNeill's countermanding order, which cancelled the Insurrection, neither force was prepared for it happening on Easter Monday instead. The British army was also caught unawares with the majority of its officers enjoying a day out at Fairyhouse Races.

While the British authorities were in possession of very definite information that arms were going to be landed from a German vessel or vessels on the West coast of Ireland, there is no evidence available to suggest that specific information was passed on to the RIC – despite claims to the contrary. [From the Fenian Rising of 1867, the RIC was always on the alert for arms being landed around the Irish coast.] The Limerick or Kerry coastlines were regarded as the most likely locations for the landing of the arms. Several British warships and some submarines were deployed off the south-west coast of Ireland in anticipation of the arrival of the German vessels but it would appear that the RIC were not informed and were not involved in any particular plan to deal with the situation when it occurred. The arrival of Casement, Monteith and Bailey, and the arrival and interception of the *'Aud'* all appear to have come as a surprise to the force.

GOOD FRIDAY, 1916 AND THE ARREST OF ROGER CASEMENT.

The events at Tralee on Good Friday 1916, were destined to have a marked effect on Head Constable Kearney, the implications of which would remain with him for the rest of his life. Traditionally, Good Friday was always a very significant day in Ireland from a religious point-of-view, when people, fasted, abstained from meat, abstained from alcohol, attended church devotions to commemorate the Crucifixion of Our Lord. It was generally observed as a day of penance and prayer. Schools were closed, most shops closed down for the day and an air of solemnity prevailed. It was one of the most sacred days in the church calendar.

Kearney later made a record of the first duty performed by him on that fateful duty:

"On the morning of Good Friday, [1916] I received a telephone message from the Sergeant in charge of Ardfert Station, to the effect that arms etc were landed on the coast in his sub-district and that three men were seen near the coast. He said that he was going out to investigate the matter, taking Constable Reilly with him.

"I sent two men to see where Stack was and whether there was any movement among the Sinn Fein Volunteers. I got in touch with the District Inspector and he took out the transport car and eight or ten cyclists to Ardfert".

When Kearney was attending to this first duty for that day, he had no way of knowing or appreciating how significant the happenings of the day were going to be for him.

Before the day ended, his life became intertwined with Sir Roger Casement and a local Republican leader named Austin Stack.

3

SIR ROGER CASEMENT

CHILDHOOD AND EARLY CAREER.

Roger David Casement was born on September 1st 1864 at Doyle's Cottages, Lawson Terrace, Sandycove, County Dublin. His father who was also named Roger was a retired army sergeant who had served with the Third King's Light Dragoon Guards in India and later in Ireland as a captain in the North Antrim Militia. The Casements were Protestant landowners in Ulster since early in the seventeenth century when they came from Ramsey in the Isle on Man. The family had originated in France. Young Roger's grandfather - Hugh Casement - was a well off ship-owner in Belfast before the Napoleanic Wars but most of his younger sons became soldiers. The most distinguished of Hugh's cousins was Major General Sir William Casement K. C. B., who was military secretary to the Government of India for twenty years and a member of the Supreme Council. He died of cholera in 1844 and is commemorated by a bust in the Calcutta Town Hall.

Roger Casement, senior, resigned his commission in the Dragoon Guards and left India in 1848. He played a role on the side of the Hungarians against the Austrians and brought a despatch to Downing Street, which resulted in the Hungarian rebels not being handed over to the Austrians. The elder Roger then went to Paris where he met up with and married an Irish girl named Anne Jephson. She came from County Wexford and was a Roman Catholic. Some time later they came to Ireland and stayed near Ballycastle, Co Antrim, at the home of Roger's [senior] brother John and he took up a commission with the North Antrim Militia. Mrs Anne Casement ceased practising the Catholic religion and consented to have her children raised in the Protestant faith. There were three boys of whom Roger [junior] was the youngest and one daughter. Roger senior died when the children were very young and Roger [junior] had only a faint memory of him. After her husband's death, Mrs Casement had Roger re-baptised into her own Catholic religion. Young Roger's older brothers Thomas and Charles, later emigrated to South Africa and Australia respectively. He kept in close touch with his sister Nina for the greater part of his life. When Roger [senior] resigned his position with the Antrim Militia, the family went to live at Sandycove, Co. Dublin.

Young Roger Casement was only nine years old when his mother died and he was taken to live with his uncle John at Magherintemple House near Ballycastle, Co Antrim where his uncle took charge of rearing him. After attending junior school, he was sent as a student boarder to Ballymena Academy, a Church of Ireland boarding school. Casement later complained about the very limited education, which he received there. He received no instruction about the history of Ireland and in fact the name of Ireland was very rarely - if ever - mentioned in the school. He stated that anything he learned about Ireland or its history was learned by himself outside of schools. He stated that:

"As an Irishman, I wish to see this state of things changed and Irish education to be primarily what that of every healthy people is - designed to build up the country from within, by training its youth to know, love and respect their own land before all other lands. Patriotism has been stigmatised and often treated as 'treason', or a 'crime' or dismissed with superior scorn as 'local'.

Roger Casement left the Academy when he was seventeen years of age and got employment as a clerk in Liverpool with the Elder Dempster Shipping Company. After three years in this post he got a job as a purser on a steamboat belonging to the company and made his first voyage to the African continent. He did return to England but was longing to get back to Africa. That continent was still being explored by people like Stanley and Livingstone and Casement got his opportunity to get back there when he joined another expedition organised by an American - General Henry Sanford - in the Congo. The Congo had become an independent state under the protection of King Leopold 11 of Belgium. Casement earned a reputation as an observant explorer and was much in demand for lectures on the subject. At this time he was an exceptionally handsome young man who looked very well but did not enjoy good health and was not very robust.

On the strength of his reputation he was appointed by the British Colonial Office as a civil servant and was appointed as a Travelling Commissioner to the Niger Coast Protectorate in 1892. The position was in fact equivalent to that of an 'intelligence officer' for the British Government in Nigeria. Three years later on June 30th 1895, he was appointed as a British Consul at Lourenco Marques, the seaport of Portugese East Africa and located on Delagoa Bay. This was a very important assignment as confrontations between the British and the Boers had already commenced. In

1898 he was transferred back to the West Coast as a consul at Loanda for the Portugese possessions south of the Gulf of New Guinea. He also held the position of Consul in the Gamboon and in the Congo Free State.

In addition to his role as Consul at these locations, he was under instructions to monitor the movement of arms and ammunitions passing through to the Transvaal. One of his primary functions was to gather and collate 'intelligence' relating to the Boers and especially to the supply of weapons to the Boers by the Germans.

He communicated sensitive material to the Foreign Office by cipher. While his reports were notably 'long-winded', they were nevertheless closely studied and given credence by the Foreign Office. He diligently kept the authorities informed about all developments. He reported on attempts made by the Boers to seduce Irish Prisoners of War, whom they had captured, to fight against England and of the attempted formation by the Boers of an Irish Brigade under the leadership of a Major McBride.

It was during these times at these locations that he became extremely interested in the welfare of the working classes in the Belgian Congo. He was not happy with what he had seen there and looked forward to getting back there at a later time to investigate what was taking place.

When the Boer War broke out he was transferred south to Capetown where he was retained until the end of the campaign because of his exceptional knowledge of the Transvaal, Swaziland and other key areas in Africa, which he had acquired from his service in the many different locations. From Capetown he continued to furnish long detailed 'Intelligence' reports to the Foreign Office and many of his reports were passed on to Lord Kitchener when he assumed control of the British forces in the war against the Boers. When the Boer War ended, he was awarded the Queen's South African Medal in recognition of the role he had played during the War.

CASEMENT'S INVESTIGATIONS IN THE BELGIAN CONGO.

Following the Boer War, he left Capetown and moved as Consul, to Kinchasa in the Belgian Congo - the transfer he had deeply longed for. From his previous contact with the Belgian Congo he had become acutely conscious of breaches of human rights and atrocities against workers being perpetrated by the Colonists and rubber producers there. He decided to investigate allegations being made and to assemble evidence relating to these problems.

From May to August 1903 he threw himself wholly into the investigation and set about doing this in a methodical fashion, working long hours late into the night, interviewing people who had limbs severed and who had suffered degradation at the hands of their employers. He was horrified by the tales, which the natives brought to him and the mutilations they had suffered. At one location in Bongandaga he found the population guarded by armed men as if they were convicts and they were kept as forced labour on the rubber plantations. Men, women and children were kept in chains. He met one boy who had both hands amputated by black soldiers on the instructions of the Belgians.

The Belgian authorities vehemently denied the abuses and the serious allegations made. King Leopold even invited Casement to join him for a social visit at Brussels, diplomatically trying to discourage him from pursuing his investigations. Casement sent regular reports on his findings back to the Foreign Office in London. Casement's authority for carrying out these investigations arose from the fact that a number of British subjects who had made their way to the Belgian Congo for employment had been caught up in the atrocities there.

At the same time, two prominent British personalities who had also become concerned with affairs in the Belgian Congo had formed the *'Congo Reform Commission'* and had put some pressure on the British Government to have the allegations investigated. This coincided with Casement's investigation.

In December 1903 he was called to London to complete his report there. He was in a very poor state of health, suffering from malaria. After completing his report he submitted it to the Foreign Office, before coming to Dublin and County Antrim for a well-earned holiday. The Report was published on the following February as a 'Parliamentary Report'. Its contents were repudiated straight away by the Belgians, but other Governments sat up and took notice of Casement's findings. The Report caused shock and horror and Casement became the centre of world attention. He was just 40 years of age at the time.

Strained relations developed between Casement and some of the Whitehall officials who were probably annoyed at Casement taking so much of the limelight, he believed that he was distrusted by some of them. He was also annoyed - that as it appeared to him - the Foreign Office was taking too soft a line on the Congo atrocities with King Leopold 11 and the Belgian authorities. A Belgian Commission of Inquiry was established to investigate the Congo atrocities but Casement had little faith that it would produce an accurate or comprehensive report. In November 1905, the Commission did publish its Report, confirming and re-enforcing all of Casement's findings. It found that the administration of the Belgian Congo was *'a system of hardly restricted savagery'*. Casement could not have been more vindicated.

In recognition of his investigative work in the Congo, he was honoured in the 1905 Honours List, when he was made a Companion of the Order of St. Michael and St. George. This was the Order to which those who gave outstanding Foreign Service were traditionally admitted. He reluctantly decided to accept the Honour but decided not to attend the ceremony to accept the Honours, he made the excuse that he was in poor health. [While in his death cell at Pentonville Prison in 1916, he was officially requested to return the insignia awarded to him when he had been conferred with the Honour.]

Casement was dogged with poor health at this time. After completing his report on the Congo he returned to convalesce in Ireland where he had many loyal friends. It was during this period that he really became interested in Ireland's history, in Irish nationalism, in the Irish language, and became engrossed in the whole Irish question. He was very much influenced through close friendships with prominent Irish nationalists - Bulmer Hobson and P.S. O'Hegarty. Mrs Alice Green, who was a well-known author and resident in London was also a close friend of his. She was also well known for her Irish sympathies and had a very strong influence on him.

It was most likely during this period of convalescence that he developed a marked hatred for Colonialism throughout the world and everything that it entailed. In his book 'Roger Casement', the author Rene MacColl states-

"There seems little reason therefore, to doubt Casement when he wrote in prison that he became an all-out Separatist in 1905 - 1906. That period he spent in Ireland after his return from the Congo, re-indoctrinated him, so to say that when he returned to active Consular duties in the service of the Crown, he was to all intents, a fifth-columnist for Sinn Fein".

His relationships with the Foreign Office continued to be strained into 1906 but he was offered a number of Consular appointments again and there was a marked improvement in his health. He was obviously caught in a quandary between returning to the Consular service and remaining on in Ireland to get more involved with Irish nationalism. In later years he admitted that the only reason he returned to Consular duties was because he wanted the money and had no other means of earning a salary at the time.

INVESTIGATIONS IN THE PUTAMAYO REGION IN SOUTH AMERICA.

On resuming his duties with the Foreign Office he was appointed British Consul to Santos in Brazil. The appointment was for the entire Brazilian State of Sau Paulo, Santos was only a base. He did not like the posting, as it was a rough location and on his return to London in the latter part of 1907 he was offered the post of Consul at Haiti. The Foreign Office changed its mind on this decision at the last moment and he was assigned to Para, which was located at the mouth of the Amazon in Brazil. He also became unhappy with this location and on December 1st 1908 he was appointed Consul General in Rio de Janeiro. This was in reality a promotion for him.

The Putamayo River Basin which covers a considerable area, was in 1909, one of the greatest rubber producing areas in the world. The local South American Indians were being exploited in the rubber production. The area was ill - defined between the countries of Peru, Columbia, Brazil and Ecuador and there was no relevant law or Government to control the situation. The British Foreign Office began to take an interest, as some British subjects were victims of the exploitation and the company against whom the more serious allegations were being made had its headquarters in London. With a view to monitoring and keeping in touch with the situation, a British Consul was appointed to Iquitos, which is a land-locked city situated close to where the Putamayo River joins the Amazon.

In mid 1910, the British Government appointed a Commission of Inquiry to investigate the alleged abuse of workers in the rubber plantations of the Putamayo region. The members of the Commission were - Colonel the Hon. R.N. Bertie, Mr L.H. Barnes, an expert on tropical husbandry, Mr W. Fox, a rubber expert, Mr E.S. Bell, a businessman, and Mr H.K. Gielgud general secretary of the biggest rubber company in the region.

Casement was appointed to assist the Commission, when he completed a holiday to Ireland in the summer of 1910.

He travelled up the Amazon on a steamboat with the members of the Commission and on reaching Iquitos stopped over there for a fortnight. There they collected evidence from some of the workers on the rubber plantations. They examined the marks and weals on the bodies of the workers who presented themselves, the victims of savage assaults by their overseers. They continued on from Iquitios by boat along the Putamayo River and visited several villages in the jungle areas. There was no scarcity of evidence about the awful brutality suffered by workers. Thousands of witnesses came forward to relate their stories and show their scars and disfigurements to the members of the Commission. Casement had seen it all before in the Congo, but was nevertheless every bit as shocked as his colleagues at what he had seen and heard.

The weather was bad, the food was unpalatable and the accommodation available to them on the small steamer, was cramped and uncomfortable. Very strained relationships existed between Casement and Mr H.K. Gielgud, who was general secretary of the principal Rubber Company - (The Peruvian - Amazon Company) - whose activities were being investigated. While at Iquitos they set up their headquarters in a hotel, but the accommodation was of poor quality. Iquitos is a very primitive city with large sprawling poverty-stricken areas. There are no roads into or out of the city and the only access available is via the adjoining Putamayo and Amazon Rivers and more contemporarily through a small airport, which has been constructed there in recent years. The city and the adjoining Putamayo and Amazon regions are particularly badly infested with mosquitoes which also makes life difficult. The carrying out of the investigation in the region must have been a great ordeal for Casement and the other members of the Commission. In mid-November 1910 the Commission started on its homeward journey via the Putamayo River and the Amazon until they reached the Atlantic Ocean. Casement and the other Commission members then left for London where they arrived in January 1911.

The Commission submitted its report to the Foreign Office, it made grim reading! It gave details of murder, floggings, torture of various kinds, beatings with tapir-hide thongs, punishment by being tied to stocks for days, resulting in some people dying due to exposure or starvation. The Peruvian-Amazon Company, which was the biggest rubber producer in the area was condemned and held responsible for most of the abuse meted out to the workers. The Report was most compelling and comprehensive and was considered very seriously by the Foreign Office. The officials were obviously very conscious of the fact that the headquarters of the offending company was located in London.

The Foreign Office directed Casement to return to Iquitos and the Putamayo region, to further check and re-confirm the facts as the Commission had found them, before the British Government would publish the Report. He arrived back in Iquitos on October 30th 1911. He re-checked and confirmed his earlier findings relating to the widespread abuse of the rubber workers in the Putamayo region. He found some small improvement in the situation, but the Peruvians were in no hurry to completely rectify the blatant abuses of human rights. Casement was disappointed that the British Foreign Office wasn't taking a tougher line with those involved.

From Iquitos, Casement went to Washington, on the instructions of the Foreign Office, and made representations there for the appointment of a United States Consul to Iquitos. He had a meeting with President Taft at the White House and on January 29th 1912 he returned again to London. In May of the same year, the Foreign Office directed him to finalise his report on the Putamayo situation, which was published on July 17th in booklet form titled *'The Blue Book on Infamies in the Putamayo'*. It sold for one shilling and five pence per copy. There was a huge demand for it and it generated a lot of publicity.

The *'Times'* newspaper devoted an editorial to it, praising the great work done by Roger Casement. The Church of England and the Roman Catholic churches joined in the condemnation of the Putamayo atrocities, some churches considered setting up Missions in the Putamayo region. Casement was hailed as a hero - receiving the highest praise in Great Britain and the world at large for what he had achieved. It must have been the highest point of his career and he was glad to achieve something worth while regarding a major problem, which had greatly troubled him.

CONFERRED WITH A KNIGHTHOOD.

In June 1911, he was conferred with a Knighthood. On receipt of the notification that he had been so honoured, he wrote in acknowledgement to the Home Secretary Sir Edward Grey:-

"I find it very hard to chose the words in which to make acknowledgement of the honour done me by the King. I am much moved at the proof of confidence and appreciation of my services on the Putamayo, conveyed to me by your letter wherein you tell me that the King had been graciously pleased upon your recommendation to confer upon me the honour of Knighthood

"I am indeed grateful to you for this signal assurance of your personal esteem and support, and very deeply sensible of the honour done to me by His Majesty.

"I would beg that my humble duty might be presented to His Majesty, when you may do me the honour to convey to him my deep appreciation of the honour he has been so graciously pleased to confer on me."

"I am dear Sir Edward, Yours etc "

His humanitarian efforts earned him world – wide acclaim and recognition.

Following the publication of the Report, he spent most of the late summer and autumn in Ireland - except for brief trips back to London. On one of these trips back to London he gave evidence before a Parliamentary Select Committee on the Putamayo atrocities. Publicity and controversy relating to the matter dragged on during the months that followed and while the British Foreign Office did endeavour to remedy the situation, the issue became a very low priority once World War 1 commenced in 1914.

Casement's health was very poor and was the cause of much anxiety to himself and to his friends. He was persuaded to attend a specialist for medical examination, who found that he suffered from a number of complications. Another specialist in Tenerieffe confirmed that it would be injurious to his health if he returned to his Consular post in Rio de Janeiro. When he reported on this, to the Foreign Office he was placed on half pay and was most displeased at the lack of generosity by his authorities.

After the holiday in Tenerieffe in January 1913, he sailed to Capetown in South Africa, with the intention of trying to sort out the financial affairs of his brother Tom, who had a history of financial mismanagement of his business enterprises there. In South Africa, he found that he had great relief from the arthritis from which he suffered and the other medical problems, which caused him so much illness and pain. He returned to London during the following May, and came to Dublin to have his portrait painted by Miss Sara Purser. He entered into further correspondence about his future, with the Foreign Office and having furnished a suitable detailed medical report, he submitted a long letter tendering his resignation from the Consular Service. He stated that his health was now so permanently impaired that he had no hope of discharging his duties as Consul General in Rio. The final paragraph of his letter read

"I have to indeed express a very keen regret at severing my connection with a Service I have for so long been associated with and still more at severing ties with persons from whom I have so often and continuously received marks of such friendship and esteem that I shall not forget ".

RESIGNATION FROM THE CONSULAR SERVICE, AND RETURN TO IRELAND.

His application for early retirement on medical grounds with a suitable pension was accepted by the Foreign Office and in 1913, Sir Roger retired from the British Consular service and he returned to Ireland.

On returning to Ireland, he found that major changes had taken place over a short period of time. The granting of Home Rule to Ireland, had become a major issue but was being strenuously opposed by the Ulster Unionists.

CASEMENT IN CONNEMARA.

RIC Constable John Feeley who was stationed at Rosmuck in Connemara [Co Galway] recorded a most amusing story about a meeting which he had with Roger Casement there in May 1913. Constable Feeley accompanied by another constable named Hodgins decided to cut turf in a bog adjacent to their barracks - instead of performing their other official duties allocated to them for the day. Turf for the barrack fire during the next winter was their priority. They were enjoying the physical exercise and they were fairly confident that the District Inspector would not be in the area on that day. On seeing a motorcar approaching in their direction, they both dived for cover in the bog and regarded their position as very perilous. They had left the barracks unmanned in contravention of the RIC Regulations. They assumed that the car driver must have been an Inspector or officer when they saw the car stop outside their barracks. They watched a tall, well-dressed man climb stiffly down from behind the steering wheel and stand for some minutes looking at the entrance to the barracks. The stranger then left the car and entered the barracks and after some minutes came out, stood at the entrance for some time and looked around him. [He had correctly expected a policeman to be in the vicinity, as barracks were never left unmanned.]

Constables Feeley and Hodgins decided that it was better to face the consequences but by this time they were reasonably confident, that the stranger was not an officer as he did not wear uniform. As the two policemen came towards him, he met them with outstretched hand and introduced himself as Roger Casement. While it was a name of international renown it was hardly known in that remote part of Ireland.

Casement told the constables that he was on a tour of the west of Ireland and thought that the police with their excellent local knowledge would be able to give him some guidance on the next stage of his journey and be in a position to give him some information about the countryside and its people. He had a very long conversation with the constables and listened most attentively as they told him about the living conditions of the people around them and that their survival depended largely on the potato crop with some people supplementing their incomes making *'poteen'* or doing seasonal work in England. In reply, Casement said it was difficult to believe that people had survived in that region for centuries. He said that the depths of poverty he had seen, confirmed his impression that the land of Connemara wouldn't feed a Russian goat and it had shocked him. He was clearly appalled at the poverty of the area.

He expressed surprise at the number of policemen assigned to the district where crime was almost non-existent. With the urgency of the journey ahead of him he parted with the constables with a wave of his hand and conveyed his best wishes to them.

John Feeley described Casement as a tall man, well groomed, with a trim beard set on a handsome face, the most striking feature of which was his eyes. Neither John Feeley nor his fellow constable, were aware of Casement's international reputation at the time. They instantly remembered him and the conversation, which they had with him on that May morning in 1913, a few years later, when they received instructions to be on the lookout for him as he was wanted for alleged treasonable activity.

JOINING THE IRISH VOLUNTEERS AND INVOLVEMENT IN IRISH NATIONALISM.

Sir Roger was upset about the developments which had taken place in Northern Ireland, the founding of the Ulster Volunteers and the great latitude given to its two prominent leaders - Sir Edward Carson and F.E. Smith [otherwise known as Galloper Smith and who ironically at the Trial of Casement in 1916 was the prosecuting Attorney General]. He was also most concerned about the fact that a huge consignment of arms had been landed there to arm the same Volunteers. He wrote anonymously in the *'Irish Freedom'* - a paper edited by Bulmer Hobson who was a well-known Irish nationalist. He immersed himself in Irish affairs and his thoughts were that a British/German war was inevitable and that when it happened, it would be Ireland's opportunity to free herself from the Saxon regime.

In November 1913, the Sinn Fein Political Committee held a public meeting at the Rotunda in Dublin. Patrick Pearse was the principal speaker. Casement was present at the meeting, which was attended by a huge crowd. The Irish Volunteer movement was founded that night. From that point onwards, several thousand young men came forward to join the Irish Volunteers. Casement was one of the first to join.

On April 24th 1914, the Ulster Volunteers landed 40,000 German rifles at the ports of Larne, Donaghadee and Bangor in Northern Ireland, they were hastily dispersed all over Ulster, to units of the Ulster Volunteers. The British authorities took no action in connection with this flagrant breach of the law, and no action was taken against the leaders. The landing of this big consignment of arms in Ulster caused consternation and generated fear amongst the southern nationalists. The leaders of the Irish Volunteers felt it imperative that they should also seek a supply of guns to be in readiness in the event of an attack being made on them by the Ulster Volunteers.

Casement played his part and used his influence to raise money for the purchase of guns in Hamburg, for the purpose of arming the Irish Volunteers. These guns and a supply of ammunition, for them, were landed in Howth, Co Dublin, in July 1914 from the yacht *'Asgard'*, which had been skippered by Erskine Childers. The total consignment of weapons landed there was 1,500 rifles and 45,000 rounds of ammunition.

Arising from his writings and open support for Irish Nationalism, the

British Government ceased to pay Casement's pension from June 1914 onwards. He had visited London in May - for the last time before arriving there as a prisoner in 1916, - to give evidence to a Royal Commission set up by the Foreign Office enquiring into the operation of the Diplomatic and Consular Service.

When the Howth gun - running took place in July 1914, Casement was in the United States raising funds for the Irish Volunteers. On July 4th he travelled from Glasgow to Montreal and then by train to New York where he made contact with the veteran Fenian John Devoy, who was a native of Kill, Co Kildare, and who had spent several years in America. He was one of the leaders of Clann - na – nGael, which was an association having very close links with the Irish Republican Brotherhood [the I.R.B.]. Devoy had supported the cause of Irish nationalism all his life, and in the United States would have been the most influential person ready to support any fund raising efforts for the Irish cause. He was editor of the "Gaelic American" newspaper. From once World War One commenced, Devoy and Casement were of one mind that ' *England's difficulty was Ireland's opportunity'*.

Casement addressed several Irish/American groups, including the Ancient Order of Hibernians, on the Irish question. He was not a good orator, but people were anxious to see him and hear what he had to say, because he was such a well-known figure at the time.

John Devoy made representations to Count Von Bernstorff, the German Ambassador to the United States, seeking the assistance of the German Government to send a supply of arms and trained military officers to Ireland. Through an arrangement made by Devoy, Casement met Count Von Bernstorff in Washington and informed the Ambassador that Irish nationalists intended to use the opportunity presented by the War, to overthrow English Rule in Ireland and set up an independent government. These were the grounds, put forward by him, for seeking the supply of arms and trained military personnel from Germany.

While in the United States in September, 1914, Casement issued a statement stating that he was one of the founders of the Irish Volunteers, he bluntly told Irishmen that they should not join the British forces to fight against Germany. This statement was published in the American press and in the *'Irish Independent'* of October 5th with Casement's signature. From this point onwards he was a 'persona non grata' with the British Government and it was alleged that the British Secret Service offered a bribe of

£5,000 to a friend of Casement, named Christensen, if he would deliver Casement into their hands.

ARRIVAL IN GERMANY.

In furtherance of Devoy's representations, Roger Casement using the name 'James Landy', with credentials and documentation given to him by Count Von Bernstorff, sailed from New York to Germany on October 15th 1914. He also intended recruiting an Irish Brigade from amongst the Irishmen who were held in Germany as prisoners of war. He hoped that the German Government would equip this brigade and provide trained personnel to support it. He was obviously well received in Germany and wrote to Eoin MacNeill who was head of the Volunteers:

"I am entirely assured of the goodwill of the Government towards our country and beg you to proclaim it far and wide. They will do all in their power to help to win our national freedom".

Despite the foregoing note of optimism to MacNeill, the German authorities adopted a very cautious approach towards Casement. They were not impressed with his efforts to raise an Irish Brigade from amongst the Irish prisoners - of - war held there.

In fact, some of the German officials suspected him of being a British agent. Despite his best efforts, he only succeeded in recruiting 53 volunteers from amongst the several hundred prisoners of war being detained. The Germans let Casement know, at an early stage, that they had no intention of sending an expeditionary force to Ireland to fight for Irish freedom. Neither would they provide an officer to lead Casement's P.O.W. Brigade to Ireland. Casement then endeavoured to obtain an American officer to lead the brigade through John Devoy, but Devoy was unable to find a suitable person to undertake the task.

Casement then appealed to Tom Clarke, a prominent Fenian and the leader of the Irish Republican Brotherhood in Dublin. Clarke succeeded in getting a man named Robert Monteith to take on the responsibility. The latter was a Boer War veteran and one of the founder members of the Irish Volunteers. As a result of his activities with the Irish Volunteers he was dismissed from his position at the Ordnance Survey Office in the Phoenix Park, Dublin. He then moved to Limerick as a full-time Volunteer organiser. When arrangements were made for him to take control of the Irish Brigade, he moved with his family to the U.S.A. and from there he was smuggled on board a ship to Scandinavia. He met up with Casement in Munich on October 24th 1915, and took charge of the Irish Brigade. He found Casement in extremely poor health and he was really appalled at his condition, he also feared that Casement was suicidal at this particular time.

The German authorities informed Monteith, that following Devoy's representations to them for a supply of arms, they were prepared to accede to that request and provide arms for the expected rebellion in Ireland. Casement was very upset and displeased that the Germans had seen fit to give this information to Monteith rather than to himself. John Devoy was informed that the Germans would send a ship to Ireland with a cargo of arms, consisting of 20,000 rifles, ten machine guns, a large consignment of ammunition and some explosives. Monteith informed Casement that a definite date had been fixed for the Rebellion in Ireland. The Germans wanted to send Casement to Ireland with the arms consignment along with fifty members of the Irish Brigade. He rejected the idea as he believed that it would result in certain death for the men. In a letter to a friend in the German Foreign Office on March 30th 1916 he wrote:

"I am in this, a passive agent, powerless to act according to my judgement and with a course of action forced upon me that I wholly deprecate. I am being used as a tool for purposes of which I disapprove, by pressure that I am powerless to combat since I am practically a prisoner ".

On April 6th 1916, Casement was informed by telegram from Joseph Mary Plunkett [one of the leaders of the subsequent rebellion in Ireland] that the Irish Rebellion would begin on Easter Sunday and that the German arms should arrive in Tralee Bay not later than dawn on Easter Saturday. Plunkett also requested the service of a German submarine, which would be needed in Dublin Bay and that it was imperative that German military officers be provided for the Volunteers. Casement prepared a reply to Plunkett, which indicated that the proposed rebellion was doomed to failure, without more assistance from the Germans. He said that the Germans were sending only a token shipment of arms to Ireland. He had looked for ten times as many rifles as were being supplied. He also said that the German Government would not send submarines or army officers. It would appear that Plunkett never received this reply from Casement.

Casement clearly realised the hopelessness of the situation at this time, and it is believed that in his desperation to halt the mission that he endeavoured to convince two people to inform Mr. Asquith, the British Prime Minister, about what was taking place.

THE ILL - FATED "AUD" GUN - RUNNING.

Casement persuaded the Germans to send him to Ireland to prepare for the landing of the arms, which were due to be landed at Fenit pier County Kerry between April 20th and April 23rd 1916. The Germans asked for an Irish pilot boat to await the arms ship at dusk, north of Innishtooskert Island, at the entrance to Tralee Bay, and to show two green lights close to each other at short intervals.

The Germans put plans for the gun - running into operation and Captain Karl Spindler was selected to command the 1,400 ton vessel, the *'Libau'*. The vessel was originally British owned and known as the *'Castro'*, before the Germans seized it early in the 1914 *l'* 18 War. Captain Spindler went to Berlin to receive his instructions and he sailed with his crew and the *'Libau'* to Ireland on April 9th.

The vessel had Norwegian 'identity' and had a cargo of timber on board, to allay any suspicions, should the vessel be intercepted or boarded. The crew wore Norwegian Navy uniforms. When out at sea, the name *'Libau'* was obliterated and replaced with the name *'Aud-Norge'* in big letters and Norwegian flags were flown. The vessel was not fitted with radio transmitting or receiving facilities. It made the voyage to Tralee Bay without interception en route.

As he entered Tralee Bay, Captain Spindler made all the necessary arrangements on board the ship for unloading the cargo of guns at Fenit pier on April 20th, by way of preparing the winches and opening the hatches etc. The *'Aud'* went well into Tralee Bay but there was no pilot boat to meet it and no signals. It cruised around all day on Thursday of Holy Week, between Kerry Head and Fenit, frequently giving the signals expected from it but got no response. It moved out into the open sea at the mouth of the bay and dropped anchor for the night near Innishtooskert. Early on Friday, 21st April, the *'Aud'* was boarded by the crew of a British warship the *'H.M.S.Shatter 11'*. Captain Spindler and his crew succeeded in 'bluffing' it out as being of Norwegian origin and being a genuine tramp steamer with a cargo of timber aboard. From the ruddy face of the boarding captain, Spindler rightly concluded that he was partial to a strong drink and a serving of several strong drinks and good quality cigars assisted in getting over any problems relating to the disguise of the vessel.

Spindler's luck did not hold later on in the day when two other British warships gave chase to the *'Aud'* but his vessel had too much speed and got away in the chase. Another British warship *'H.M.S. Bluebell'*, took up the pursuit and directed Captain Spindler to proceed to Queenstown [now Cove, Co Cork]. The *'Aud'* slowed down considerably and was ordered by the *'Bluebell'* to increase its speed. As they approached the entrance to Cork Harbour, Spindler ordered his crew to don their German uniforms and to raise the German flag. Explosives and incendiary devices which had been strategically dispersed throughout the 'Aud's cargo were ignited and the resultant explosions shook the vessel from stem to stern before it disintegrated, taking its cargo of timber, 20,000 rifles, ten heavy machine guns, a large quantity of ammunition and explosives to the bottom of the Irish Sea, just outside Cork Harbour. Captain Spindler and his crew took to the lifeboats and raised the white flag before being taken into custody by the crew of the *'H.M.S. Bluebell'*. There were no casualties amongst the crewmembers. With the scuttling of the *'Aud'* and its cargo, the two-year long saga, of raising money to buy the weaponry and in convincing the Germans to bring the consignment to Ireland, ended dramatically and quickly at the mouth of Cork Harbour.

Captain Karl Spindler and his crew of twenty-one were taken into custody, spending the next two years in Britain. He spent most of his internment at Donington Hall. In July 1917, he escaped from the internment camp with another German officer who was also interned there at the time. Even though much thought and planning had been put into the daring escape, they were re-captured within a few days and returned to Donington Hall. As experienced by many German prisoners of war detained in England at that time, they found the internment very difficult - particularly in relation to the very poor quality of the food received. In accordance with the provisions of the Hague Convention of 1918, Captain Spindler and the other internees were exchanged for other prisoners and were transferred to Holland. They had completed over two years in captivity.

CASEMENT'S ARRIVAL IN IRELAND.

While the doomed voyage of the *'Aud'* was taking place to Fenit, Roger Casement acquired a submarine to bring him to Ireland, to make arrangements for the landing of the arms. The vessel was the German submarine 'U20'. He decided to take Captain Robert Monteith and Sergeant Julian Beverly - whose real name was Daniel Bailey - with him. The latter was a native of Dublin, who had served in the Royal Irish Rifles and who had been taken prisoner by the Germans in September 1914. He held the rank of private in the British Army, but was made a Sergeant when Casement formed the Irish Brigade in Germany. The 'U20' sailed from Wilhelmshaven on April 12th 1916. After two days, the vessel developed engine problems and had to return to port at Heligoland. Casement and the crew then transferred to another submarine the 'U19'.

Bad weather was encountered on the voyage and the 'U19' took five days to reach the West Coast of Ireland. The accommodation on board the submarine was very cramped and had bunks and space for only four naval officers, but there were now seven on board. Casement had very little sleep during his twelve nights on board the submarines. He was seasick for most of the voyage. The German naval officers did what they could to relieve Casement's discomfort, trying to cheer him up and giving him breadcrumbs and coffee. He was too weak to crawl through the hatch to take fresh air and the foul air and engine noise of the submarine were difficult to contend with. Bailey was also sea - sick during the journey. The *'Aud'* was already outside Tralee Bay when they arrived there, but as the 'Aud' had no radio equipment there was no contact between the vessels.

The German skipper of the 'U19' later recounted the final part of his voyage into Tralee Bay :

"When darkness set in, proceeded in to Loop Lighthouse. Lighthouse 11 p.m. abeam. Up to 12 o'clock, fierce squalls hindering manoeuvring for the time being. After midnight, weather and visibility improved with the rising moon. With boat clear for submergence, made for the pre-arranged rendezvous with steamer. One mile north west of Seven Hogs [Tralee Bay]. Neither pilot boat nor other vessel in sight. There remained no other alternative than landing with dinghy in Ballyheigue Bay. First, made for high-lying coast of Kerry Head, then entered bay as far as diving draught allowed. Launched dinghy. About 2.15 a.m., the dinghy with three Irishmen aboard set out for flat shore. Sea perfectly calm, little groundswell,

no wind, pale moonshine. After launching dinghy, immediately left bay by westerly course".

The 'U19' arrived off Banna Beach in the early hours of Good Friday – 21st April. A small boat [currently in preservation and on display at Ballyheigue Maritime Museum, Co Kerry] was launched through the conning tower of the submarine. Casement, Monteith and Bailey came ashore on to Banna Beach in the little boat and as they did so, the boat capsized, resulting in the clothes of all three occupants getting wet. They had no change of clothes. The beach was deserted as it was early a.m. John McCarthy, a local man, saw the boat and footprints of the three men on the beach shortly after 2 a. m. At Casement's subsequent trial, he gave evidence that he had gone to pray at a local Holy Well [which he had never visited previously] when he saw the boat and footprints on the sand. Mary O'Gorman, a young servant girl on a local farm, saw the three men - Casement, Monteith and Bailey - passing the farmhouse where she worked at 4.30 a.m. She brought the incident to the notice of a farmhand Tom Madden, who was having breakfast at the time.

Casement was in very poor physical shape following the submarine voyage and a decision was taken that he should remain in hiding in an old ring-fort, known locally as McKenna's Fort at Currahane, near Banna Beach. Monteith and Bailey decided to walk to Tralee, to get transport for Casement's conveyance from the ring-fort. Monteith had been in the Tralee area previously in the course of his activities as trainer of the Irish Volunteers.

Casement later wrote :

"When I landed in Ireland that morning I was happy for the first time in a year. Although I knew that this fate awaited me, I was for one brief spell happy and smiling once more. I cannot tell you how I felt. The sand-hills were full of skylarks rising in the dawn - the first I heard for years. This was the first sound I heard as I waded through the breakers and they were rising all the time to the old rath [fort] at Currahane. All around were primroses and wild violets and the singing of the skylarks in the air and I was back in Ireland again".

ARREST OF CASEMENT AND BAILEY.

Monteith and Bailey reached Tralee town, which is six miles from Banna Beach at 7 a.m. on that Good Friday morning. They did not know the identity of the local Volunteer leaders, nor where they resided. They took a local shopkeeper named George Spicer, who was open for the sale of newspapers into their confidence and shortly afterwards, got fixed up with a meal and a change of clothing. George Spicer sent a message to Austin Stack, the leader of the local Volunteers about the arrival of the two men, who wanted to see him. Stack was very slow in arriving and a further message had to be sent to him. When Stack arrived, Con Collins of Newcastlewest, Co. Limerick, who had been staying with him overnight accompanied him and it emerged that Con Collins knew Monteith very well. When Monteith and Bailey had related their story to Stack and Collins, a motorcar was procured for the purpose of collecting Casement from McKenna's Fort and Bailey went with Stack and Collins to the Banna Beach area. Due to a number of mishaps, search activities and checks being conducted by the Royal Irish Constabulary, the search for Casement proved fruitless. Stack, Collins and Bailey then went towards Ballyheigue in the motorcar and Bailey was left at a 'safe house' near Kilmoyley, where he stayed for the night.

On the following day - Easter Saturday - Bailey was arrested by the RIC near Abbeydorney and was taken to the local RIC station. While there, he offered to talk to Sergeant Restrick [RIC] in return for his immunity. District Inspector Frederick Britten of Tralee, travelled to Abbeydorney to interview him at 4 p.m. and Bailey gave him a complete account of how they had arrived at Banna Beach by submarine and about the arms ship expected to arrive at Fenit over the weekend with arms, ammunition and explosives, as well as details of the planned rebellion expected at the weekend. He made a long statement to D. I. Britten. Bailey was the man who completed the 'jig-saw' for the RIC and tied up all the strange events that were happening over the Easter weekend. District Inspector Britten conveyed the information received by him from Bailey by telephone to Dublin Castle.

Bailey was detained in custody and went on to trial at the Old Bailey, after he had given incriminating evidence at the Casement trial. The Volunteers thereafter regarded Bailey as 'traitor'.

[For further information relating to D. I. Britten – see Appendix A.]

Robert Monteith stayed in Tralee overnight on Friday night and on Saturday night, he attended a meeting of the local Volunteers at their headquarters in *'The Rink'* in Tralee, which was about 300 metres from the RIC police headquarters. Austin Stack had been arrested during the afternoon when he called to Tralee RIC Station. Paddy Cahill who was Adjutant of the Tralee Volunteers, refused to take charge of the Volunteers in Stack's absence and suggested that Monteith should do so. Despite the latter's natural objections to doing so, he was prevailed upon to take charge of the Volunteers from Tralee and adjoining areas. For Monteith who was a virtual stranger in the town, the decision was indeed a strange one and he found himself in a very difficult situation. He was not aware of the final plans, which had been prepared over several weeks prior to that relating to the expected landing of arms at Fenit and their subsequent dispersal. The final arrangements had been made by Stack and kept secret by him and he was now in custody. Monteith failed to locate any boatman to take a boat out to Tralee Bay to act as pilot boat for the arms shipment. There was only one map of the Tralee area available and this was out of date. There were about 500 military personnel and 200 armed police in the area at the time. Neither was he aware of what final plans the Volunteer Headquarters in Dublin had for the expected Rebellion.

Early on Sunday morning he sent out scouts to Fenit and Ardfert, to look out for the arms ship and arranged for other volunteer scouts to patrol Tralee town. Contingents of Volunteers marched in from Dingle [30 miles away] and Ballymacelligott, in accordance with arrangements made by Austin Stack earlier in the week.. Lieut Patrick Whelan of the Limerick Volunteers, brought word that Volunteer H.Q. in Dublin had called off all activities for Easter Sunday. To justify the mobilisation of the Volunteers who numbered about 300, they were drilled in a nearby field until darkness fell. The different contingents were then dismissed and directed to return to their bases. Monteith knew that the RIC and military were looking for him and he handed back control of the Volunteers to Adjutant Paddy Cahill. Monteith left *'The Rink'* in disguise, marching with the Ballymacelligott Volunteers and stayed in Ballymacelligott overnight. He remained in hiding in different locations for some time in Counties Kerry and Limerick before being successfully smuggled on board a ship leaving for the United States, he was never caught up with by the British authorities or charged with any offence.

John McCarthy who had seen the abandoned boat and footprints on the sand on Banna Beach early on Good Friday morning, returned to the scene later in the morning, accompanied by his neighbour Pat O'Driscoll. He found three revolvers and a tin box containing 900 rounds of ammunition near the abandoned boat. When on his way to Ardfert Creamery later on in the morning, he reported what he had found at the RIC station in Ardfert. From there, Sergeant John Thomas Hearn and Constable Robert Larke cycled to Banna Beach to check the abandoned boat. In the course of local enquiries, the policemen heard that Mary O'Gorman had seen three men coming from the area where the boat was abandoned before dawn that morning. They realised that this was no ordinary case of a boat being abandoned or washed up by the tide and Sergeant Hearn returned to his station to collect his carbine [rifle] and to get assistance. Constable Larke remained with the boat to preserve the scene. Sergeant Hearn accompanied by Constable Bernard O'Reilly returned fully armed to the area to continue the search for the strange men.

Casement had spent almost twelve hours in McKenna's fort when Constable O'Reilly found him hiding there at 1.20 p.m. The constable called Sergeant Hearn to his assistance, while keeping Casement covered with his carbine. Casement assured him that he was not armed and by way of explanation for his presence there, stated that he was out fishing and got lost in the fog. He gave his name as *'Roger Morton'* and his address as *'The Savoy, Denham, Buckinghamshire, England'* and stated that he was an author. He rather foolishly stated that he had left Dublin by train at 8 a.m. that morning - making it impossible for him to be in Banna Beach by that time. He had no documentation on him to verify his identity. Sergeant Hearn was not convinced by any of Casement's replies, he observed that the legs of Casement's trousers were wet and that he had sand on his shoes, he decided to take Casement to Ardfert RIC station for questioning.

Sergeant Hearn got a local boy named Martin Collins, who happened to be on the road at the time with a pony and trap, to convey Casement to Ardfert as he [Casement] was very weak and barely able to walk. En route to Ardfert they stopped at the house where Mary O'Gorman worked, she confirmed that Casement was one of the three men she had seen earlier that morning, coming from the area where the boat had been abandoned. Young Collins had observed Casement dropping some pieces of paper on to the ground from behind his back, before he got into the trap. He later returned to that spot, retrieved the torn pieces of paper and took them to the RIC station at Ardfert. These pieces of paper later turned out to be a

Code, which Monteith had given to Casement, to which a lot of attention was paid in Casement's subsequent trial. Sergeant Hearn formally charged and arrested Casement as follows -

"In the name of His Majesty, King George the Fifth, I arrest you on a charge of illegally bringing arms into this country, contrary to the Defence of the Realm Act".

District Inspector Frederick Britten of Tralee, directed that Casement should be removed to the RIC Headquarters Station at Tralee.

A horse-drawn sidecar, which had been despatched from the RIC H.Q. in Tralee, was used to remove Casement in the custody of two armed RIC men to Tralee shortly before 3 p.m. on that afternoon. It was a six - mile journey from Ardfert to Tralee. At the latter station, District Inspector Britten questioned Casement for some time but he did not disclose his identity nor did he give any information of an incriminating nature to the District Inspector. Casement was clean-shaven, and at this time the police were clearly ignorant about his identity, there was no indication or clue as to who he really was or what his exact mission was. In the course of a careful search of Casement's clothing, a German rail ticket, for a rail journey between Berlin and Wilhelmshaven was found. This document also became an exhibit at the subsequent trial.

4

AUSTIN STACK AND THE RISE OF THE VOLUNTEERS IN KERRY.

AUSTIN STACK'S CHILDHOOD AND EARLY CAREER.

Austin Stack was born at Ballymullen, Tralee, Co Kerry, on December 7th 1879. His full baptismal name was Augustine Mary Moore Stack. He had five sisters and two brothers, he was the third eldest. The family moved to another house in the locality when he was ten years old. He received his primary education at the Moyderwell Convent School and at the Christian Brothers Schools at Edward Street, Tralee. His father Moore Stack worked as a law - clerk with Maurice J.Horgan, Solicitor, Tralee. Moore Stack [Austin's father] had strong nationalist sympathies and in 1881 he was jailed for one year for offences connected with the Land War. In 1889, when Austin was ten years old, the family was hit by tragedy, when his mother died. After her death the family moved again to a smaller house at Pembroke Street, Tralee. Part of this house was run as a shop.

The family found it difficult to make ends meet, as Moore Stack had become unemployed as a solicitor's clerk and had gradually become an alcoholic. When aged fourteen-and-a-half years, Austin left school and got a job as a solicitor's clerk with John O'Connell, Solicitor, Nelson Street, Tralee. The girls in the family kept the home together but when they emigrated to the U.S.A. Austin and his brother Nicholas, went in to lodgings at Strand Street, Tralee. They were the only two members of the family left in Ireland. Some years later, Austin changed lodgings to the home of Miss Elizabeth Slattery, Rock Street, Tralee. He resided at this address from 1912 until his arrest on Good Friday 1916.

As a young man, he was described as being shy and reserved. Under his father's influence he joined the local Young Ireland Society and the Irish National Foresters. Studying history was one of his great hobbies. He was interested in gymnastics and in the games promoted by the Gaelic Athletic Association. In 1901 he was co-founder of the John Mitchel Gaelic Athletic Club in Tralee town, becoming its first secretary. The club won the County Kerry Senior Football Championship for eight years in a row from 1902 until 1909. He was selected on the County Kerry Senior

Football team in 1902. He was on the All-Ireland Kerry winning teams of 1903 and 1904 and captained the 1904 County team to All-Ireland victory. He became well known all over Ireland through his Gaelic football activity. As well as being an active Club Secretary and player, he also became involved in the administration at county level and was secretary of the County G.A.A Board from 1904 to 1908.

During the early 1900s he was involved with the Tralee Branch of the Gaelic League. He was sworn in by Cathal Brugha as a member of the *'Irish Republican Brotherhood'* [the I.R.B.] in 1908 and from then onwards was the 'head centre' - or chief organiser - for County Kerry. With others, he continued to recruit, secretly, for the organisation and by 1913 had ten 'centres' with ten members in each 'centre' in the county. They were visited occasionally by Cathal Brugha and Major John McBride who were leaders of the I.R.B. but there was little work or responsibility for them during the early years of the organisation. He was also a member of the Irish Club in Tralee, which promoted the use of the Gaelic language and Irish culture.

Following a decision taken by Professor Eoin MacNeill, Patrick Pearse and others in Dublin, in November 25th 1913, to form the Irish Volunteers, a meeting was held in the Tralee County Hall on December 10th 1913, to consider forming a branch of the Irish Volunteers in Tralee. A further meeting was held to accept recruits for the organisation and Austin Stack was one of the first to join. With other members of the I.R.B., he had been very instrumental in getting recruits for the new Volunteer organisation. Big numbers enrolled from Tralee town and its outskirts, and it was necessary to form four companies to cater for the town area. Branch members of the Fianna Eireann organisation, which had existed in Tralee since 1911, also joined the Irish Volunteers. Each volunteer contributed one old penny weekly. They met regularly for drilling, parades, some firearm training and route marches. Concerts and fund-raising events were held to raise funds. Around the end of January 1914 they acquired an old roller-skating rink at Basin View, Tralee, for their meetings and this became the permanent home for the organisation and was known as *'The Rink'*.

HEAD CONSTABLE KEARNEY'S OBSERVATIONS ON THE VOLUNTEER ACTIVITIES.

Head Constable Kearney who had arrived in Tralee before the formation of the Irish Volunteers later recorded the origin and growth of the organisation as follows:-

"In 1912 -'13, the question of Home Rule for Ireland was much debated in Parliament. All the people throughout the country were much keyed up over the question. The R.I.C also followed the debates in Parliament with the utmost keenness. Almost to a man, the rank and file were followers of John Redmond M.P. the head of the Nationalist Party.

"The Liberal Party were in office and their leader Mr Asquith K.C. was the Prime Minister. Mr Churchill was a Minister in the Government. If my memory serves me right he was the First Lord of the Admiralty.

"The Irish Nationalist Party, I believe to a man were true Imperialists and loyal to the King and Empire.

"There was at this time a small clique in Ireland of Clann-na-Gael who were Republicans. But there were never more than thirteen on the police list, which was known as the 'B' List. They were non-entities.

"Arthur Griffith tried to form a party called Sinn Fein at this time, on the Hungarian principle to abstain from entry to the English House of Commons. He was a candidate for election in Co Leitrim, I believe, and the candidate opposing the Nationalist was completely defeated.

"Sir Edward Carson was the leader in Northern Ireland who strongly opposed Home Rule. Eventually early in 1914 the Home Rule Bill was passed in the House of Commons and the House of Lords for the whole of Ireland. The overwhelming majority of the people in Ireland were satisfied with it.

"Now an extraordinary thing happened. Sir Edward Carson K.C. and 'Galloper' Smith - afterwards Lord Birkenhead - two potential Prime Ministers, landed a cargo of guns from Germany into the Port of Larne for the purpose of arming the Orangemen of Northern Ireland to oppose by force the Home Rule Bill.

"The arms were quickly distributed all over Ulster and training in their use became the order of the day. There is no doubt whatever about it that the Ulster Volunteers were determined to a man to fight to prevent this Act

of the Imperial Parliament becoming the law of the land in Ulster. It was strange. To me and the R.I.C. generally, whose duty it was to enforce the law as we found it, whether the people liked it or not - we as a Force did our duty, except in this particular case in the North.

"The cargo of arms from Germany were landed and distributed without any apparent interference by the police. As a matter of fact, the District Inspector who was in charge of Larne - although passed over long before this for incompetence - was promoted subsequently to be County Inspector. Why? He failed in his duty. Out there was an old saying in the R.I.C. 'Watch how the cat jumps'. If this happened in Cork or any port in the South, well there would have been lives lost and the arms and ship captured. Of course any one with half an eye saw there was one law for the North and another for the South. If determined steps were not taken in such circumstances in the South, the police authorities concerned and proved to have neglected their duties would simply be wiped out of the service. Not so in the North. Why?

"A Royal Irish Constabulary officer said to me 'Oh Carson and Smith are wonderful, we won't have Home Rule now and our jobs are safe'.

'Do you really believe that now, 'I asked.

'Of course I do – don't you'?, he said

'Do you think that that an Act of Parliament passed in the British House of Commons and House of Lords is not going to be enforced because two men, Carson and Smith arm a crowd of hooligans in the North with German arms to prevent its enforcement'

He hummed and he hawed, but could give no answer.

I asked 'Well if the Home Rule Bill is thus prevented from becoming – as it should be now - the law of the land, I at all events never read nor heard anything like it in British History. A precedent will be established which is likely to have many repercussions'

'Well' he said 'What's going to happen now anyway?'

'The South' I said 'will certainly arm now'.

'Oh we won't permit them' he replied.

'What' I said 'we won't permit them but we permitted Ulster and what is sauce for the goose is sauce for the gander. We certainly would prevent them from arming if Ulster had not already armed'.

'Do you think the South will arm '? he asked

'Yes' I replied 'within a few weeks there will be thousands of Volunteers armed in the South'.

"I was quite right. In a few weeks time thousands of National Volunteers were in military training all over the South. Arms were coming into the country from many sources. John Redmond introduced some from Italy and Mr Childers [an Englishman] landed a cargo at Howth.

"In Tralee, the volunteers were a splendid body of men and on many occasions I drilled them and taught them how to use their guns. Regular, or rather ex Regimental Officers all over the country - both North and South - in command on both sides.

The National Volunteers were fitted out with a light green uniform. They looked very smart and it was quite an easy matter to train them as soldiers. They were full of enthusiasm and the national spirit was never so high throughout the country.

"If the North attacked, well we in the South would have done our duty and none more so than the R.I.C. who of course saw that 'right' was on this side – the enforcement of an Act of Parliament".

DEVELOPMENT OF THE VOLUNTEERS FROM 1914.

There was no scarcity of young men to join the Volunteers in Tralee or Co Kerry, and their greatest display of strength and numbers was evident at the big parades which were held regularly. On June 14th 1914, a parade of about 2,000 Volunteers, drawn from Tralee and the other towns and villages in North and West Kerry, paraded in Tralee, the parade was reviewed by Captain Maurice Talbot Crosbie of Ardfert [a member of the local aristocracy and a former Captain in the British Forces].

Patrick Pearse, who was deputising for Professor Eoin MacNeill inspected a parade, which was held six weeks later. A month further on - on July 27th - there was another parade of about 700 Volunteers. This parade was to celebrate the Howth gun -running, which had taken place on the previous day, when a consignment of arms and ammunition for the use of the Volunteers was successfully landed from the yacht *'Asgard'*, under the command of Erskine Childers. A further small consignment of arms and ammunition was landed from another yacht at Kilcoole, Co Wicklow on August 1st 1914.

Austin Stack was deeply involved with the Volunteers in Tralee and Co Kerry, from the outset. Due to his popularity as a Gaelic Athletic player and administrator, and the fact that he was an All-Ireland Gaelic football winning captain, he was looked upon by all those around him as being a leader of men. He was instrumental in organising the Irish Republican Brotherhood and the Volunteers. By the end of July 1914, he was openly regarded as being the leader of all the Tralee Volunteers.

From the commencement of the First World War the recruiting of young men for the British Forces became an issue. The Volunteers from Tralee and elsewhere, objected to men joining these forces. Nevertheless, the initial recruiting campaign was a resounding success according to Head Constable Kearney.

"Recruits rolled in, in large numbers to join the Royal Munster Fusiliers. The Home Rule Bill was shelved till after the War. This of course had a reaction amongst the people. It affected recruiting for the army in no small way. Many of the sensible people shook their heads and said 'Well! It is another case of leaving Ireland in the lurch'.

John Redmond M.P., the veteran leader of the Irish Party at the Westminster Parliament made a speech at Woodenbridge, Co Wicklow on September 24th 1914, in the course of which he urged all the National Volunteers to fight for Britain in the War. Professor MacNeill and other officers of the Volunteer movement rejected the call and about 11,000 volunteers from around the country sided with them. About 70,000 remained loyal to John Redmond and these became identified as the 'National Volunteers'. Those who stayed with MacNeill became known as the 'Irish Volunteers' or more commonly the 'Sinn Fein Volunteers'. Many of the Volunteers in Tralee and County Kerry led by Austin Stack sided with MacNeill. The drilling, training and parading of the Irish Volunteers under Stack continued in Tralee and throughout Kerry during the remainder of 1914 and through 1915.

The RIC Confidential Report furnished for Co Kerry in respect of 1914 stated that:

"The National Volunteers at the beginning of the year had a membership of 4,202 of whom 1,008 were Sinn Feiners. At the end of the year the membership had fallen to 2,800, including 273 Sinn Feiners. In the interval, the

Irish Volunteers had come into existence, and at the end of December, they had a membership of 960. The National Volunteers were inactive during the year and membership of the body was merely nominal. On the other hand, the Irish Volunteers showed great activity, especially during the latter part of the year and allied themselves to a certain extent with the labour party. On 31st October a public meeting was held in the town of Tralee to protest against the dismissal of Mr J.O'Connor, a prominent Trade Unionist and Sinn Feiner, by a local business man, for an anti-recruiting speech made by him on the previous Sunday. W.P.Partridge of Liberty Hall, was brought down specially from Dublin to speak at the meeting. He made a very violent anti-recruiting speech on the occasion, and started a campaign to form a local branch of the Transport Union in connection with which he subsequently held a number of meetings. The visits of Partridge led to considerable unrest amongst the labouring classes at Tralee and Fenit. Arising out of the movement a number of workmen were dismissed from an establishment in Tralee for their Sinn Fein tendencies".

Sean McDermott, one of the leading members of the I.R.B and the Irish Volunteers addressed the Volunteers in Tralee in November 1914. Following that meeting, he met with Stack and all the I.R.B. officers from the area. He told them, that he had more confidential matters to relay to them. He told them -

"Nationalism as known to Tone and Emmett is almost dead in the country and a spurious substitute, as taught by the Irish Parliamentary Party, exists. The generation now growing old is the most decadent generation nationally since the Norman invasion and the Irish patriotic spirit will die forever unless a blood sacrifice is made in the next few years. The spark of nationality left is the result of the sacrifice of the Manchester Martyrs nearly half a century ago. It will be necessary for some of us to offer ourselves as martyrs if nothing better can be done to preserve the Irish national spirit and hand it down unsullied to future generations".

The Irish Republican Brotherhood was the main organisation involved in organising the Irish Rebellion. It was a very militant organisation and had its roots in the unsuccessful Fenian Rebellion of 1867. Its numbers were limited, but it diligently nurtured the Irish Volunteers along the same path, to make a force with numbers when the time came.

Patrick Pearse was in Tralee one month later, inspecting a parade of about 500 Irish Volunteers in the Sports Field at Tralee. The Manchester

Martyrs - William Allen, Michael Larkin and Michael O'Brien, who were executed forty-eight years earlier, for the shooting of a policeman in Manchester, whilst trying to effect the rescue of Fenian prisoners - were being commemorated on that occasion. In February 1915, Earnan De Blaghd, [Ernest Blythe], inspected a drill session of the Volunteers at *'The Rink'* and said that they were the best Volunteers he had seen up to that time, complimenting the leader Austin Stack and his Adjutant Paddy Cahill.

A section of the National Volunteers [who had sided with John Redmond M.P.] remained in existence in Tralee, and at different locations in County Kerry in late 1914 and through 1915, but their numbers gradually dwindled, they had very few firearms and were badly equipped. During 1915, 178 of the National Volunteers in Kerry joined the British forces and 354 others joined who were not Volunteers. At the St. Patrick's Day Parade in 1915, about 300 Irish Volunteers turned out and they were fully armed with rifles and shotguns. About 100 National Volunteers paraded on the same occasion, but they had few firearms and were not turned out as well. A local Member of the British Parliament – Mr Tom O'Donnell – who had a great loyalty to John Redmond, did everything he could to promote the National Volunteers in Tralee and West Kerry, by holding meetings and campaigning for recruits. He met with huge opposition from the Irish Volunteers led by Austin Stack. Despite his best intentions and loyalty to Redmond, Tom O'Donnell eventually became ostracised and lost his battle to promote the National Volunteers.

In September 1915, Stack and other officers of the Irish Volunteers from Co Kerry, participated in a training camp near Athlone, Co Westmeath. Volunteer Officers from other counties also attended - including some who would become well known as national leaders all over Ireland, within a few years, and others who would face execution after the 1916 Rebellion. Patrick Pearse visited Tralee shortly afterwards, and appointed Austin Stack as Brigadier over all the Kerry Volunteers. He told Stack that a Rebellion had been decided upon. It was also decided at that meeting that having considered all the port facilities in County Kerry, Fenit port [situated six miles from Tralee] would be the most suitable location to bring arms ashore for the Rebellion.

Some employers in Tralee town dismissed employees who were actively involved with the Irish Volunteers. Austin Stack lost his Government post as a part-time tax collector in March 1915. However, he did retain his position as a senior law - clerk in Dr O'Connell's Law Office in the town.

Head Constable Kearney was obviously keeping a close eye on the development and progress of both the Irish' and 'National' Volunteers through 1914 and 1915 and from his view of the situation he summed it up as follows:-

"A breach came in the National Volunteers. The followers of John Redmond, notwithstanding the shelving of the Home Rule Bill still with him regarded the Home Rule Bill as just a postponement of the measure.

"But a strong element was at work which eventually disrupted the Volunteers The Sinn Fein party formed their own contingent in Tralee and Austin Stack was appointed Commandant. The National Volunteers still carried on and many of them joined the British army.

"Often I watched both Volunteer groups on their route marches. Strange in Tralee, the National Volunteers were men of splendid physique - somewhat older than the Sinn Fein Volunteers who on the whole were of much poorer physique than the National Volunteers.

"We - the R.I.C. - were really brothers-in-arms of the National Volunteers and as time went on, the Sinn Fein Volunteers became sour and bitter towards us. Their numbers too increased and they took as strong a hand as they could against recruiting for the British Army.

"The National Volunteers gradually decreased in numbers. But on the other hand, those who had not enlisted in the British Army were staunch supporters of the Empire at war with Germany.

"The Sinn Fein Volunteers continued training – and for the most part were well –armed - much better armed than the National Volunteers who had old Italian rifles – practically of no use whatsoever. These rifles were known as 'John Redmond Rifles' and the Sinn Feiners held them up to ridicule.

"The Sinn Feiners were mostly armed with Martini Henry rifles, grooved for the .303 cartridges and each had a bayonet. Their uniforms consisted of a green tunic and trousers, valise, haversack and the usual peak cap. Each volunteer had two hundred rounds of ammunition. Their turn - out on route marches was smart and did make a 'good show' with their piper's band. In Tralee alone there were about 150 Sinn Fein Volunteers and in the country around there were about 600 strong.

"The Sinn Fein organisers sent two Belfast men to organise Kerry. Both

I understand had been Orangemen but were converted [really so] to Sinn Fein. They were undoubtedly men of character and determination. It was fun to watch old Sergeant George Neazer shadowing them when they'd visit Tralee. They would turn a corner quickly, George would stop up and look around - not one in sight. Then a low whistle or a sharp shout from the opposite direction from which George was looking and there were the two heads peeping around the corner, which George had just left. It was a game of 'Hide and go seek'. Much to George's delight I stopped the 'shadowing' and this gave him a rest.

"*They were active, extremely popular with the Sinn Feiners and more thorough and successful in their organisation - much more so than we would wish. Both of them studied the Irish language and could speak it - I was told - very fluently.*

"*Ernest Blythe, a Methodist was really 'Number One'. The other, Alfred W. Cotton was Church of Ireland. There were many Protestants in the movement and as far as the police knew they were sincere in their convictions. Mr Blythe took part in the Dublin Rebellion of 1916 and was subsequently Finance Minister in the Cosgrave Government*".

THE BUILD - UP TOWARDS 1916.

The number of Irish Volunteers continued to grow in County Kerry into 1916 and by the spring of that year there were six battalions, totalling 600 men in the district. The number of rifles held by the Irish Volunteers at this time was almost 400. On February 26th [1916], Patrick Pearse visited Tralee and reviewed a parade of about 250 Volunteers in the Sports Field. Later on the same day he delivered a lecture at 'The Rink' on the '*The Nature of Irish Freedom*'. On the same day he told Stack and Fr. Joseph Breen, C.C. - a priest who acted as Chaplain to the Volunteers - at a private meeting of the plans, which had been made by the Irish Republican Brotherhood, for an Insurrection in April. He also informed them that there would be a landing of arms at Fenit either on Easter Sunday or Easter Monday and that the Tralee Volunteers would be responsible for seeing that they were landed safely and distributed amongst the Kerry Volunteers and to the Volunteers from the adjoining counties.

At the St Patrick's Day parade in Tralee, the Volunteers paraded in full strength. Towards the end of March – just a month before the Easter Rising - Stack took his Adjutant Paddy Cahill into his confidence. He told him that a Rebellion was planned for Easter Sunday 23rd April and that a consignment of arms were to be landed at Fenit Pier on the same night and he outlined to him how the arms were to be distributed. He cautioned Cahill that no shot was to be fired before then to ensure that the authorities would not be put on their guard. Stack swore Cahill to secrecy, but he did not divulge the detailed plans he had personally made for the final operation of landing the arms and distributing them.

Stack went to Castlegregory [on the south side of Tralee Bay] to organise the manning of a pilot boat, to guide the ship bringing the arms consignment from Germany into Tralee Bay and to Fenit Pier. He also arranged for the collection of two signalling lamps from Sean McDermott in Dublin. Miss Kathleen O'Brien brought the lamps to Tralee. Arrangements were also made to have a wireless transmitter and receiver set up at Ballyard near Tralee for the purpose of communicating with the '*Aud*' as it entered Tralee Bay. Michael Collins along with others made this arrangement during the week prior to Easter. Had the latter temporary wireless station been put in place, it would have been a pointless exercise as the 'Aud' had no wireless transmitter or receiver.

During late 1915 and the early months of 1916, Austin Stack put a massive effort into the recruiting, drilling, parading and training of the Irish Volunteers in North and West Kerry. He also managed to acquire firearms to the point - where according to the confidential Police Reports submitted by the County Inspector of the RIC in Tralee to Dublin Castle - that the Volunteers were armed with 396 rifles and 273 shotguns. The increased Volunteer activity came under the close scrutiny of the RIC and regular confidential reports were furnished on a monthly basis. Stack's movements were also closely monitored and reported on during this time and while the extent of his involvement in the organisation was known to the RIC he was never arrested or brought in to the police station in Tralee for questioning before Easter 1916. Other high-ranking members of the organisation had been arrested for miscellaneous breaches of the '*Defence of the Realm*' Act and they served terms of imprisonment during the same period.

In relation to the months leading up to Easter 1916, Head Constable Kearney made the following observations about the Sinn Fein Volunteers and their leaders:

"The Sinn Fein Volunteers still retained their numbers. There was no falling off but at the same time they were losing any little popularity which they had.

"James Connolly - a noted Labour Leader - from Dublin, at this time visited Tralee and addressed a public meeting in the Town Square in Tralee. He was a good speaker with plenty of logic. I remember one sentence of his speech "Let those who hold any land or property in the Empire - I say let them fight for it - but you have or hold nothing, why should you fight?" Connolly was a bold determined character who feared nothing. His speech had an effect. Recruits as a result of Connolly's speech joined in some numbers the Sinn Fein Volunteers.

"The Sinn Fein Volunteers were almost to a man those who were 'Have Nots' while on the other hand the National Volunteers were those who 'Have'.

"From week to week they became more efficient, more well - equipped and certainly showed up well in long marches and military manoeuvres. To the R..I..C. they were sour and cheeky. They certainly had 'Heart' but the point was what of their leader?

"Cahill who was Stack's second in command was also a dour determined character. But to the police it seemed doubtful whether he knew how far the movement would take him. However, the police had no doubt of his courage – but his initiative was said to be small indeed. Nevertheless he was a man to be reckoned with.

"O'Connor was quite in the dark as to the future or where he was going. This didn't matter as he was no leader of any consequence. He lacked the essentials of leadership.

"Stack was efficient, but the point was, would he act when the 'crucial time' came. He would, if he hadn't a yellow streak. To me, he seemed cool and determined, a man of action - with little to say, which meant he was a good conspirator. Of course, a leader like him was really sitting on a gunpowder barrel, which may blow up at any time, and therefore, he must be prepared to take the consequences. He must have known the position, otherwise he'd be a fool. From all of this, it would appear that he was prepared to sacrifice his life unless at the last moment his heart failed him.

"To me anyway at this time, I was certainly of the opinion that he was a born leader and that he had made up his mind to face the consequences *whatever they'd be – death or otherwise.*

"Therefore, he was a dangerous man and everything pointed him out as a clever and bold conspirator. I certainly at this time had a great deal of respect for him."

Little did Kearney know or conceive at this time, what destruction and upset Austin Stack would bring on him and his family six years later.

THE FINAL PREPARATIONS BY THE KERRY VOLUNTEERS FOR EASTER WEEK.

Austin Stack presided at the weekly meetings of the Volunteers in Tralee on the 10th and 17th April 1916. Arrangements were made for the mobilisation of all Volunteers in Tralee and in North and West Kerry for Easter Sunday. The plans discussed related to the taking over of Ballymullen Army Barracks in Tralee, the RIC barracks, the post office and Telegraph centre and the take-over of the railway station. Train drivers and firemen were being organised to take a train to Fenit Pier, to collect the bulk of the arms being landed there and convey them by train to Limerick. Lots of arrangements were made but due to Stack's over zealousness about keeping things, secret the arrangements made were very loose in nature. And there was a marked absence of specifics. The train drivers, firemen and railway signalmen would have had the most critical role in any planned operation, but a meeting with them was only arranged to take place on Easter Sunday morning. Due to the developments over the weekend the meeting did not take place.

In fairness to Stack and the other Volunteer leaders in Tralee, it appears that, at no time had they any advance warning or prior notice about the arrival of Casement, Monteith or Bailey in a German submarine at Banna Beach or in County Kerry.

The arrival of the submarine with Casement, Monteith and Bailey was a surprise element and had not been planned for.

On Good Friday morning, while Stack was having breakfast at his lodgings with a friend - Mr Con Collins, from Newcastlewest, Co Limerick, - who had arrived in Tralee on Holy Thursday night, a messenger arrived who was the son of a shopkeeper named Spicer from Dominick Street, Tralee. The messenger told him that a man who had given his name as Murray and another man were in his father's shop at Dominick Street and wanted to see Stack urgently. Stack told him that he would be there in about an hour. The distance between Stack's lodging and Spicer's shop would have been about one quarter of a mile. When young Spicer told Monteith that Stack would be there in an hour, Monteith sent him back to Stack, to tell him that he should come immediately. [Stack later explained that he feared that the situation might have been a trap for him.] Stack and Collins arrived at Spicer's shop some time later and Con Collins - who was a member of the I.R.B and a Volunteer officer - recognised Monteith immediately. Over the next hour Stack and Collins conversed with Monteith and Bailey in private, the latter two related their account of landing at Banna Beach from a German submarine earlier that morning and that Casement was still in hiding at Banna Beach.

Stack later wrote about what Monteith had told him:-

"Monteith told me what purported to be the view of Casement with regard to the Rising itself, and this was that the attempt would be pure madness at the moment, that he had determined to come to Ireland to put his views before the leaders at home, and that if he failed to persuade them he would do his duty as an Irish Volunteer and go out and fight with the others".

The R.I.C. Station at Moyvoughley where John A. Kearney was born.

The Old school at Moyvoughley where John A. Kearney's mother taught.

R.I.C. Constable Thomas Kearney – father of John. Circa 1868

John A. Kearney as an R.I.C. recruit.

John A. Kearney, following his promotion to acting Sergeant.

John A. Kearney, following his promotion to Head Constable.

At the front – Mary Catherine Kearney, wife of John A. Kearney.
Back row – Tom Manning, British Army Medical Corps 1914 - 1918 and later member of the R.I.C., brother of Mrs. Kearney; Isobel Manning, sister of Mrs Kearney and Head Constable John A. Kearney.

The old Tralee R.I.C. Barracks at the commencement of it's demolition, October 1983.

The Officer's Mess at The Depot, Phoenix Park as it is at the present time.

John A. Kearney as a District Inspector in Boyle.

86   *District Inspector John A. Kearney*

Tralee R.I.C. station party in 1916. H/Constable John A. Kearney is seated at the left of front row.

Austin Stack

TELEGRAMS: SCRIPT HOLB LONDON
TELEPHONE: 4582 HOLBORN

4 Raymond Buildings
Gray's Inn
London W.C.

6th June 1916.

J. Kearney, Esq.,
   Head Constable, R.I.C.,
      Tralee,
         Co. Kerry. Ireland.

Dear Sir:-

    I thank you for your letter of 2nd inst. and have duly received Sir Roger Casement's watch and returned it to him. I, of course, quite appreciate your position in the circumstances of the case.

                Yours faithfully,

                G. Gavan Duffy.

Copy of letter from George Gavan Duffy to John A. Kearney acknowledging receipt of watch which Sir Roger Casement left behind in the Kearney home.

Casement in his thirties.

Sir Roger Casement, centre right, clean shaven, on board the submarine U20 in April 1916. With him are Captain Robert Monteith, second from left and Daniel Bailey, third from left, along with German naval officers.

District Inspector Frederick A. Britten, Tralee.

The take-over of Boyle R.I.C. barracks by the Irish Republican Police following its evacuation by the R.I.C. in February 1922.

> Rialtas Sealadach na hÉireann
> (Irish Provisional Government)
>
> Halla na Cathrach
> Baile Átha Cliath
> 3rd Feby. 1922
>
> Sir,
>
> The Irish Provisional Government are setting up a Committee for the purpose of drafting a scheme for the organisation of a new Police Force.
>
> Your name has been suggested to the Government for membership of this Committee and I shall be glad to learn whether you would be willing to serve.
>
> The first meeting of the Committee will be held at Room 85, Gresham Hotel, Dublin, on Thursday 9th inst., at 7 o'clock p.m.
>
> (Sgd) Micheál O Coileáin
> Chairman of the Provisional Government.
>
> J. Kearney Esq.
> Royal Irish Constabulary.

Copy of letter from General Michael Collins sent to District Inspector Kearney inviting him to assist with the setting up of a new Police Force.

94 *District Inspector John A. Kearney*

The first recruits for the 'Civic Guards' parading at the temporary Ballsbridge Depot in February 1922.

Three of John A. Kearney's sons in British army uniform.
Left to Right:-
Shane, [London Irish Rifles]. Killed in action in Germany in 1945. Aged 26.
Thomas, [The Irish Guards] Died 2000, aged 85 years.
Brendan, [The Irish Guards] Killed in active service in England, 1943. Aged 30.

5

THE EVENTS OF GOOD FRIDAY AND EASTER SATURDAY, 1916

THE DETENTION OF ROGER CASEMENT AT TRALEE.

Good Friday morning, was the start of a very busy day and night for Head Constable Kearney. Members were coming and going to the station and reporting on the results of tasks, which had been allocated to them. All members of the station party had been called on duty. He was monitoring all the reports and directing operations in Tralee station. In the early afternoon, word was received from Ardfert that a man had been arrested at Banna Beach and brought to Ardfert RIC station. District Inspector Britten directed that the arrested man should be brought to Tralee for detention.

The man - then unknown - was brought to Tralee on a horse - drawn sidecar accompanied by two members of the RIC. He arrived in the station there at about 3 p.m., Kearney received the prisoner at the station and was immediately struck by his very poor physical condition. He was haggard, tired and dishevelled in appearance and suffering from diarrhoea. The prisoner gave his name as *'Richard Morton'*, a writer, from *'The Savoy, Denham, Buckinghamshire, England'*. There was no suspicion at this time, that he might have been Sir Roger Casement.

Kearney was so struck by the dilapidated and abject condition of the prisoner, that he gave directions to his sergeants and barrack orderly that the man should not be put in the cell at the station, but should be detained in the station billiards room. The latter room was situated to the right rear of the entrance hallway of the station, immediately past the dayroom [or public office]. A fire was lit in the room to make the prisoner comfortable. The entrance hallway and billiards room, were located on the ground floor of the station at street level, with direct access from High Street.

District Inspector Britten had an interview with the prisoner late in the afternoon, but he made no incriminating statement to the D. I., persevering with giving his name as *'Richard Morton'*, and that he was a writer by profession. During a search of the prisoner's overcoat, the D. I. found a rail sleeping - car ticket for a journey from Berlin to Wilhelmshaven in Germany. It was dated for April 1916 and the D. I. later gave evidence of this find at Casement's Trial.

It continued to be a busy afternoon for Kearney, following the arrival of the prisoner. On receiving word that Con Collins - who had been spoken to at Stack's lodgings earlier in the day by Constable Neazer - was in a local public - house, Kearney went there with other members of the force and arrested Collins. He was brought to the RIC station where he was searched and a revolver and ammunition taken from him. He was placed in the station cell.

From the moment that Kearney had spoken to the prisoner [who gave his name as Morton] on his arrival at Tralee station, he instinctively knew that this prisoner was no 'common lawbreaker' or ordinary individual. He kept him under observation and studied him during the afternoon. While he attended to other matters, he racked his brain in trying to figure out what the prisoner's real identity might be. While no photograph had ever been published of Sir Roger Casement, without his famous beard, Kearney had a hunch that the mystery prisoner might be Casement. As an avid reader of newspapers, with an extensive knowledge of world affairs and of Roger Casement's exploits and fame, he became more convinced that it was he. He searched for and located an old newspaper, which had Casement's photograph and concluded that by covering up the beard, the photograph bore a striking resemblance to the prisoner. Based on his suspicions, he felt obliged to facilitate the prisoner in every way and to make him as comfortable as possible. Keeping the prisoner in the station billiards room with a comfortable fire would have been totally in breach and in conflict of the very strict rules for the treatment and safe-keeping of prisoners which was specified in the RIC Code. Kearney had made his decision to detain him there solely on compassionate grounds, as he felt great sympathy for him.

DR MICHAEL SHANAHAN, VISITS CASEMENT.

Kearney was obviously concerned about the state of Casement's health and had much sympathy for his plight, and, with the consent of the prisoner, decided to call in Dr Michael Shanahan, a local general practitioner to examine him. In an interview with Rene MacColl, author of 'Casement', Dr Shanahan described his visit:-

"At 6 p.m. on the night of that Good Friday of 1916, the police sergeant

came round to tell me that they had a commercial traveller over at the lock-up who had 'got into trouble' and was in need of medical attention. I went along and found a clean- shaven man of distinguished appearance sitting over a smoky fire in the policemen's billiards room. He looked jittery and exhausted. When I went to examine him, two policemen remained in the room. I ordered them outside and closed the door after them. The man then whispered to me that he was Casement, and expressed the hope that I was in sympathy with the Irish cause, which of course I said I was. Casement said that he was exhausted "after twelve terrible nights in a U-boat". He did not definitely say that he wanted to be released but the impression I got was that I should tell the people outside that he was in the barracks and that he had no other purpose in his mind, only that he might be released which was quite an easy matter at that time. The barracks door was wide open and half a dozen men with revolvers could have walked in there and taken Sir Roger away".

"As Dr Shanahan left the barracks, the Head Constable, Kearney - 'an astute man' as Dr Shanahan recalls - stepped up to him and showed him a newspaper cutting of Casement as he normally was, complete with beard. Kearney, narrowly watching the doctor, put a piece of paper across the beard in the photo and asked Shanahan whether the top part of the face did not remind him of the man in the lock-up. Loyally Shanahan replied no. But, 'I could see that Kearney knew that the man he had inside was Sir Roger Casement; but even so, the prisoner was under no heavy guard'.

"Next, Shanahan rushed about Tralee trying to incite the local Irish Volunteers into a rescue attempt, but without avail. To Shanahan's consternation, the local men shrugged off all his plans, saying merely that the man in jail was 'some Norwegian sailor'. 'In very plain language,' the doctor told the leaders of the Volunteers what he thought about their attitude, but they refused to budge. Some time later, Shanahan was told that they knew perfectly well that it was Casement who was at the barracks, but they did not want to risk doing anything which might set the Rising off at half-cock".

THE ARREST OF CON COLLINS AND AUSTIN STACK.

In the late evening, the prisoner Con Collins, requested the RIC to send word to Austin Stack that he wanted to see him in the RIC station. His request was acceded to and a member of the force located Stack and passed on the message to him. When Stack came to the station, Kearney arrested him and found a number of incriminating documents in his possession. Stack was detained in the kitchen of the station, which was located on the ground floor - at the opposite end of the hallway to the billiards room. He then organised a search of Stack's lodgings by other members of the station party and they reported back with more incriminating documents, which they had found there.

Having attended to the foregoing matters, Kearney had some more time to talk with Casement who still had not revealed his true identity. At about 9 p.m. Fr Frank Ryan, O. P. who was attached to the local Dominican Priory located less than one hundred yards from the station, was asked by a member of the RIC to call to the station. The decision to call the Dominican priest was taken at the prompting of Kearney and after Casement had agreed to have him called. Details of this visit are again given by Rene MacColl in his book 'Casement:-

"About 9 p.m. a Dominican priest, Father Ryan, came along to the police barracks in answer to a request by the prisoner for spiritual guidance [the R.I.C considering that they very strongly suspected Casement's identity, and realising the importance of their catch, were remarkably accommodating] - Father Ryan too saw Casement in private and was also told of his identity. After a brief talk about such spiritual problems as were on his mind,, Casement, according to the next day's Dublin 'Evening Mail', told the Father that he wanted him to go to the Volunteers and urge them to keep quiet; to tell them that the Rebellion would be a hopeless failure because the help on which the Irish counted would not be forthcoming.

"Father Ryan protested, according to the newspaper account, saying that he was a priest and not a political go-between. But Casement pleaded with him, saying 'Do what I ask and you will bring God's blessing on the country and on everyone concerned'. Father Ryan, after giving the matter thought, decided that it would indeed be the best thing to convey the message to the Volunteers and thus perhaps to be the means by which bloodshed and suffering might be avoided. 'So I saw the leader of the Volunteers in Tralee and gave him the message'. He also informed the Head Constable in Tralee of the steps he had taken and his reasons for doing so.

"When the 'Evening Mail' story broke the next day, they got a telegram

from Fr Ryan which said that he had given no interview to 'any pressman anywhere'. The Mail published this telegram as requested, but thoughtfully pointed out that the Father might well have been unaware that he was talking to a newspaper reporter when he said what he was alleged to have said".

When it emerged as the late evening wore on that the prisoner in custody was most likely Sir Roger Casement, District Inspector Britten called to see him again and sympathised with him saying:

"I think I know who you are, and I pray to God it won't end the way of Wolfe Tone"..

KEARNEY TAKES CASEMENT TO HIS PRIVATE HOME.

Early that night, Kearney took Casement from the billiards room to his private family quarters upstairs on the first floor of the station. When he asked Casement if he was hungry - Casement replied that he was 'starving'. When asked what he would like to eat, he said *'I would love nothing better than a good steak'*. It being Good Friday - a day of fast and abstinence in all Catholic households - and it was also in the pre - domestic refrigerator era, Mrs Kearney went to the local butcher shop, which she frequented almost on a daily basis. She obtained what was described as a 'fine steak' and cooked it for Roger Casement who relished it.

The members of the Kearney family described Casement as being a lovely, refined gentleman. He took some of the Kearney children on his knee and spoke to them about the schools they attended, the games they played at school and about the poetry they learned. This took place in the family kitchen/living-room and Casement settled in as if he was one of the family. One of the children - Margaret Mary Kearney, [later Mrs Clery] - spoke about this experience up to the time of her death in 1997, of Casement jogging her up and down on his knee. She was most likely the last person alive to have known or physically met Sir Roger Casement.

While with the Kearney family, Casement was given an opportunity to wash and freshen-up in the Kearney bathroom, he was given a linen face towel [which had been hand-woven by Mrs Kearney's grandmother from flax] to facilitate him with his wash. That face towel which measures 27 inches by 24 inches, was never subsequently used by the Kearney family, but was retained safely by them as a keep - sake. It is still in the safe - keeping of a Kearney family member. Casement was insisting on giving something to the Kearney family as a token of his appreciation for the kindness bestowed on him, but Head Constable Kearney and his wife courteously declined any such offer. Casement was in the Kearney home for about two hours and relished his meal, which was the first palatable and substantial meal, he had in two weeks.

Before Kearney left the married quarters with Casement that night, Kearney's children distinctly remembered hearing their father advising their mother, not to allow the children out of the quarters for the rest of the night, as he expected an attack to be made on the station before morning. In compliance with his instructions, their mother locked the entrance door to the quarters and for a considerable period into the night they recalled her sitting on the floor of the kitchen with her back to the locked entrance door. They eventually fell asleep and found that Casement was again in their accommodation for breakfast on the following morning.

KEARNEY KEEPS CASEMENT COMPANY THROUGHOUT THE NIGHT.

Kearney sat with Casement in the station billiards room throughout the night. The front door of the RIC station was unlocked and there were few RIC men on duty in the building. Casement was not handcuffed while in custody and the door leading to the billiards room was unlocked. For the remainder of his life, Kearney always claimed that Casement was there to be rescued that night and that two men carrying revolvers could have rescued him. It has always been acknowledged that there would have been little trouble in effecting a successful rescue of Casement and Kearney had no intention of obstructing any effort which might have been made to do so.

Sometime before twelve midnight, Kearney sent Constable Clancy to the West End Hotel, [now 'Val's Bistro and Bar'] at Bridge Street, Tralee, to obtain a whiskey for Casement. The hotel was owned by Patrick and Margaret O'Connor and its bar was the one most frequented by the RIC personnel in Tralee. Their daughter Maggie was in charge of the hotel on the night. She recalled Constable Clancy calling to the premises for the whiskey. He ordered a bottle of stout for himself and asked for a half-whiskey *'for a prisoner in the barracks, who was very distressed and who would hardly last until morning'*. On hearing of the plight of the prisoner, she insisted on handing over a full glass of 'Jameson' Whiskey. The cost of the drink was six old pence, but she refused to take the money from the constable. It wasn't until the following morning that Maggie O'Connor became aware that the prisoner was Roger Casement. The whiskey was probably served to Casement as a 'hot whiskey or punch' rather than in its raw state. This was certainly his last 'Irish Whiskey'.

Casement took Kearney very much into his confidence, as they talked through the night. This is evident from notes which Casement gave to his Counsel, Serjeant A.M Sullivan, K.C, after the first day of his trial at Bow Street, London, on May 16th 1916.

He wrote -

"The Chief Constable at Tralee was very friendly to me. It was he got me the priest, and I said a lot of things to him during the night. Many of these things were in confidence, as at that time, I was bent on taking the poison I had, and wanted this friendly man to tell all my friends after - it was the following Wednesday evening, 27th April, I first tried to rub the poison, curare, into a cut I made in my fingers at the Tower, and thought surely I would go that night".

The only motive that Casement could have for giving this note to his Counsel, is that he wanted the Counsel to know that Kearney treated him very well. He obviously did not want his Counsel to make any allegations of ill - treatment or misconduct against Kearney or the RIC relating to his detention in Tralee, in the course of the forthcoming trial.

Casement probably 'bared his soul' to Kearney in the course of the conversation which they had through the night. It can be taken that much of the conversation was of an academic and intellectual nature, wide ranging on Irish, British and world affairs. It would have been difficult to find in the whole of the RIC force, a man of Kearney's calibre or knowledge who would be as well versed in these matters. He was aware of Casement's background, of his activities and reputation in the interest of human rights throughout the world. He had an exceptionally good knowledge of Irish and British affairs and was well able to converse on any subject. He realised only too well what Casement's fate was likely to be, and in later years he made no secret of the extent of the sympathy, which he had for Casement and the predicament in which he was then in.

Kearney would not have condoned Casement's activity in conniving with the Germans - the 'arch enemy' of the British Empire. Despite his strong sense of Irish nationalism, his loyalty to the British Government and the Empire could not be questioned. On the other hand, he would have the highest personal regard for Casement's activities in Africa and South America and his extraordinary humanitarian work for basic human rights. He found Casement -*"To be a very pleasant person, genteel, and very polite"*, but, for whose cause he had no sympathy in any way.

Casement said that he *'said a lot of things'* to Kearney that night, but to Kearney's eternal credit he never disclosed publicly what Casement had said to him in confidence. He certainly never disclosed the details to his children and it is doubtful if he ever told his wife anything about it. He never betrayed the confidence which Casement had placed in him. He was not aware that Casement had poison [curare] concealed on his person. It is believed that Casement had the poison in a small phial concealed in the hair of his head.

The prisoner was seated in an easy - chair in the billiards room. At no time during his detention did he come in contact with Stack or Collins, who were both detained overnight in the station.

On the following morning - Easter Saturday - Kearney again took him to the family married quarters, where Mrs Kearney cooked breakfast for him. He washed and shaved in the family bathroom.

TRANSFER OF ROGER CASEMENT FROM TRALEE TO DUBLIN AND LONDON.

Instructions were received at the RIC station from Dublin Castle that Casement was to be removed to Dublin under escort early on Saturday morning. Kearney selected Sergeant James Butler - a very sound and reliable member of the force - to perform the escort duty to Dublin. Sergeant Butler and two constables escorted Casement, on foot, through Tralee town to the local railway station, to meet the 10.30 a.m. train to Dublin. Casement was not handcuffed as he walked through the town with his escort. Only Sergeant Butler travelled as escort on the train. In addition to his duty in escorting Casement he also carried three bags containing firearms and the other exhibits which had been found in and near the abandoned boat at Banna Beach. He also carried a parcel, which contained three overcoats found at McKenna's fort in Currahane.

Sergeant Butler and Casement travelled in a private carriage and when the train stopped at Killarney, Casement sought permission - which was given - from the Sergeant to buy a newspaper. At that station the local Head Constable of the RIC, came to the carriage door and said to Sergeant Butler

"Did you hear what happened the two lads at 'Puck"?

When Sergeant Butler replied that he had not, the Head Constable said

"They ran into the tide and were drowned".

After leaving Killarney, Casement began to cry and cried for some time. He then turned to Sergeant Butler and said -
"Where is Puck, is it near Castlemaine Bay "? When the sergeant told him that it was, Casement said,

"I am very sorry for these two men. It was on my account they were there. They were two good Irishmen".

Casement obviously assumed that the two casualties of the drowning accident were Monteith and Bailey. On arrival at Mallow, Sergeant Butler asked Casement if he had been there before and Casement replied

"Yes. I know Blackwater well".

On arrival in Dublin, Sergeant Butler escorted Casement to Arbour Hill Military Detention Barracks, where the prisoner was taken over by Sergeant Major Whittaker. Sergeant Butler also handed over the three bags and parcel to him. Casement was again thoroughly searched at Arbour Hill and after very little delay there, he was conveyed under escort to the mail boat at Dunlaoghaire, en route for London. He was conveyed by an escort under the command of Sergeant Bracken of the Military Foot Police based at Ship Street, Dublin. Casement was taken via Holyhead to Bow Street Police Station in London, where he was handed over to the London Metropolitan Police, under Inspector Joseph Handcock, of the London C.I.D.. The latter received him from Sergeant Bracken and conveyed him in the first instance to New Scotland Yard and finally from there to the Tower of London.

On Saturday 21st April, the *"Kerry Evening Post"* carried the story that a stranger of unknown nationality had been arrested, not far from where a collapsible boat was found between Barrow Harbour and Banna Beach.

It stated that according to local rumours, he was no less a personage that Sir Roger Casement. It stated that the arrested man *'was taken under a strong escort'* to Dublin on the 10.30 a.m. train that morning. The Dublin *"Evening Mail"* of the same day, carried the story relating to the interview which Fr Frank Ryan O. P. had with Casement.

In retrospect, it seems extraordinary that a high profile prisoner like Casement should have been escorted to Dublin by only one sergeant, who was also carrying three bags and a large parcel. It has to be considered whether this was another opportunity presented by Kearney and/or the RIC to facilitate the rescue of Casement from custody.

CHARGING OF AUSTIN STACK AND CON COLLINS.

Following the safe departure of Casement to Dublin, the attention of the RIC then turned to Austin Stack and Con Collins, who were detained in custody in the station. They were brought before a Resident Magistrate and charged with being involved in a conspiracy to illegally import arms into the country. They were remanded in custody to the County Jail at Ballymullen,Tralee, to which they were removed under escort, later on that afternoon.

EASTER WEEK AND ITS AFTERMATH.

During the following two weeks there was an intensive round - up of Sinn Fein Volunteers in the Tralee area and several arrests were made. These arrests were made by the RIC with backup from the local military. In *'Tans ,Terror and Troubles'*, T. Ryle Dwyer describes one of these arrests –

"Prominent Sinn Feiners were arrested around the county. 'I am sorry I have come to arrest you' Head Constable John A. Kearney said when he arrived at M. J. O'Connor's home on May 8th 1916. O'Connor was taken to the R.I.C station and charged with 'being engaged in a conspiracy to land German arms in this country'. After being formally charged, he was escorted by an R.I.C sergeant and three constables on foot through the Green and to the county jail in Ballymullen, on the other side of the town. Joe Malinn who had just been arrested on the same charge, was with

him".

A total of twenty-four Sinn Fein Volunteers were arrested during the round - up in the Tralee area, while another thirty-seven were arrested elsewhere in the county. Nineteen of the Kerry prisoners were conveyed to Richmond Barracks in Dublin.

Mr Asquith, the English Prime Minister came to Dublin specially on May 12th, to personally assess the situation relating to prisoners who were being held at the time. He instructed the military to properly assess each prisoner and to send to England, only those against whom there was a real case to be met. The majority of the Kerry prisoners were released under this order but the nineteen prisoners held at Richmond Barracks were taken to England by boat and lodged in Wakefield Prison on May 24th.

The following men from Castlegregory, Co. Kerry who were rounded up in the weeks following Easter Week, 1916, were tried by Court Martial and 'Found Not Guilty' -

John Brown, Michael Duhig, James Kennedy, Michael McKenna, Daniel O'Shea, and Abel Mahon,

Fionan Lynch, Cahirciveen, was tried by Court - martial and 'Sentenced to Death' but this was later commuted to 10 years Penal Servitude.

Austin Stack, Rock Street, Tralee, was tried by Court - martial and sentenced to Penal Servitude for Life.

In Kerry, the events of Easter weekend and the Dublin Rebellion brought mixed re-action amongst the people. Prisoners being conveyed from the RIC station to the County Jail on foot, were cheered and wished well by onlookers. Most Revd Dr Mangan, the Bishop of Kerry, condemned the rebels and their activities, from the pulpit of Killarney Cathedral. He said that he was filled with horror and dismay at their actions. He denounced Casement as 'a traitor to his country' and he continued -

"The situation that has been so unexpectedly created demands that I, as the spokesman of the Catholics of this diocese, should give public expression to their strong disapprobation of the action of some misguided men, who, if they had their way, would plunge this country into all the horror of civil war". [It was from the same pulpit that Bishop Moriarty - then Bishop of Kerry - condemned the Fenians following their ill-fated insurrection of 1867 when he said that *'hell was not hot enough'* for those who had been involved].

Tralee Urban District Council adopted a resolution, condemning the Easter Week Rising.

John Kearney's observations in relation to that particular period were:

"There was no doubt whatsoever about it, that the vast majority of the Irish people at this time were opposed and strongly opposed to the attitude of Sinn Fein. Even during the Rebellion and up to the time of the execution of the leaders of it, the Irish people were thoroughly ashamed of what had happened and looked upon the rank and file as deluded fools of the hot - headed leaders.

"Many representatives and otherwise of the people of Kerry, called to our Barracks and protested against the Rebellion. There was no doubt whatever about the sincerity of these people. They deplored in all seriousness as to what happened and heartily condemned the action of the hot - headed leaders. Many of these men were officers of the National Volunteers and I was offered the service of one hundred of these Volunteers in the event of us being attacked.

"That was the attitude at this time of the Kerry people in general".

CASEMENT'S POCKET WATCH.

When Casement was in Kearney's home on Good Friday night, he wanted John and Mrs Kearney to accept some gift or token from him, in appreciation of their kindness and generosity towards him, but the Kearneys courteously declined to accept anything from him. After Casement had left for Dublin on Saturday morning, the Kearneys discovered that Casement had left his pocket watch - which appeared to be a valuable one - behind. He most likely left it behind on Saturday morning when he had breakfast in Kearney's home and used the bathroom facilities. There was little doubt about Casement's motive in deliberately leaving the watch behind, in Kearney's home. He had left it as a gesture of his appreciation, for what the Kearney's had done for him.

The finding of the watch created a quandary for Kearney. Had it been left behind in the station proper he would have no trouble in returning it to Casement via the County Inspector's office and the Inspector General of the force. The situation was more difficult, seeing that Casement had left it in Kearney's private quarters. He could not report this fact through 'official channels' as he was in breach of the strict regulations relating to the custody of prisoners by reason of having Casement in his private home while in custody. When a few weeks had elapsed and details of Casement's defence counsel was published, Kearney sent the watch by Registered post to Mr George Gavan Duffy, who was a junior barrister assisting Serjeant Sullivan in defending Casement in London. He obviously explained to Mr Duffy the circumstances that gave rise to the finding of the watch and the personal complications for himself surrounding its finding.

On June 6th 1916, Duffy acknowledged receipt of the watch and confirmed that he had had handed it over to Casement. The following is a copy of the letter received by Kearney from Duffy:-

4 Raymond Buildings,
Gray's Inn,
London W.C.
6th June 1916.

J Kearney Esq,
Head Constable R.I.C.,
Tralee,
Co Kerry.
Ireland.
Dear Sir,

I Thank you for your letter of the 2nd inst. and have duly received Sir Roger Casement's watch and returned it to him. I, of course, quite appreciate your position in the circumstances of the case.
Yours Faithfully,

G. Gavan Duffy.

Kearney's efforts to have the watch safely returned to Casement indicated the level of his honesty and integrity. Casement had left the watch for him in good faith and as a token of his appreciation for what he and Mrs Kearney had done for him, but Kearney felt obliged to return it.

Casement however, was not prepared to let the matter rest or leave Kearney's generosity to go without reward. Despite the turmoil which surrounded him and his inevitable trial and fate, he subsequently managed to have his cigarette lighter forwarded to Head Constable Kearney as a keep - sake. John A. Kearney retained this and he regarded it as a precious possession during the remainder of his lifetime. It is now in the careful custody of a member of his family. The lighter measures 2.5 inches by 1.5

inches and is a dull silver colour.

Casement also left a detached shirt collar behind in the Kearney home and another member of the Kearney family retains this. This was probably 'accidentally' left behind.

THE COURT-MARTIAL OF STACK AND COLLINS.

Head Constable Kearney travelled to Dublin in mid June, along with other police and civilian witnesses to give evidence at the Courtmartial of Austin Stack and Con Collins. He had arrested both at Tralee on the previous Good Friday evening. The Court - martial lasted for two days.

It was a General Court-martial, held at Richmond Barracks in Dublin on Friday 16th June 1916, for the trial of Austin Stack and Con Collins. The charges against the accused were:-

1. 'That in or about the month of April, 1916, they conspired and agreed with certain other disloyal and disaffected persons to bring about a rebellion in Ireland, and to spread disaffection amongst the civil population of the country, such act being of such a nature as to calculated to be prejudicial to the public safety and defence of the realm, and being committed with the intention and for the purpose of assisting the enemy'.

2. 'That, in or about the month of April, knowing, or having reasonable grounds for supposing, that certain persons, by name Monteith and Bailey, were then engaged, contrary to the regulations for the defence of the realm, in the importation of arms and ammunition into Ireland, without previous permit of the competent military or naval authority - which said arms and ammunition, as they [the accused] well knew, or had reasonable grounds for supposing, were intended to be used in aid and in furtherance of the rebellion in Ireland, - they did harbour the said persons, Monteith and Bailey, such act being calculated to be prejudicial to the public safety and the defence of the realm, and being committed with the intention and for the purpose of assisting the enemy'.

Major General Lord Cheylesmore, KCVO, presided, and Mr Kenneth Marshall was Judge Advocate. Major E. G Kimber, DSO, conducted the prosecution. Mr E.J. McElligott, K.C. and Mr Arthur Clery instructed by Mr John O'Donnell, Solicitor Tralee, appeared for the accused.

Major Kimber stated the case for the prosecution and described Stack as being a well known commander of the Irish Volunteers and Collins as a clerk in the employment of His Majesty, in the Dublin Post Office. He went into great detail about the events in Tralee and Ardfert, the arrest of Casement, Monteith and Bailey and the capture and scuttling of the *'Aud'*. In various ways he indicated the role played in the whole affair by Stack and Collins and quoted from different documents found in their possession which were incriminating in nature.

The following witnesses were called to give evidence:-

1 Frank Goodwin, of Scraggen Point, Castlegregory, who stated that he watched a strange boat in Tralee Bay on Good Friday. The boat was painted black and had a black funnel that had a white band on top of it. Two flags were painted on her sides, they were Norwegian flags.
2. John McCarthy, Currahane, Ardfert who had located the boat on Banna Beach.
3. Mary O'Gorman, who had seen three strange men coming from the direction of the abandoned boat.
4. Sergeant Thomas Hearn, Ardfert, who arrested Casement and found miscellaneous items of evidence.
5 Constable Bernard Reilly, Ardfert, who corroborated the evidence of Sergt. Hearn.
6 Constable William Larke, R.I.C Ardfert, who found articles at Banna Beach.
7 Sergeant Daniel Crowley, Ballyheigue who gave evidence of seeing Stack and Collins and others in Moriarty's motorcar at Banna Beach.
8 Maurice Moriarty, Tralee, who was driver of the motorcar which conveyed Stack and others to Banna Beach in search of Casement..
9 Constable George Neazer of Tralee who said that Collins gave him his correct name address when he questioned him on Good Friday afternoon.
10. Signalman Waghorne of *'HMS. Bluebell'* who gave evidence about the interception of the 'Aud' and the sinking of the vessel outside Cork Harbour.
11. Constable McKeown of the Dublin Metropolitan Police who said that he had seen Con Collins at the shop of Thomas Clarke in Dublin who was a leader of the Sinn Feiners and who was recently executed.
12. Mr S.J. Harrison a senior official at Dublin G.P.O. gave details of Con Collins' service in the General Post Office.
13. Constable Daniel Coffey of Dublin Metropolitan Police, gave evi-

dence that he had seen Collins on several occasions associating with prominent Volunteer leaders in Dublin.
14. Mr John Dempsey, a diver employed by the Admiralty at Queenstown [now Cobh] who gave evidence of his observations and details of the weapons found by him when he dived to inspect the wreck of the *'Aud'*.

Kearney gave his evidence to the Court-martial. He said that he had known Austin Stack for three years and that he was the commandant of the Volunteers in Tralee. The witness said that he had met Con Collins in Tralee on the night of April 20th. Collins told him that he had been for a drive to Ardfert, Ballyheigue and Causeway with a man named Mulcahy of Mountjoy Street, Dublin, whom he had met once or twice before and Mr Austin Stack. Collins also said that he had been stopped and searched several times during the day. The witness arrested Collins on a charge of conspiracy to land arms and he [Collins] made no further statement. He searched Collins who handed him a revolver and sixty-one rounds of ammunition. Collins said that he usually carried the weapon in Dublin, because he was often out late at night and early in the morning. The prisoner also had £35.00 on him and a soldier's English - German dictionary. At the police station, Collins said that he wanted to see Stack, and Stack was sent for.

When Stack came to the station he arrested him. He asked the witness [Kearney] if he was serious in arresting him. He searched Stack, found documents on him and other documents were found at his lodgings. Among those was a map of Tralee, showing the post office, the railway station, the G.P.O. store at the station, and other leading places.

H/Constable Kearney said that he also found a paper, on which was written a form of oath as follows:

'I swear in the presence of God that, if I become a member of the Irish Volunteers, I will do all in my power to assert the independence of Ireland, keep the secrets of the organisation, and obey the commands of my superior officers'.

He also found a letter addressed to Stack from the Irish Volunteers in America, which contained the phrase:

'The news from Ireland that recruiting is a failure is very gratifying, and has given us renewed hope '.

The letter was signed Patrick Griffin. There was also a letter from a person in British South Africa, in which occurred the statement:

'Now is the moment for Young Ireland to assert itself'.

There was a bundle of letters, all directed to Stack on matters relating to the Volunteers, from members of the body in Dublin such as Bulmer Hobson and the late P.H. Pearse.

In cross-examination it was put to H/Constable Kearney,

'You will agree that the newspaper cutting which Major Kimber read in his opening statement is a very brutal document?' I should say so.

'Did the prisoner tell you that it was an extract from 'The Review of Reviews of February 1910?' No.

'Or that article in the Review professed to give the very words as the sentiments of Admiral Lord Fisher? Yes, he said they were the words of Lord Fisher.

'Did you confirm that as being cut out of the 'Review of Reviews' of February 1910? "No".

A copy of the magazine was handed to the witness and at counsel's request, he read from the article giving a character sketch of Lord Fisher, the part quoted by Major Kimber in his opening statement.

Austin Stack did not give evidence at the Court-martial but he handed in a statement that was read by the President. In the statement, Stack said that he had always been a believer in the right of Ireland to self-government. When the Irish Volunteers were formed with the object which their constitution states - namely to defend and maintain the rights and liberties of the threatened, by a rising of the armed Volunteers of Ulster - he became an active Volunteer. When compulsory service was proposed, he was preparing to resist it, by means similar to those that the Ulster Volunteers used against Home Rule. He continued, an ardent worker in the Irish Volunteers up to the date of his arrest. As to Monteith and Bailey, these men may have come to Tralee from some part of Ireland, or from Timbuctoo, or from somewhere else, as far as he could see.

The President read a statement that had been handed in by Con Collins. He said that he had been in the service of the Post Office since May 1902. In April of this year he was spending his annual leave in Limerick and Kerry, Limerick being his native county. On April 20th he went to Tralee, where he had been accustomed to go for a number of years, to spend a portion of his holidays in visiting friends. He had no knowledge of any contemplated landing of arms on the Kerry coast, or at any other time. He had not been a member of any Volunteer force, for upwards of eighteen months. As to his alleged connection with Monteith or Bailey, he knew nothing of them, and they might have come to Tralee from Dublin or Cork, or any other part of Ireland, for anything he knew to the contrary.

Mr Michael Flavin, M.P., Mr Thomas O'Donnell, M.P., Mr D.J. Liston, Solicitor, and Revd. Father O'Quigley of the Dominican Order, each gave Stack a very high character reference.

Mr Thomas Buckley, a member of Limerick County Council and Chairman of Newcastlewest District Council, gave evidence of Collins' good character.

Mr Browne, who was in charge of the Accountant's Department at the GPO, said the accused, Collins, was a member of the staff, and was a steady man who did his business satisfactorily. Until March 1915, there was no record against him. At that time, it came to the notice of the Secretary, that he was connected with the Irish Volunteers, and he was warned under threat of instant dismissal to sever his connection with that, or any other, political movement with which he might be connected. He was, witness thought, reminded of that warning once since March 1915. Since then, the Department had no information that he had not kept his promise, to leave the Volunteers.

The result of the trial was announced in a report from the Military Headquarters on Thursday 22nd June 1916 as follows:

'Austin Stack and Cornelius Collins were tried on the 15th and 16th June instant. They were found guilty of complicity in the attempt to land arms and ammunition in Kerry, and of conspiring to bring about a rebellion in Ireland. They were sentenced to penal servitude for life, which was confirmed by the General Officer Commanding-in-Chief.

Stack never denied that he had the incriminating documents in his possession when he went to Tralee RIC barracks on the Good Friday evening nor did he challenge their alleged incriminating contents. He had been reminded by his Adjutant - Paddy Cahill - to ensure that he had nothing incriminating is his possession before he went to the barracks. The fact that Stack went to the barracks at all and that he had these documents on him has always been the subject of debate and controversy.

Fr J. Anthony Gaughan, biographer of Austin Stack, in his book *"Austin Stack: Portrait of a Separatist"* [Page 62] comments on Stack's extraordinary action :-

"The only plausible reason which can be given for Stack's going to the police - barracks and certain arrest was that he wished to ensure that the British Forces would not be placed on the alert. Few people, however, would find this very convincing. And yet it is significant that the Irish Volunteer leadership found no fault with him for his actions during Holy Week, 1916. He had not even to suffer the indignity of presenting himself before an official inquiry as had the leaders of the Cork Brigade".

There was no further contact between Stack or Collins with Kearney from the completion of their court – martial, until they made false allegations against him in Dail Eireann in February 1922.

THE ROYAL COMMISSION OF INQUIRY INTO THE 1916 RISING.

Kearney did not attend the Royal Commission of Inquiry into the Irish Rebellion and the facts surrounding it, which opened at the Royal Commission's House, Westminster in London on Thursday 18th May 1916. The events of Holy Thursday, Good Friday and the Easter weekend in the Tralee area, figured large in the proceedings at the Inquiry.

Evidence relating to this and to County Kerry in general, was given to the Inquiry by County Inspector M.O.H Hill of Tralee. In the course of his lengthy evidence, he stated that the Sinn Fein movement first came to prominence in Kerry in October 1914, after Mr John Redmond had announced the decision of the Nationalist Party to support the war. At a meeting in Tralee that month, it was decided that Mr Redmond's policy should be adopted. Others decided to remain loyal to Mr John MacNeill's party in Dublin. The Sinn Fein party produced a Union Jack, which they waved in the face of the Redmondites, and afterwards burned. Then green flags were produced and waved. He estimated that there were 646 Sinn Feiners in the county after that. On November 30th, he estimated that the strength of Sinn Fein in the county was 1,041 persons. Up to October, 1914, nearly everyone in Kerry was in favour of winning the war, and assisted the police in hunting up spies. But after that, all that stopped. In February 1915, the number of branches of Sinn Fein had increased to seven with a membership of 1,039. In April, the number had increased to 1,044, which was due to the activity of Ernest Blythe, an organiser who came to Kerry during the month. In May, the number was 1,060 and Blythe and a man named Cotton were very active in organising work.

County Inspector Hill, then outlined how the number of Sinn Fein Volunteers decreased over a few months, for different reasons, but by November 1915, it was back up to 1,143 members and by the following month it was 1,233. He related a story about the Sinn Feiners having a meeting with the Listowel Race Committee on October 8th. They got the Committee to rescind a decision that they had taken some time previously, to give one penny out of every shilling of their receipts to the 'Royal Munster Fusiliers Fund'. The Sinn Fein delegation demanded that the Race Committee should give that one penny to the Irish Volunteers. The Race Committee agreed to comply with the request but they rescinded that decision some time later.

He also gave evidence about the activities of Cotton, who was employed in the local Labour Exchange in Tralee and stated that he left Kerry on 27th March 1916 after being served with an order to do so. He named the various leaders of the I.R.B. and Irish Volunteers who had come to Tralee and Kerry, at different times leading up to Easter 1916. He stated that Austin Stack was the principal man in the movement in Kerry and said that he had been arrested on Good Friday 1916.

He read from a lengthy document, which detailed all the events of Holy Thursday and Good Friday relating to the 'Aud' and to the arrest of Roger Casement and the other arrests which followed in Tralee. He gave details of the shooting of two policemen – both of whom were injured - near Firies over the same period.

Owing to the general state of unrest and the rumours which were flying at the time, he asked the officer in charge of the military troops in Tralee, if he could send some soldiers to assist the police where necessary, but the officer told him that there were none to spare. He got in communication with the General Commanding at Queenstown, and he promptly sent 100 soldiers by train. They arrived in Tralee at 5 a.m. on 22nd April. On the 21st he had also wired for extra police for Tralee and they came in from outlying areas. He placed extra men in Waterville and at Valentia to protect the cable stations.

When asked by the Chairman of the Inquiry if there had been any Rising in Kerry, he replied that there had not and he attributed this to the arrest of Casement and local leaders, the arrival of extra troops from Cork and the extra police drafted in. He said that Austin Stack was in charge of everything and when he was arrested, the Irish Volunteers who were assembled in Tralee became nervous. Those who were from the country gradually returned home. In reply to a question he said that 316 Sinn Fein Volunteers had assembled in Tralee on Easter Sunday.

He agreed that the question of conscription had a lot to do with the Sinn Fein movement saying that their numbers largely increased over the period.

He said that he never expected danger from the Redmondite Volunteers, but did from the Irish Volunteers. Although he did not expect a Rising, he knew there would be great danger in the case of a German invasion. The railway lines and the telegraph wires would be cut, and it would be difficult for the military to operate. There were only four young priests connected with the movement. Several Parish Priests prevented the formation of Sinn Fein branches. Out of a population of 165,000 in the county there were only a little over 1,000 Sinn Feiners.

In reply to questions, he said, that it would be difficult to know if some people were Sinn Fein or Redmondite Volunteers. He agreed that it was possible, that some of them may not have been too sure themselves, and said that many Sinn Feiners were insulted when they were referred to as MacNeillites.

When questioned about the arrival of the 'Aud' he agreed that it was intended to land the arms by force. He said that there was a large number of Volunteers assembled in Tralee to receive it, but his idea was that the ship came in a day or two too soon and that it was 'unpunctual'.

When questioned about the manpower available to him on the occasion, he said that in the whole county he had 338 men before the war, but this had been reduced to 272. He had only thirty men in Tralee at the time.

The extent of the evidence given by C.I. Hill was considerable, due to the events that had occurred in Tralee and County Kerry. Evidence, was also given by the County Inspectors from Kilkenny. Wexford, Cork, Clare, Galway East and Galway West in respect of activities within their counties over the period and by Sir Neville Chamberlain, Inspector General of the RIC.

The Inquiry published its report on June 20th 1916. It made no criticism of the RIC in Kerry or how the affairs of Holy Week were handled there. It was highly critical of the British administration in Ireland for having let the situation deteriorate so badly in the lead up to 1916. At the conclusion of the report it stated:-

"We are, however, of the opinion that the Chief Secretary, [Mr Birrell] as the administrative head of Your Majesty's Government in Ireland is primarily responsible for the situation that was allowed to arise and the outbreak that has occurred.

"Sir Matthew Nathan assumed office as Under - Secretary to the Irish Government in September 1914, only. In our view he carried out with the utmost loyalty the policy of the Government, and of his immediate superior, the Chief Secretary, but we consider that he did not sufficiently impress upon the Chief Secretary during the latter's prolonged absences from Dublin the necessity for more active measures to remedy the situation in Ireland, which on December 18th last, in a letter to the Chief Secretary, he described as 'most serious and menacing'.

"We are satisfied that Sir Neville Chamberlain, the Inspector General of the Royal Irish Constabulary, and Colonel Edgeworth - Johnstone, the Chief Commissioner of the Dublin Metropolitan Police, required their subordinates to furnish, full and exact reports as to the nature, progress and aims of the various armed forces in Ireland. From these sources the Government had abundant material on which they could have acted many months before the leaders themselves contemplated the actual rising.

"For the conduct, zeal and loyalty of the Royal Irish Constabulary and the Dublin Metropolitan Police we have nothing but praise.

"We do not attach any responsibility to the military authorities in Ireland for the rebellion or its results.

"As long as Ireland was under civil Government, those authorities had nothing to do with the suppression of sedition. Their duties were confined to securing efficiency in their own ranks and to the promotion of recruiting, and they could only aid in the suppression of disorder that duly called on the civil power. By the middle of 1915, it was obvious to the military authorities that their efforts in favour of recruiting were being frustrated by the hostile activities of the Sinn Fein supporters, and that they made representations to the Government to that effect. The general danger of the situation was clearly pointed out to the Irish Government by the military authorities, on their own initiative, in February last, but the warning fell on unheeding ears".

On Saturday 28th May 1916, another serious incident occurred in Co Kerry, about 10 miles south of Tralee town while two police constables were on duty between Farranfore and Firies villages. They were Constables Michael Clery and Thomas McLoughlin. They were allegedly following a man named James O'Riordan as he walked from Farranfore towards his home at Firies. He suddenly drew a revolver that he had in his possession and without warning fired at point blank range at the two constables. Both were seriously wounded. Before the shooting took place, the constables had been engaged in putting up proclamation notices. A widespread search was carried out for the attacker but he was never located and absconded to America.

For the two or three months after Easter 1916, Head Constable Kearney and the RIC in Tralee had a very busy time as a result of the fall-out from the events of Holy Week and the Easter weekend. There were several arrests and searches for suspects, the collation of evidence and the work that followed in the preparation of files for the Crown Solicitor. These were followed by the various trials and court-martials. It was August before the situation returned to any degree of normality.

THE TRIAL OF ROGER CASEMENT.

The Trial of Sir Roger Casement for high treason opened before three judges and a jury in the Royal Courts of Justice in London on June 26th 1916. The Lord Chief Justice of England, Viscount Reading, presided. The prosecution was led by The British Attorney General, Sir Frederick Smith - a former leader of the Ulster Volunteers. Serjeant A.M. Sullivan, K.C., led the defence. Several police and civilian witnesses from the Tralee/Ardfert area attended and gave evidence.

Kearney was not a witness in the trial of Roger Casement nor did he travel to London for the event. He had not in fact been involved in the investigation of the case against Casement. With his wife, he took a very keen interest in the progress of the trial and they both deeply grieved for Casement after he had been condemned to death and while he awaited for his appeal proceedings and ultimate execution.

The trial attracted considerable interest in Ireland, Great Britain and internationally.

A number of books written about Casement give much detail about the Trial and evidence given at it. Rumours began to circulate during the trial relating to diaries being located belonging to Casement. It was alleged that these diaries contained references that strongly indicated that Casement had been engaged in homo-sexual activity. These diaries which became known as 'The Black Diaries' have since been the subject of controversy amidst allegations that they had been forged. On the balance of probability, the diaries were genuine. The British authorities with a view to blackening Casement's character disclosed their existence, perhaps in an effort to have a plea of 'guilty but insane' entered by his defence.

The jury returned a verdict of 'Guilty' on the treason charges against Casement on June 29th. Addressing Casement, the judge said –

"Sir Roger David Casement, you stand convicted of high treason. What have you to say for yourself why the Court should not pass sentence and judgement upon you to die according to the law ?

In reply, Casement made his speech from the dock, which ranks amongst one of the great speeches made in such circumstances. The Chief Justice then condemned him to death by hanging.

Immediately afterwards, Private Julian Daniel Bailey, was brought into the dock and charged with treason and pleaded 'Not Guilty'. Then to the surprise of everybody in the Court, the Attorney General stated that he was offering no evidence against Bailey who was accordingly acquitted by direction of the Chief Justice and he was discharged.

Casement's defence team lodged notice of Appeal against his conviction. Many prominent people including *'The Irish Party'* made numerous appeals on Casement's behalf, to the English authorities. There was no reprieve for him and on August 2nd he was notified that he was to be executed on the following morning. He was received into the Catholic Church on the same day and the execution went ahead on August 3rd as arranged. A group of people congregated outside Pentonville Prison when the execution was due to take place. When word got out that the execution was over, a cheer went up from the crowd and they dispersed. Casement's body was buried in quicklime within the prison confines. After several years of agitation and appeals for the return of his body, his remains were repatriated to Ireland in 1965 and after receiving a State funeral he was re-interred at Glasnevin Cemetery in Dublin.

REWARDS FROM THE 'IRISH POLICE AND CONSTABULARY RECOGNITION FUND'.

The outstanding police work performed by Officers and members of the rank and file of the RIC was assessed by the committee of the 'Irish Police and Constabulary Recognition Fund' following the Easter Rising of 1916 and one year later, awards and presentations were made to each member of the force who had been involved.

On Thursday 17th May 1917, at the Royal Irish Constabulary Depot in the Phoenix Park, Dublin, ninety officers and men of the RIC and Dublin Metropolitan Police were presented with certificates of honour for their conspicuous service in the suppression of the 1916 Rebellion. Sir Maurice Dockrell on behalf of the 'Irish Police and Constabulary Recognition Fund' made the presentation. Mr Richard Orpen RHA of the Royal Hibernian Academy designed the certificate. Each certificate was neatly framed and was worded as follows

'Presented in recognition of service to the State during the Sinn Fein Rebellion of 1916 by the Executive of the Irish Police and Constabulary Recognition Fund'.

Along with the certificate of honour, each policeman present [other than officers] was presented with a £5. 0s 0d in scrip of the War Loan.

The following members of the RIC from County Kerry were amongst the RIC personnel present from other centres and they received their Certificates and £5. 0s 0d worth of War Stock :-

Sergeant Daniel Crowley, Ballyheigue; Acting Sergeant Bernard Reilly, Ardfert; Constable George Carter, Causeway and Constable Patrick O'Connell, Tralee.

The following RIC Officers from County Kerry were amongst a number of officers who were awarded certificates of Merit by the Committee of the 'Irish Police and Constabulary Recognition Fund':-

County Inspector H.O.H Hill, Tralee; District Inspector E.A. Britten, Tralee, and District Inspector John A. Kearney, Boyle, Co Roscommon who was Head Constable at Tralee during the 1916 Rebellion.

None of the three officers were in attendance at the ceremony in the Depot on May 17th 1917.

The following members were also awarded Certificates of Merit and £5.00 War Stock, but they were not in attendance. They were:-

Sergeants R.A Crawford and Thomas O'Rourke, Tralee; Sergeant

Thomas J Hearn, Ardfert; Sergeant Patrick Brennan, Causeway; Sergeant Thomas Rahill, Farranfore; Acting Sergeant E.J.McKenna, Tralee; Constable George Neazer, Tralee; Constable Michael J. Dowd, Brosna and Constable James Donovan, Ballinillane.

6

A CATALOGUE OF DISASTERS IN CO.KERRY DURING HOLY WEEK, 1916

THE EARLY ARRIVAL OF THE '*AUD*'.

The H.Q. officers of the I.R.B., the Irish Volunteers and the Tralee/Kerry branches of the I.R.B/ Irish Volunteers, understood and believed that the '*Aud*', with its shipment of arms and ammunition, was to arrive in Tralee Bay on Easter Sunday night, or early on Easter Monday morning. All the arrangements put in place were geared towards the arrival of the ship on those days.

On April 6th, Roger Casement while in Germany, was informed by telegram, from Joseph Mary Plunkett [one of the leaders of the Irish Rebellion], who was then in Berne, Switzerland, in connection with the arms shipment, that the Irish Rebellion would begin on Easter Sunday 1916. He told him, that the German shipment of arms, should arrive in Tralee Bay not later than dawn on Easter Saturday.

The official message, sent initially, by the German authorities to John Devoy in America via the German Embassy in Washington read:

"Between 20th and 23rd April in the evening, two or three steam trawlers could land 20,000 rifles and ten machine guns with ammunition and explosives at Fenit Pier, Tralee Bay. Irish pilot boat to await the trawlers at dark, north of the Island of Innishtooskert at the entrance to Tralee Bay and show two green lights close to each other at short intervals. Please wire whether the necessary arrangements in Ireland can be made secretly through Devoy. Success can only be assured by the most rigorous effort".

This offer was accepted by the I.R.B. Military Council and was obviously acted upon, seeing that arrangements were made to obtain two signalling lamps and a suitable pilot boat, but the instructions relating to the dates of arrival, were obviously not adhered to.

In *"The Mystery of the Casement Ship"*, the author, Captain Spindler outlined the specific orders which he had received in relation to the trip:

"On April 4th 1916, I received my secret orders that were given in great detail. For obvious reasons, of course, I am unable to give here the actual

wording of these instructions, but I do not think that I can be held to be guilty of an indiscretion by quoting the following passages from Section 111 that deals with the carrying out of my task.

1. *Leave port in due time that the vessel arrives in Fenit Harbour in the days from April 20th at the earliest and April 23rd at the latest.*

2. *In accordance with arrangement a vessel to pilot the steamer is to lie in wait in the days from April 20th to April 23rd at the entrance to Tralee Bay near the Island of Innishtooskert. This vessel is to be recognised by day by one of the crew wearing a green sweater and at night by two green lanterns shown intermittently, so that they are not visible from the shore.*

"*Both of these parts of my instructions thus indicated beyond any shadow of doubt that I had to be lying-to in Tralee Bay in the time between Holy Thursday [April 20t^{h}] and Easter Sunday [April 23rd] in order to land my arms and ammunition at this spot, and that I was to expect there, within that period of time, an Irish pilot boat to be recognised by distinctive markings. This fact is of quite special significance for me personally as I never received any other instructions regarding the time at which I was able to make the delivery and I was unable to receive any later instructions because my ship was without wireless installation and consequently all my means of communication were cut after I had left German waters.*"

On 14th April, Philomena Plunkett, arrived in New York with a message for John Devoy, from the I.R.B.:

"*The arms must not be landed before the night of Easter Sunday the 23rd. This is vital. Smuggling impossible*".

John Devoy passed this message to Von Papen [the German military attache in the United States], who had it sent by wireless to Berlin on April 15th. The 'Aud' was then six days out at sea and had no wireless. It is difficult to accept that some word was not sent back to the I.R.B., that the 'Aud' could not be contacted and that the original arrangements should stand.

The alternative view, is that the I.R.B., carried on with the amended date arrangement, on the assumption that Captain Spindler, and the crew of the '*Aud*', knew about the new date for the landing arrangements.

The inevitable result of the date change, for the arrival of the arms at Fenit, ensured that the venture was never going to be successful.

THE *'AUD'* IN TRALEE BAY.

The *'Aud'* was clearly visible from the shoreline in Tralee Bay, during the afternoon of Holy Thursday. It was loitering around during the afternoon, and several people saw it. An eyewitness, Mr Dan Crowley of Fenit, related several decades, later that he saw the strange ship 'hanging around all evening' in the Bay. He said that it was a dark coloured ship, possibly completely black in colour. It spent a good deal of time between the Maharees islands and Fenit pier. It did not come all the way into Fenit Pier, but was not very far out - maybe a half-mile. He knew that it was not a British warship, and it was not like any of the ships that regularly frequented Fenit. He said that a lot of people saw the ship, and were wondering about it.

At the Court-martial of Austin Stack and Con Collins, Mr Frank Goodwin, a boat pilot residing at Scraggen Point, Castlegregory, gave evidence that he had seen the strange boat in the Bay. He described it as being painted black, with a black funnel, which had a white band on top of it. Two flags were painted on its side in the Norwegian colours.

One cannot but sympathise with Captain Karl Spindler, and with the twenty-one members of his crew, who found themselves in this precarious predicament, which he later described, in detail, in his book *"The Mystery of the Casement Ship"*, in which events unfold as follows :

"By 4.15 p.m. we were at the very spot - exactly a mile north - west of Innishtooskert, a long low-lying island which was entirely uninhabited.

"Now for it. With eager expectation we awaited the men who were to meet us here, and on whom the successful conclusion of our mission now depended. For the last half-hour we had had hanging from the bridge-rail the signal agreed upon with Casement.

"Now with the naked eye and then with our glasses, we scanned the surroundings. Nothing to be seen. Nothing moving in any direction. Not a boat on the water or any sign of life. The whole neighbourhood seemed to be dead. As there was no appreciable current here in the inner part of the bay, I lay-to temporarily with the engines stopped. When another ten minutes had elapsed and still nothing was to be seen, I began to feel a little uneasy. A quarter of an hour went by and from moment to moment our anxiety increased. We waited and waited with beating hearts, silently hoping that the next few seconds would see our wishes fulfilled. In vain,

The stillness remained absolute.

"*Slowly the minutes slid away. The half-hour's grace agreed upon was nearly up. I got my secret orders and read them through once more. There could be no doubt, I was at the right spot and exactly at the right time. But where were the Irish?*

"*The half- hour was up. I considered for a few moments what I should do.*

"*Turn back? No. Under no circumstances would I give up the game as long as any possibility remained of carrying out a landing. But how to carry it out? To run in, in full daylight without having established communication with Casement or any of his people would be foolish. I might just as well make the British a present of the munitions. Another point was that, according to my chart, the channel beside the pier was only six feet deep at low tide, so that if I were obliged to blow up the ship to prevent her falling into the hands of the enemy, hardly half of her hull would be under water!, I had no way of knowing then that my chart was not correct, and that the channel was, in fact nearer sixteen feet at low water.*

"*It looked to me as if something had gone wrong. On the slopes of Kerry Head, the northern buttress of Tralee Bay, and in several other places, clouds of smoke were rising from the hills. Could these be warnings intended for us? But if so, where the deuce were the men who had lit them. How could I know then, that it was the practice to burn furze bushes at that time of year?*"

With his crew, Captain Spindler pondered on the many things that might have gone wrong. They gave serious consideration to every possible eventuality, which had resulted in the fact, that there was no pilot boat and no signals. Spindler continues:

"*I had abandoned the idea of leaving the bay again and returning after dark as being too suspicious a manouevre. On the other hand, to continue to lie here indefinitely would also be likely to awaken suspicion. I, Therefore decided to explore the inner part of the bay.*

"*At half-speed I headed for the shore between Fenit and the Hog Islands. While working slowly round the north point of Innistooskert some of these smaller islands lying behind it came into view. Some of these seemed to be inhabited, but none of the inhabitants was to be seen. We could now also see the first signs of Fenit, a little pier with a lighthouse. Behind it rose* the masts of one or two small sailing vessels, and to one side a number of brick buildings - the village. The whole thing had a depressing look for us. The only imposing feature in the picture was the ring of high, bare hills, which surrounded the bay. Nothing whatever to attract our interest - stay, what was that? Was there not a man standing on the pier? There certainly was! At the base of the flagstaff, from which was hung the folds of the British ensign stood a marine with his rifle over his shoulder.

"In striking contrast to his warlike exterior, the marine seemed to take no notice whatever of us, though we were now lying as large as life only a few hundred yards before him.

"We looked in vain for further marines, or any indication of the proximity of a large military force. Did they want to lure us into a trap?

"The pier was now so close to us that with the glasses we could make out every object upon it: so, of course, everything on board could be seen with equal clarity, if anybody was watching us. I, therefore, turned gradually away towards the north to have a look at the flat coast below Kerry Head. Perhaps, I might there find an opportunity to get in touch with the Sinn Feiners. After we had steamed all round the upper part of the bay, however, all hope of this kind had to be abandoned. Though we showed our signals more and more boldly as time went on, no one took the slightest notice of us. The situation became more and more extraordinary. For two solid hours we had been cruising about in the bay. It was beginning to grow dusk and there had not been the slightest sign from the land. The fact that no one had taken the slightest notice of our presence, or of our peculiar behaviour, confirmed me more and more in the theory that there was some kind of a concealed trap. Neither I nor any of my men found it possible to believe that the British really took us for a harmless trader - as afterwards proved to be the case.

"With these unpleasant thoughts running through our minds, we were glad when night fell and darkness shielded us from inquisitive glances. Instead of flags we now used a green light which we showed at short intervals both towards land and sea. Hour after hour passed and nothing happened. Darkness reigned everywhere, even in the village. Only on the pier there burned a small green light – the pier-head light intended to show incoming vessels the entrance to the harbour. From time to time we imagined we saw a signal light in one of the houses to the south - east; but always the glasses showed that we were mistaken.

"As midnight drew near, it became noticeably brighter – no wonder, for towards one o'clock the moon would rise. I approached the pier once more, this time to within six hundred yards, and, at the risk of discovery, showed my green light once again. Then, when this last attempt proved fruitless, I steamed slowly back to the rendezvous off Innishtooskert. Cautiously we felt our way along the cliffs to the anchorage. So still was the night, that even on the forecastle the stroke of our propeller blades could be clearly heard. It must have been an hour and a half after midnight when the anchor rattled down into the depths and we brought up in the shadow of Innishtooskert, in what seemed to us a hiding-place well screened in every direction".

Captain Spindler arrived at the following conclusions for the failure of the mission:-

1. The time fixed for the landing was changed at the last minute by the principals in Dublin, when there was no possible chance of communicating this alteration of plans to the *'Aud'* and the German submarine.
2. The Supreme Council in Dublin, did not take steps to see that the German ship received timely notification of this alteration, consequently no preparations were made in Tralee for the reception of the arms. If the Council had no means of getting confirmation, then it was all the more its duty to give orders for preparations to be made at Fenit for the reception of the arms ship between April 20th and 21st.

It is remarkable that no Volunteers, at either side of Tralee Bay, reported the presence of the strange ship, or raised any suspicions about it. Neither had any observations of the strange vessel, been reported by any member of the RIC, attached to the maritime stations located around Tralee Bay.

When the Tralee Volunteers heard rumours on the following day that a strange ship had been seen near Fenit, Quartermaster Billy Mullins was despatched to Fenit to make enquiries. He travelled on his bicycle and spoke to two men there, who worked on the pier. They confirmed to him that they had each been watching the ship. He reported back to the Volunteer headquarters at 'The Rink' and he concluded that -

"From that moment, all the years of planning started to go astray".

THE SUSPENSION OF VOLUNTEER TRAINING CAMPS AT BANNA BEACH.

On a number of weekends prior to Easter 1916, the Irish Volunteers from Tralee and Kerry, took part in training camps amongst the vast sand hills and beach at Banna. The Royal Irish Constabulary were at first very suspicious about these camps, but having visited them on a number of occasions and finding nothing illegal taking place, they ceased to pay attention to them and did not see them as a security risk.

These camps had been organised principally by Alfred W. Cotton. He had joined the Irish Republican Brotherhood while still in his teens. He was active in the Gaelic League and he helped to establish the Sligo Battalion of the Irish Volunteers. He became its secretary, while working in the civil service in Sligo. He came to Tralee in 1914, to work in the local Labour Exchange, and was appointed captain of the Tralee Volunteer Cycle Corps. He was dismissed from his employment in 1915, because of his Volunteer activities. He became a full-time organiser and instructor for County Kerry with the rank of vice-commandant of the Tralee Battalion of the Irish Volunteers and brigade adjutant.

Prior to Easter Week of 1916, the training camps were maintained with a view to assisting with the landing of arms at nearby Fenit. Unemployed Volunteers, would go to the camp on Friday or Saturday mornings, while the Volunteer Cycle Corps from Tralee would travel there on Saturday or Sunday mornings. Cotton later stated that *"the time was spent mainly in bathing, playing games and generally enjoying themselves. The Volunteers carried arms but there was little display of military activity"*.

He later explained:

"As these camps had ceased to be of interest to the RIC, I intended that on Good Friday a small but effective armed force of Volunteers would be encamped there to deal with any emergency which might arise and to have them on the spot when the arms ship arrived. But unfortunately this intention was not carried out, for while on a visit to Belfast in March 1916, I was served with an order under the Defence of the Realm Act forbidding me to return to the Counties of Cork and Kerry and confined me strictly to the city of Belfast."

Despite the exclusion order, Cotton intended to return to Kerry for the Easter weekend, but was advised by I.R.B. leader Sean McDermott, against doing so and to sever all connections with Kerry, until the Rising had taken place. He later commented:

"I thought of what would have happened had a party of Volunteers been in camp close by when the ship arrived and if Casement and his comrades had found our men ready to give immediate assistance when they came ashore. However, there was no weekend camp and I remember that Mc-Dermott did not like the idea of that camp. He seemed to think it would be dangerous. I was quite confident that it would not arouse suspicions. I don't think he was satisfied, and orders may have been given to cancel any such arrangement".

Had there been a camp over that weekend, those attending may very well have been in a position to assist Casement, Monteith and Bailey, when they landed or they may have spotted the *'Aud'* loitering around in the Bay, on Good Friday.

THE DROWNING TRAGEDY AT KILLORGLIN ON GOOD FRIDAY NIGHT, 1916.

The *'Aud'* was not fitted with a wireless transmitter or receiver. Considering the sensitive mission in which the vessel was engaged, it is difficult to understand why this should be so. Neither the I.R.B. nor Volunteers, were aware of this. At his home in Larkfield House, Kimmage, Dublin, Joseph Plunkett one of the leaders of the I.R.B. and Volunteer movements, who was an amateur 'radio ham' made several attempts in the weeks leading up to the Rebellion, to make contact with the *'Aud'*, through transmitting equipment which he had set up in his back garden. The results were negative.

The establishment of a temporary wireless station at the home of John P.O'Donnell, Ballyard, near Tralee was the brain - child of Michael Collins and Sean McDermott of Volunteer H.Q in Dublin. It was arranged that Con Collins, who was a post office official in Dublin and a native of Newcastlewest, Co Limerick, and who had a knowledge of wireless operation was sent to Tralee to take charge of the temporary transmitting station. He travelled to Tralee on Holy Thursday, where he was met by Austin Stack. He was arrested in Tralee on Good Friday and later stood trial with Stack.

Michael Collins and Sean McDermott selected five Volunteers at the

Dublin Volunteer H.Q., to organise the setting up of the wireless station. They were Cornelius Keating and Denis Daly who were natives of Cahirciveen, Co Kerry, Donal Sheehan of County Limerick, Charles Monahan of Belfast and Colm O' Lochlainn of Dublin. The plan was that they would 'acquire' the essential wireless equipment from Maurice Fitzgerald's Wireless College at Cahirciveen. It was then to be brought, to a predetermined location between Tralee and Castlemaine, on the Saturday morning, where it was to be handed over to Tralee Volunteers, organised by Austin Stack. They were to bring it to Ballyard and set up the temporary station there.

The five Volunteers received their final instructions from Sean McDermott on Holy Thursday night at No.44, Mountjoy Square, Dublin. They travelled by train to Killarney on Good Friday, where they arrived at 8 p.m. Outside Killarney town, two motorcars driven by Tom McInerney and Sam Windrum, picked up the Volunteers. They proceeded to Killorglin, where McInerney sought directions for Cahirciveen. McInerney's car proceeded on, but took a wrong turning on the edge of Killorglin town. The car drove off Ballykissane Pier into the River Laune, which was in high tide at the time. Local people rescued McInerney, but Keating, Monahan and Sheehan were drowned. The three deceased men became the first victims of the Easter Rising.

McInerney was arrested by local members of the RIC, who came on the scene and he later stood trial. The mission may not have succeeded in any case, as the RIC at Cahirciveen were maintaining a permanent checkpoint, at the Killorglin entrance to the town. This was an on-going security measure, related to the protection of the trans-Atlantic cable station on Valentia Island.

While the entire episode, which resulted in tragedy, indicated the lengths to which the I.R.B. and Volunteers had gone in making plans, it turned out to be a futile exercise, because the organisers did not have the correct date for the arrival of the *'Aud'*, which in any case, had no wireless equipment. The *'Aud'* had already spent the previous day - before the Volunteers arrived from Dublin - cruising around Tralee Bay, looking for the pilot boat, which was to meet it and for the pre-arranged signals.

THE TIP - OFF FROM NEW YORK TO THE BRITISH AUTHORITIES.

On Wednesday 19th April 1916, the United States Secret Service raided the German Embassy offices at New York. There they discovered a copy of the message, brought by Philomena Plunkett to John Devoy, from the I.R.B. in Ireland. The U.S. Secret Service, transmitted the message to the British authorities in London. Ironically, it was accepted that the raid made by the U.S. Secret Service, on the German Embassy, was illegal and contrary to International Law. The raid on the Embassy had probably come about as a result of suspicions held by the U.S.A. authorities about the German bona - fides at the time, when America was seriously considering entering the Great War against the Germans.

This timely tip - off to the British authorities, gave the British Navy ample opportunity to despatch a number of warships to the west coast of Ireland, more particularly to the Kerry coast, which would have been regarded as the most likely landing place.

Furthermore, the naval service - despite the other calls on its service in connection with the Great War - took on the policing and interception of the arms shipment on its own, without the apparent involvement of the military in Ireland, or the Royal Irish Constabulary.

7

PROMOTION TO DISTRICT INSPECTOR AND TRANSFER TO BOYLE

PROMOTION TO DISTRICT INSPECTOR.

Head Constable Kearney was promoted to the rank of Third Class District Inspector on August 19th 1916. He was fully qualified for his new rank and was one of the senior Head Constables in line for promotion. His promotion came as no surprise to his colleagues or to those who knew him well.

Only a small number of men from the rank and file of the RIC reached the officer rank of District Inspector. Fewer still made the rank if they happened to be Roman Catholics. From the introduction of the Cadet system in the RIC in the early 1840s, entrance to the Cadetship was gained through a competitive examination and afterwards by the nomination of the Viceroy. Those selected then underwent a six -month officers' training course at the Depot in the Phoenix Park. During that period they became members of the Officer's Mess, which was the exclusive Club reserved for officer rank within the Depot complex. The training course was similar in content to that for army cadets, at the military academies, with the addition of instruction in Law, accountancy and RIC Regulations.

It was generally accepted that considerable influence was brought to bear on the making of the appointments, resulting in the majority of those selected being from families of the Anglo/Irish ascendancy or from prominent English families. The average age of Cadets was 20 - 21 years, those joining from Great Britain invariably had a University Degree. Before sitting for their examination in Dublin they came to Ireland and attended 'cramming schools', for some months. Having served for some years and gained operational experience as District Inspectors, a good number went on to receive appointments as Resident Magistrates. In fairness to those appointed to the latter positions, they proved most successful in that role and were fair and open in their administration of the law. Some of those not appointed as Resident Magistrates went on to become County Inspectors with responsibility for the policing of a particular county - with the exception of counties Cork and Tipperary, which were each divided in two, having a County Inspector in charge of each division.

In a feature titled *'The R.I.C., a plea for Reform'* in the *'Constabulary Gazette'* of 1907, it was stated that -

"If a constable by sheer worth became a District Inspector, he was branded as 'a ranker'. Only by a miracle could a constable ever rise to the rank of County Inspector. By the time his elevation on seniority became due, he had reached the age of retirement".

This was a good assessment of the situation, as so few men had succeeded in making it to officer rank from the lower ranks.

John A. Kearney was forty-five years of age when appointed as District Inspector. He attained the promotion through his seniority in Head Constable rank and on the recommendations of his senior officers, as to his efficiency, good health, and all round suitability for the higher rank. The proudest day of his career - and life - occurred, when on his promotion, he received the 'officer's sword' which was a symbol of his office, at a ceremony in the RIC Depot, Phoenix Park, Dublin. He was then introduced to the other officers in the force, and was invited and welcomed to dine with them at table in the Officer's Mess by the Inspector General of the RIC, Brigadier General John A Byrne. The latter, by co-incidence happened to be the only Inspector General of the RIC to have been of Roman Catholic persuasion. This was John A. Kearney's formal introduction to his office. He must have been a very proud man, considering his fairly average background and that so few officers had made the rank from the lower ranks of the force. He gained it solely on merit.

TRANSFER TO BOYLE, CO ROSCOMMON.

He was transferred from Tralee to Boyle, Co Roscommon, and appointed as District Inspector in charge of Boyle District. His appointment was a very popular one and his allocation to a busy district such as Boyle was a tribute to the confidence, which his superiors had in his ability. First appointments as District Inspectors, were usually made to the more remote or less important districts.

The newly promoted District Inspector was genuinely very sorry and very sad at leaving Tralee. He loved Kerry and never made any secret of the fact. He loved the people of Kerry, holding them in very high regard and he never failed to praise their generosity and kindness, at every opportunity, which presented itself. Despite the tragedy which later befell him and which was orchestrated by a Kerry man, he never once waivered from these views and opinions of Kerry and its people, until his death.

Mrs Kearney, also had a great affiliation and love for Kerry and its people. She was born at Lyreacrompane RIC station where her father was a sergeant. In her childhood she had lived at Cloghane in the Dingle Peninsula and at Killorglin, when her father served at these stations. She was extremely happy growing up there and attending the local schools. In later life, she always reminded her children about her happy times there and about the beauty of the county. She was again very happy, while residing with her husband and family in Killorglin and Tralee.

There were eight children in the Kearney family at this time, five of them were attending the local primary schools in Tralee. They were happy in their schools and with their friends. Leaving Tralee was a big upset for them, and the journey by train from Tralee to Boyle was a long and lonely one.

On a professional basis, Kearney was a loss to his officers in Tralee and to the rank-and-file members throughout the RIC District. He was a tower of strength in their eyes. He was extremely competent, very firm but fair when dealing with subordinates and always maintained the highest standards of efficiency and integrity. They were sad at his departure. Members of the legal profession in the town, with whom he had a lot of contact in the course of their work in the Petty Sessions, also regretted his departure.

At the opening of Tralee Petty Sessions on 26th August 1916, glowing tributes were paid to the newly appointed District Inspector on his promotion.

Mr Wynne, Resident Magistrate, stated that he had only heard of D. I. Kearney's promotion on the previous day. He said that he had only one regret and that was, that District Inspector Kearney was leaving them, but that their regret was his gain. He proposed a resolution congratulating him on his well-deserved promotion. Mr R. Fitzgerald, J.P. seconded. He said that if he were to mention all the useful duties that Inspector Kearney had performed, they would probably be detained a long time. He said that he had come to Tralee with a high reputation and felt that his police records would, no doubt, mention all his services and experiences. He said that in his forty years experience he had never met a better officer. He said that

D. I. Kearney had earned the respect of all classes, discharging his duties without favour or affection. He was sorry that he was going from them, and wished him success in his new career.

Mr T. P. Liston spoke on behalf of the legal profession and associated himself with the resolution. He said that during his experience, since Head Constable Kearney came to the town, a better or more courteous officer, could not have been connected with the Force. He had performed his duty with satisfaction to everybody who had come in contact with him.

Mr Quinnell, Solicitor and Mr. Farrell, Solicitor, also associated themselves with the remarks of the Resident Magistrate.

District Inspector Britten of Tralee, returned thanks, on behalf of District Inspector Kearney. He had been closely associated with him for years and knew him to be a courteous and sterling officer. He said, that he was sorry for losing him, and was proud of his promotion.

SERVICE AT BOYLE.

D. I. Kearney, Mrs Kearney and their family moved to Boyle and took up residence in a detached house named *'Abbey Villa'*, just outside the town. From the point of view of his family, it was a major move for their school-going children, who had to transfer to new schools. The house was a substantial one, and had a separate 'maid's quarters'. They had far more space in their new home, and much more privacy compared with their earlier life in the fairly confined quarters on the first floor of a busy police station.

The Kearneys were also in a position to employ, a maid, to assist with the household duties, she resided in the house with them. One of the more humorous stories from the family's residence at Boyle, relates to one maid employed there. She was partial to alcoholic spirits. D.I. Kearney had made a sizeable seizure of 'poteen' [illicit spirits] and had retained a generous sample for production as evidence in court proceedings. Before the court took place, the maid had located the sample and consumed it. She refilled the container with water - leaving Kearney empty-handed for his court case.

The Kearneys became very settled in their new surroundings and some members of the family retained very pleasant memories of their six-year stay there. They got on well with everybody, until the events of 1922 'changed everything'.

At Boyle, Kearney was a highly respected officer. He maintained his high standards of efficiency, running an excellent Police District. He was popular with those with whom he came in contact, and was regarded as being a very humane individual. He had a close friendship with Percy French, the poet and songwriter. Up - grading to Second Class Inspector came to him on November 23rd 1917 - a little more than one year from his initial appointment as District Inspector.

Tragedy again struck the family shortly afterwards on January 6th 1918, when his daughter Ethna - aged fourteen years - died. She was the first child of his first marriage to Bridget Wallace. She was a much-loved and popular member of the Kearney family, and had made a huge contribution to the family by assisting in the rearing of the seven younger children. The fact that her mother had died at a young age, when Ethna was only four years old made her death all the more difficult for John A. Kearney to accept. She died as a result of peritonitis, which had by co-incidence also caused the untimely death of her mother. Ethna was interred at Boyle.

THE WAR OF INDEPENDENCE, 1919 TO 1922.

When the War of Independence commenced in 1919, D. I. Kearney found himself trying to cope with the situation amongst a much depleted RIC strength in his District. This situation was due to the fact that so many RIC men had joined the British forces during World War One and were never replaced. When the War ended, only about one third, of those who had originally joined the armed forces, were in a position to rejoin the RIC - the remainder having been killed or so badly injured that they were unable to resume duty.

From the time that Constables O'Connell and McDonnell were shot dead by Dan Breen and other members of the I.R.A. at Soloheadbeg in South Tipperary, on January 21st 1919, many RIC. men, who were eligible for pension, retired from the force. This created more gaps in the strength, which could not be filled, because recruits could not be trained quickly enough and there was a natural 'slow-down' on the number of young men wishing to join.

On the arrival of the *'Black and Tans'* in Ireland, to supplement the strength of the RIC in April/May 1920, Boyle District got its quota of members from this new source. While Kearney was glad to obtain assistance in his efforts to maintain law and order, he was not enamoured by the quality of the new arrivals. They were all former British soldiers, who had fought through the World War. The majority had never worked at any employment, other than being soldiers. Many were shell-shocked or suffering from other after effects of the War. Their standard of discipline was poor, and they had no knowledge or experience of policing. In general, they fell far short of the very high standards, which Kearney normally expected, from the men under his command. He allocated the newcomers to different stations around his District and ensured - in so far as it was possible to do so - that when on duty, they were always accompanied by a member of the RIC or under the direct supervision of a sergeant.

He made no secret of the fact that he never trusted the *'Black and Tans'*.

In July/August 1920, another force - the *'Auxiliaries'* - arrived in Ireland and a detachment of one hundred officers and men, with a supply of vehicles and armoured cars were allocated to Boyle. They took up occupation in the military barracks in the town and operated over a wide area throughout North Roscommon. Through a liaison officer, they maintained daily contact with the RIC. The Military Barracks, was the most substantial and prominent building in the town, and had been central to the history of the Boyle area for many years. It had also been an important recruiting base for the British armed forces. Another claim to fame attached to the building was that the Barrack Adjutant serving there in the early 1900s was Major C. J. O'Sullivan. His daughter Maureen O'Sullivan - the well-known Hollywood actress was born there in 1911. She was involved in the making of over 30 films as well as the popular *'Tarzan'* series with Johnny Weismuller. She married John Farrow, who died in 1963 and was mother of film actress Mia Farrow.

There was also a contingent of regular British army personnel, based permanently in the town, at the time. The RIC in Boyle had a close liaison with them, and there was a particularly close friendship between D.I. Kearney and the commanding officer - Col. Pilkington.

D. I. Kearney was an *'Irish nationalist'* at heart, all through his life. He was sickened by what was taking place, and every death in the struggle for independence - irrespective of which side it was on - was in his view one death too many. When compared with many other parts of Ireland, there were probably fewer deaths in the Boyle area by comparison, during the War of Independence. Kearney played his part in endeavouring to keep the casualties to a minimum, in the area under his control.

Like many other District Inspectors of the time, Kearney was not spared from tragedies relating to the loss of members of his District personnel during the period. According to *"Police Casualties in Ireland 1919 to 1922"* by Richard Abbott, the following were the most notorious tragic events which occurred in his District between 1919 and 1922.

1. On September 1st 1920, five RIC men were making their way on bicycles from Ballaghadereen, Co Roscommon, to attend Frenchpark Petty Sessions, when they were ambushed at Rathnacross. Constable Edward Murphy was killed outright, Constable Martin McCarthy, was seriously wounded and died the next day. Murphy was a single man who had just turned twenty-four on 24th August 1920. He was from County Mayo and had two years' service, having been a farmer before he joined the RIC. Constable McCarthy was twenty-eight, single, and from County Clare. He had eight years' police service, and was also a farmer before joining the force.

2. On 22nd March 1921, an RIC party was cycling from Keadue to Ballyfarnon to investigate a raid on the Post Office. When the patrol reached Blackwood it was attacked. Constables William Devereux and Michael James Dowling were killed outright and Sergeant Reilly was wounded. Constable Devereux was a fifty - seven year old married man, and a native of Roscommon. He would have had thirty - nine years police service on 11th April 1921. Constable Dowling was thirty and single, from Co Wicklow. He had seven and a half years police service and had been a grocer's assistant prior to joining the RIC Sergeant Reilly recovered from his wounds.

3 On May 23rd 1921, an extraordinary event occurred at Frenchpark, in the Boyle RIC District when three constables were reported missing. They were:- Constable Michael Dennehy, aged 27 years, single and a native of Cahirciveen,Co. Kerry. He had been stationed in Roscommon. Constable James Evans, aged 23 years, single and a native of Co Offaly. He was also stationed at Roscommon. Constable Robert Buchanan, aged 21 years, single and native of London. He was stationed at Roscommon. {He was a 'Black and Tan'.] The RIC and the military made intensive searches and enquiries to locate the missing constables, but they were never located and appeared to have disappeared without trace. It was presumed that they had been captured by the I.R.A and executed.

4. One month later, on June 16th 1921, another member of the RIC was re-

ported missing at Frenchpark station. He was Constable Harold Round, aged 23 years. He had been married on February 10th 1919 and was a native of the Lancashire in England. He was also a 'Black and Tan'. Again, extensive searches were made for him and despite these and numerous Enquiries, he was never located. In his case, it was also presumed that he had been captured and killed by the I.R.A. and his body disposed of.

5. On the 6th of the same month, another constable accidentally lost his life at Ballaghadereen. He had been on sentry duty at the barracks there. As he came off duty he was unloading his rifle when it went off and seriously wounded him. He died from his injuries four days later. He was Constable George Southgate, aged 23 years and a native of England.

These were very traumatic events for D. I. Kearney, like many other District Inspectors, who had similar unfortunate and regrettable tragedies amongst their District personnel at the time, he found himself trying to comfort widows, children and immediate relatives of the deceased men. In many cases there were problems in trying to recover the dead bodies of RIC men, and preparing them for burial. A major problem for RIC officers at the time was in acquiring coffins for the funerals of RIC men, as the boycott on the RIC prevented carpenters and undertakers from providing coffins for them. There was also a problem in obtaining hearses, to remove the remains for a funeral service. In at least one case in County Roscommon, the RIC were forced to commandeer a hearse, which they drove themselves to have the body of an RIC man killed by the I.R.A., returned to his native place for burial.

In several cases, members of the force were interred in local cemeteries, as their remains could not be taken back to their native places. Any funerals, which did take place, had to have strict police security in some parts of the country.

The deaths of the RIC men under his command grieved D. I. Kearney. It was a very worrying time for the wives and families, of those who were serving in the force at the time and this created extra pressure on the members. As a number of District Inspectors had been singled out for assassination, and were shot throughout the country, those who held the rank, had to be extremely careful about their own personal safety.

During his service in charge of Boyle District, he was commended by the Inspector General of the RIC in June 1918 receiving three Favourable Rewards - *"for his determination and ability in coping with a state of law-*

lessness in County Roscommon".

In 1919 the Lord Lieutenant specially commended him for his police work, in a raid for arms at Woodbrook. In February 1920, he received a further 'Favourable Reward' for *"Good Police Duty relating to a raid for arms".*

RESCUING A PRIEST FROM THE BLACK AND TANS.

A local priest, Fr Michael Brennan, spoke out very strongly about the Black and Tans in the course of a Sunday sermon. He was later kidnapped by a number of Black and Tans and taken to a remote area, where they intended to shoot him. On hearing of the incident, Kearney rounded up a number of RIC men and led them in hot pursuit to where the priest was being held. He challenged the Black and Tans about their actions and managed to get Fr Brennan away safely. The priest stayed in a 'safe house' for some days. Kearney insisted in the Black and Tans returning to Boyle, with him, so that they could not continue their search for Fr. Brennan. The priest was very grateful to Kearney and there was little doubt but that he would have been killed but for the courageous action taken by Kearney and the RIC men with him.

SAVING REPUBLICANS FROM DEATH.

During the War of Independence, there was an 'Active Service Unit', of the Irish Republican Army in Boyle. Niall Harrington, a native of County Kerry, with a few others who were not natives of the Boyle area assisted the local I.R.A. unit there, in enforcing a 'boycott' relating to the supply of goods by local shopkeepers to the RIC and Auxiliaries. This was part of a nation - wide campaign carried out by the I.R.A., and it was more successful in some parts of the country than others. Boycotting in Ireland, was a tactic inherited from the previous century and had its origins in Co. Mayo, where an infamous landlord named Boycott, was in serious dispute with his tenants, eventually becoming the victim of a 'successful' campaign of social ostracism. It was revived again by Sinn Fein in 1917, as a weapon against people who did not vote for Eamon De Valera, in the County Clare bye-election.

In April 1919, Dail Eireann, on the proposal of Eamon De Valera, approved the boycotting and 'social ostracism' of the Royal Irish Constabulary. De Valera made a very long and emotive speech, during which he said:

"It is scarcely necessary to explain what is meant by this motion. The people of Ireland ought not to fraternise, as they often do, with the forces which are the main instruments in keeping them in subjection. It is not consistent with personal or national dignity. It is certainly not consistent with safety. They are spies in our midst. They are England's janissaries. They are the eyes and ears of the enemy. They are no ordinary civil force, as police are in other countries. The R.I.C., unlike any other police force in the world, is a military body, armed with rifle and bayonet and revolver as well as baton. They are given full licence by their superiors to work their will on an unarmed populace. The more brutal the commands given them by their superiors, the more they seem to revel in carrying them out, against their own flesh and blood be it remembered.

"Their history is a continuity of brutal treason against their own people. From their very foundation they have been the mainstay of the privileged ascendancy and the great obstacle to every movement for social as well as for national liberty. I need not remind you of their record during the tithe and land wars or of their recent outrages at Ballybunion for which not a man of them has been punished. Punishment by their British masters - not likely. They are patted on the back, praised and encouraged. The British Minister, McPherson, to whom they are most directly responsible, speaks of their wonderful fidelity - there have been no Curragh mutinies in the R.I.C. - and promises that he and his Government will back them up, with all their resources, in everything they do and in every action they take. Very well, they have undoubtedly merited the praise of their paymasters, but the Irish people have a duty to themselves.

"If Mr McPherson may incite the police, the Irish people, as an organised society, have a right to defend themselves. The social ostracism which I propose, and which I ask you to sanction, is a first step to exercising that right. These men must not be tolerated socially, as if they were clean, healthy members of our organised life. They must be shown and made feel how base are the functions they perform and how vile is the position they occupy. To shun them, to refuse to talk or have any social intercourse with

them, or to treat them as equals, will, give them vividly to understand how utterly the people of Ireland loathe both themselves and their calling, and may prevent young Irishmen from dishonouring both themselves and their country by entering that calling".

Niall Harrington and two of his I.R.A. friends, were located at their separate lodgings and mysteriously beaten up by armed men in uniform. They could have been shot but escaped with their lives.

In later years, Niall Harrington, wrote his memoirs which were published as *"Kerry Landing"* and in which he referred to the above, and other incidents:-

"It was disquieting that the raids should have taken place on a night when three of the four of us who had received threatening notices could be found at home by the R.I.C.

"Years afterwards, Pat Delahunty told me in the course of a letter that, as Brigade I.O. [Intelligence Officer], he got occasional information from District Inspector John Kearney of the R.I.C. who was then stationed in Boyle. Some time after the raids by the masked R.I.C. men, he received a note from Kearney advising him to clear out of town and to tell Feely and Harrington to get out also. 'I met Kearney later' he wrote, 'and he told me that Colonel Sharpe, who was in charge of the Auxiliaries [in Boyle] intended to shoot us as a reprisal for the boycott'. Kearney had entered Irish history some four years earlier when, as head constable in Tralee, he had custody of Roger Casement after his arrest at Banna Strand on Good Friday 1916. He claimed after the Truce that he would have facilitated the rescue of Casement by the Kerry Volunteers if an attempt had been made. Be that as it may, it is beyond question, that he was in contact with I.R.A Intelligence during the 1920-21 period..

"It was evident that the R.I.C. had a great deal of information about us and our movements. There was no question of withdrawing the boycott and little prospect of enforcing it either. In fact, our immediate concern was how to avoid arrest, if not a bullet. Jim Feely went on the run. He was well placed to do so for he had the support of his family and their many relations and connections. In a sense, I was but a bird of passage in Boyle and could not count on such aids to freedom and a ripe old age".

The foregoing confirms that D. I. Kearney saved, at least, the lives of Harrington, Feely and Delahunty through his passing on of vital information to Delahunty, to the effect that they had been singled out for retaliation by the Auxiliaries. Theirs were probably not the only lives saved by him, during the War of Independence.

Further to the recollections of Niall Harrington, Pat Delahunty - the I.R.A. Intelligence Officer for North Roscommon, in a letter to Mr Desmond Fitzgerald, a Minister in the Irish Government in the 1920s, confirmed the fact that D. I. Kearney had passed on confidential information to him during the War of Independence.[The letter is among the Fitzgerald Papers].

While he passed on information to I.R.A Intelligence, it was solely to prevent more individuals being needlessly killed, or summarily executed by the Auxiliaries or the Black and Tans. He was obviously carrying out his administrative duties in a manner, which met with the approval of his superiors, because on January 18th 1921, he was appointed a First Class District Inspector. He remained as District Inspector in charge of Boyle District until his disbandment from the RIC on April 5th 1922.

Due to his unquestioned 'nationalist' feelings, the efforts made by him to prevent needless deaths, and his commitment to his work and profession, he clearly 'walked a very thin line'. While he did take precautions about his security and safety during his time in Boyle, he was reasonably confident that his life was not in real danger. His family did not receive any threats or upset from Republicans, while they went about their ordinary lives attending school etc, but they were always very anxious about their father's safety. Seventy years later they recalled the precautions being taken in their home, with all doors being locked and secured, and they were strictly warned not to open letters or parcels delivered at their home.

From July 11th 1920 when the Truce came into operation, things became quieter from an RIC point of view, with only routine police duties. The exceptions were occasional crimes being committed by criminal gangs, who had firearms available to them, and who were taking advantage of the lull in activities to enrich themselves. All members of the RIC accepted that their disbandment was inevitable. Those who did not have the required number of years in service for pension eligibility, concentrated their minds very much on negotiating a suitable pension when they left the Force. In this they were reasonably successful, but it was a difficult struggle. D. I. Kearney, would have had the required service in the force to merit a pension, but not the maximum amount.

A number of the smaller RIC stations in Boyle District were closed down during 1920 and 1921, and the personnel from those were allocated to Boyle. Following the Truce, Kearney was keenly aware of the breakdown in law and order, which followed the failure of constitutional politics. He sympathised with the efforts being made by a 'rather shaky' Dail Eireann, to establish a system of order in the new fledgling nation.

RIC Deputy Inspector General C.A. Walsh, put preliminary arrangements in place, to have the RIC disbanded not later than 31st March 1922. On March 15th, Michael Collins who had become alarmed at the deteriorating state of law and order in the country, requested the Chief Secretary to have the disbandment of the RIC postponed indefinitely. This request was considered by the British Government, but was not acceded to, on the grounds that it was not in conformity with the terms of the Treaty.

REPRESENTING HIS FELLOW RIC OFFICERS.

During the period from 1919 until the disbandment of the RIC, D. I. Kearney along with D. I. John Conlon were elected by their fellow officers to represent them on the RIC Representative Body. In the ordinary course this would not have been an onerous task but during these critical years it carried much responsibility and a lot of work. Members were very conscious about the uncertainty of their future and from once the Truce was agreed, they knew that their fate was doomed and that a date would be fixed for their disbandment.

The Representative Body met on a regular basis in the library at the RIC Depot in the Phoenix Park. During 1921 they were meeting almost on a weekly basis and there was a huge sense of urgency about these meetings. The main concern amongst the force related to the question of Pensions or what the amount of the pensions would be on their disbandment. A very big number of members had short service in the Force [these did not include the Black and Tans or Auxiliaries]. In the ordinary course, those who fell into this short service category would be entitled to negligible pensions. While the British Government admitted in principle that it had a *"debt of honour"* to the Royal Irish Constabulary, the Representative Body found itself making very little progress throughout 1921. Assurances were given but there was nothing specific offered or agreed. The Body had several meetings with the Under Secretary Mr Andy Cope and with other officials at Dublin Castle. The Body was basically seeking an addition of 12 to 15 years to the actual service of members with short service so that they could qualify for a decent pension.

Eventually the Representative Body decided to travel to London for a meeting with Sir Hamar Greenwood in October 1921. D.I.s Kearney and Conlon led the delegation, which also included representatives of the Dublin Metropolitan Police. The meeting was a fruitful one and the Rep. Body succeeded in getting 12 years added to the actual service of all members, thereby bringing all members with long service up to a full pension and those with shorter service qualifying for a reasonably good pension. The outcome was a satisfactory one. When the formal proceedings were over, Sir Hamar Greenwood and his wife hosted a dinner for the Representative Body members in the Pall Mall Restaurant at the Haymarket. While the Representative Body members were in London, the Irish Parliamentary delegation under Michael Collins was also there in negotiations connected with the Irish Treaty.

Both delegations met and D. I. Kearney came into personal contact with Michael Collins.

As a representative for his fellow officers, the second half of 1921 was a particularly difficult time for Kearney. Commencing with a particularly critical meeting at the Depot on July 26th, it became a frenzy of activity with meetings and representations until the Force finally disbanded.

8

ORGANISATION OF A NEW POLICE FORCE – THE 'CIVIC GUARD'

AN INVITATION FROM GENERAL MICHAEL COLLINS.

Everybody knew that a new police force would be put in place to replace the RIC. There was no definite indication as to whether the new force would be drawn from the existing *'Republican Police'*, the disbanded RIC, or whether a fresh start would be made with recruits being enlisted from every strata of society. On January 28th 1922, Michael Collins, informed the Provisional Government that a police organising committee was being formed.

Apart from the meeting, which D. I. Kearney had with Michael Collins in London in October 1921, it has been suggested that while serving at Boyle he was also in direct communication with Michael Collins. The latter was Director of Intelligence for the I.R.A. and the most prominent nationalist figures in Ireland during the War of Independence. There is no documentary evidence available to verify this. Kearney did not speak about having such contact later in life. He never made any secret of the great regard and respect, which he had, for Michael Collins. His family recalled his grief when Collins was assassinated on August 22nd 1922 and of the great affection, which he held for the memory of Collins, right up to his own death. He was in enforced exile in England when Collins was shot and if circumstances had been different he would most certainly have come to Ireland for his funeral.

In early February 1922, John A. Kearney was still carrying out his duties as the RIC District Inspector at Boyle, when he received the following letter:

Rialtas Sealadhach na h-Eireann,
[Irish Provisional Government],
Halla na Cathrach,
Baile Atha Cliath.
3rd February 1922.

Sir,
The Irish Provisional Government are setting up a Committee for the

purpose of drafting a scheme for the organisation of a new Police Force. Your name has been suggested to the Government for membership of this Committee and I shall be glad to learn whether you would be willing to serve.

The first meeting of the Committee will be held at Room 85, Gresham Hotel, Dublin on Thursday 9th inst. at 7 o'clock p.m.

Signed :
Micheal O'Coileain.
Chairman of the Provisional Government.

To :
J. Kearney Esq., D.I.,
Royal Irish Constabulary,
Boyle,
Co Roscommon.

He was naturally chuffed at receiving this invitation from Michael Collins, and without hesitation took up the offer, and the great challenge, which he knew lay ahead. He was confident that with his vast experience in policing he could make a substantial contribution to the formation of the proposed new police force. He attended the meeting at the Gresham Hotel, as requested.

Eamon Duggan, Minister for Home Affairs obtained clearance from Under Secretary Cope in Dublin Castle, for serving members of the RIC to attend the inaugural meeting at the Gresham Hotel.

Present at the Gresham Hotel on the night of February 9th were: Michael Collins, Chairman of the Provisional Government; General Richard Mulcahy; Eamon Duggan, T.D. and Minister for Home Affairs; Michael Staines T.D. and General Eoin O'Duffy.

The following high-ranking I.R.A. officers were in attendance:- Brigadier Michael J. Ring T.D. from West Mayo; Colonel Patrick Brennan, T.D. from Meelick, Co Clare, and Jeremiah Maher, Intelligence Officer who was formerly an RIC Sergeant. I.R.A.Commandant Martin Lynch from Co. Laois, joined the group some days later.

The following RIC members attended :- District Inspectors John A. Kearney, Boyle; Patrick Walsh, Letterkenny; Thomas McGettrick, Howth and Patrick Riordan, Cork. Head Constables James Brennan, RIC Depot and J.P. Foley, Musgrave Street, Belfast.

Sergeants Michael McCarrick, Letterkenny; John Galligan, Carrick on Shannon; Edmund Prendeville, Clonmel; Matthias McCarthy, Chichester Street, Belfast and Patrick Harte, Roscommon.

From the Dublin Metropolitan Police, Inspector Michael Kelly of Donnybrook and Constable Thomas Neary of Kevin Street Station, attended.

Former DMP Sergeant Edward Broy and former RIC Sergeant Thomas J. McElligott were also in attendance.

Also there, was a 'P.O'Shea' - whose identity has been lost to the mists of Irish history.

CHAIRING THE SUB-COMMITTEE ON ORGANISATION.

On the proposal of Michael Collins, Richard Mulcahy chaired the proceedings. He outlined the objectives of the meeting and gave a broad outline of the type of force which it was hoped to establish. He proposed that Michael Staines, T.D. be appointed as Acting Chairman, on the grounds that he [Mulcahy] already had too much work on his hands, relating to army business. This move effectively placed Michael Staines as the designated head of the new police force.

Michael Collins did not actively participate in the affairs of the meeting, but listened attentively to all the proposals and suggestions made.

Those assembled worked into the early hours on the morning of February 10th. Many proposals were made, and a lot of business was transacted. The following sub-committees were set up:-

Organisation of the new police force -
District Inspector John A. Kearney, Chairman; H/Constable James Brennan; Sergeant Michael McCarrick; Sergeant John Galligan and Inspector Michael Kelly, DMP.

Training of the new force:-
Sergeant Edmund Prendeville, Chairman; D.I. Patrick Riordan; Sergeant Matthias McCarthy and Constable Thomas Neary, DM P.

Recruiting for the new force :-
Head Constable J.P. Foley, Chairman; Thomas J. McElligott and P.O'Shea.

Conditions of service:-
District Inspector Thomas McGettrick, Chairman; Sergeant Patrick Harte

and former Sergeant Edward Broy.

Finance Code Committee:-
Sergeants Michael Cormack, Patrick Harte, Edmund Prendeville and D.I. McGettrick.

District Inspector Patrick J. Walsh was appointed as adviser to Michael Staines.

Riordan, Shea, Foley and McGettrick dropped out of their sub-committees at an early stage, and their overall contribution to the task in hand thereafter, was minimal.

Thomas J. McElligott resigned at an early stage from his sub-committee. While in the RIC he was involved in controversy relating to the setting up of a Police Union for the RIC and DMP. He later took the anti -Treaty side in the Civil War and was interned for some time.

The sub-committee established to produce a Finance Code, for the new force, failed to produce one, and it was a number of years later, before the first official *'Garda Siochana Finance Code '* came into being. All other sub-committees worked exceptionally hard at the tasks allotted to them. They were very enthusiastic, and had a great commitment to their work

SUBMISSION OF PRELIMINARY REPORT TO THE PROVISIONAL GOVERNMENT.

Within one week, the sub-committees submitted their preliminary reports, which were collated by Michael Staines and D. I. Patrick J. Walsh and submitted by way of a comprehensive thirty-one page document, to the Provisional Government, by Staines on February 17th. The report provided for a *'People's Guard'* type of police force, consisting of 4,300 men organised throughout the twenty-six counties [excluding the Dublin Metropolitan Area] in twenty-one Divisions. It made recommendations in relation to the uniform to be worn and the recruiting and training of the new force. The rates of pay were to be on a par with those of the RIC, and a recruiting officer to recruit new members was to be appointed at each county headquarters.

It recommended that recruits should be drawn from:- serving army officers; constables of the Irish Republican Police; members of the RIC and DMP who had been dismissed on conscientious grounds; civilians, and members of the RIC and DMP following their disbandment. All promotions in the new force would come from the rank-and-file members of the new force and there would be no cadets.

It was also recommended that the members should be lightly armed, with a Webley revolver.

The sub-committees continued with their work, and on February 27th a more comprehensive report was submitted to the Provisional Government. This report dealt with the essential qualifications for new recruits, the procedures for recruiting and an agreed formula of the proposed Oath of Office, to be taken by each member.

The final report of the Police Organising Committee was submitted and approved by the Provisional Government on March 3rd. The Government deliberated on a name for the new force and the title of *'Civic Guard'* was agreed upon. A headline in the *'Irish Independent '* of March 7th, read:-

"AN IRISH CIVIC GUARD. A SCHEME COMPLETED.
COMPOSITION OF THE NEW FORCE".

This appears to be the first time that the title of the new force was published. The feature included all details about the proposed composition of the new force, the system and arrangements for recruiting, essential physical and educational requirements and how promotion within the force would operate etc. It gave a comprehensive account about the framework of the new force, and when compared with the actual report submitted, the information in the newspaper was very accurate.

The final paragraph of the feature reported that on the previous day, a party of RIC men handed over 26 Ford cars, 4 Crossley tenders and 2 Crossley touring cars to the new *'Civic Guard'*.

[By co-incidence, the adjoining column of the paper carried a plea from the Irish Hierarchy, relating to the current crime wave and the duty of the public to co-operate in full with 'Peace Officers' in trying to curb the serious crime problem prevailing at the time.]

SERVICE AT THE BALLSBRIDGE RECRUITING DEPOT.

Kearney worked very hard as Chairman of his sub-committee and in the submission of its reports relating to the 'Organisation of the Force'. After submitting the interim and final reports there were on-going matters to be attended to by way of a follow up, and he carefully and diligently dealt with these. Due to his considerable experience in policing and his very sharp intellect, he was very much in demand for advice and guidelines, by some of the other personnel involved.

In the course of these endeavours, he remained in Dublin for the duration of his work and only made a few visits to his home in Boyle. In March his wife gave birth to a baby daughter named Dympna. He returned home for a few days for the event and to attend to his domestic affairs including the Baptism of their new baby.

During the early months of the new force, Michael Staines was given a free hand by the Provisional Government to make many of the essential arrangements. In this he received a lot of guidance and assistance from his adviser District Inspector Patrick Walsh. There was no possibility of the RIC Depot at the Phoenix Park nor any of the British military barracks in Dublin City becoming available to train recruits. The Royal Dublin Society premises located at Ballsbridge, was acquired as a temporary training depot. An undertaking had to be given that the premises would be vacated before the Spring Show.

Before recruiting actually began, four prospective candidates had already made their way to the R.D.S. on February 21st to join the new police. Others who arrived on the following days, and who were considered eligible were retained and given some work to do at the depot, until attestations actually got under way.

Mattresses and bedding were obtained for the new recruits from British military barracks within the city, where troops were gradually being disbanded. By the end of March, seven hundred recruits for the new force occupied the main exhibition hall in the building.

The formation of a Mess Committee to organise the feeding of the new police recruits at the R.D.S. in Ballsbridge was one of the first priorities. Michael Staines was elected as President of the Committee, Kearney was elected Vice-President.

The other members of the Mess Committee were Michael J. Ring, Martin Lynch and Edmund Prendeville.

With Staines' involvement in so many aspects of the organisation as well as his role as a T.D., most of the organising work to arrange food and mess requirements fell on Kearney's shoulders. When recruits began to arrive in late February, food was available for them - even though it may not have been of 'five star' quality. Catering equipment consisting of emergency field kitchens was obtained from one of the Dublin military barracks that was being evacuated.

EMPLOYMENT OF APPOINTMENT OFFICERS.

Twelve *'Appointment Officers'* were employed by the Organising Committee to travel around the country for the purpose of enlisting recruits for the new force. They were paid £7. per week plus travelling expenses. Six 'Assistant Appointing Officers' were also employed at a wage of £4. 10s. per week. No sooner had recruiting got under way, than serious problems became evident which would also have serious repercussions in the months ahead. From late February onwards, the appointed recruiting officers in each county were being antagonised by the anti-Treatyite elements in their respective parts of the country. Gregory Allen in his book *"The Garda Siochana"* summarises what happened at this time:

"The brigade recruiting officers became the first target for the opponents of the new state. They were arrested, kidnapped, held in custody and threatened, attempts were made to extract pledges of neutrality from them. The recruits themselves were held up, turned back, arrested and threatened with the most severe penalties. The object was to strangle the infant Garda at its birth. In September, Assistant Commissioner Patrick Brennan who was in charge of recruiting asked for a supply of plain envelopes for use in areas controlled by the Irregular forces to protect the identity of the candidates."

Those opposed to the Provisional Government, maintained their campaign to disrupt the recruiting procedures, and to discourage eligible young men from joining. Genuine young men who wanted to join, had, in many cases, to travel to railway stations several miles from their home, to prevent their identification, by the Irregulars, who certainly would have prevented them from joining the Civic Guard.

The sub-committee on training pointed out the necessity for a comprehensive training programme for the new recruits. The need for a strict code of discipline was also emphasised. Recruits who displayed initiative and intelligence, in the early stage of their training were appointed as company orderlies, and drill and classroom instructors. The only training material available relating to police duties were old *'Manuals of Law and Police Duties'* left behind by the RIC. Much of the time was taken up with drill and physical training instruction. Training went on in a fairly haphazard manner, into late April, when the recruits had to evacuate the R.D.S. before the Spring Show and move to the Kildare Military Barracks in Kildare town.

APPOINTMENT OF MICHAEL STAINES AS COMMISSIONER AND OTHER OFFICERS.

On 10th March, Michael Staines, was officially appointed as Commissioner of the Civic Guard, by the Provisional Government, Colonel Commandant Patrick Brennan T.D. was appointed as Depot Commandant. On March 27th, Brennan was promoted to Assistant Commissioner with responsibility for recruiting, finance and discipline. [Brennan was the former Commanding Officer of the East Clare Brigade of the I.R.A.]. On the same day, RIC Sergeants Galligan and McCormack were appointed as assistant storekeeper and accounting officer respectively.

The official records of appointments made at the time are not available but it is accepted that the two RIC officers - Kearney and Walsh - who remained on to assist with the setting up of the new police force following the completion of the report, were to be appointed Superintendents at the earliest opportunity with a promise of higher ranks to come. District Inspectors McGettrick and O'Riordan had left when the report on the organisation of the new force was completed. Neither Kearney nor Walsh returned to active duty in the RIC following their arrival in Dublin on February 9th. It has been frequently stated that Kearney held the rank of Assistant Commissioner or Deputy Commissioner in the Civic Guard, but it can be taken that he never held either of these ranks. District Inspector Patrick Walsh was promoted to the rank of Deputy Commissioner on April 6th - the day following his disbandment from the RIC. This was the second highest rank in the force - next to Commissioner Staines and more senior to that of Assistant Commissioner Brennan.

By May 1st, the following appointments had been made and approved of by the Provisional Government:-

Matthias McCarthy and Michael McCormack, promoted Chief Superintendents.

Edmund Prendeville, John Galligan, Jeremiah Maher, James Brennan, Patrick Harte, Bernard O'Connor and Robert McCrudden, all promoted Superintendents.

The foregoing had all been members of the RIC.

The following former Volunteer/I.R.A officers were appointed on the same date:-

Patrick Brennan, to Assistant Commissioner
Michael J. Ring, to Chief Superintendent.
Martin Lynch, Sean Liddy, John Keane, Francis Burke, Daniel Hallinan, Patrick Kelleher and John J. Byrne, to Superintendent rank.

Thomas Neary, formerly of the DMP was also appointed as a Superintendent.

Former RIC men got most of the senior ranks, and received a greater number of appointments than the former Volunteer officers. This situation became a bone of contention amongst the former Volunteer/I.R.A men, and it contributed significantly to the later Mutiny at Kildare.

The appointments by the Provisional Government of the former RIC men were understanable, as it had already taken a firm decision to have the new force under the control of experienced and professional police or military personnel. Michael Collins and the other senior members of the Cabinet, were determined to stick with this decision.

DISAPPOINTMENT FOR DISTRICT INSPECTOR KEARNEY.

The major surprise, was that the name of D.I. Kearney did not appear amongst the list of those promoted. On seniority, experience, professionalism and commitment, he would - with the exception of District Inspector Patrick J. Walsh - have been very far ahead of those who had been promoted. The notable absence of his name from the Promotion List, indicated that he was no longer in favour with Commissioner Staines, who obviously had capitulated to those who had persevered with lies and false allegations against him.

FORMATION OF A 'DISSIDENT COMMITTEE' AMONGST THE RECRUITS AT BALLSBRIDGE.

Early in March, a dissident committee was formed amongst the recruits in training and on March 14th, Patrick Brennan, who was Depot Commandant at the time, met a deputation from the committee. The deputation aired its grievances about the appointment of former RIC men to high - ranking posts in the organisation. Brennan told them that the appointment of the RIC advisers was only a temporary measure and this satisfied the members of the deputation.

The foremost activist amongst the recruits, in the creation of dissension, spreading of false rumours about Kearney and promoting a general anti - RIC campaign within the Ballsbridge Depot was, Thomas P. Daly, a native of County Cork. As a result of claims made by him relating to the prominent role he had played in General Tom Barry's famous Fighting Column in West Cork, he was placed in a position of trust at the training depot, when appointed as head of the depot defence unit. [His claim to notoriety as one of Tom Barry's great fighting men later failed to stand up to scrutiny.] He subsequently created major problems for the organisation, and the members who conducted the Inquiry into the Kildare Mutiny concluded that he had been 'planted' amongst the recruits as an agent for the Irregular or anti-Treaty forces led by Rory O'Connor. His objective in being in the new force, was clearly to de-stabilise it in any way possible.

A *'CLARE CLIQUE'* BECOMES EVIDENT AMONGST RECRUITS AND STAFF.

During the early months of recruitment, County Clare got more than its fair share of recruits, resulting in about one third of those in training being from that county. This was due in no small way to the considerable influence held in the new organisation by former Volunteer/ I.R.A Officers Patrick Brennan [Assistant Commissioner], Sean Liddy, Sean Scanlon and Patrick Haugh. This led to the development of a *'Clare clique'* within the organisation, it became very evident and pronounced a few months later, while the Kildare Mutiny raged.

9

STACK'S CAMPAIGN AGAINST KEARNEY AND THE 'CIVIC GUARD'

AUSTIN STACK'S CAREER - 1916 TO 1922.

John A. Kearney had no contact with Austin Stack - or Con Collins - from the time that their Court-martial concluded in June 1916. Both were then sentenced to Penal Servitude for Life. On being sentenced they were both committed to Mountjoy Prison, and after a few days there, they were transferred to Dartmoor in England. At Christmas 1916, Stack was transferred to Lewes Prison near Brighton. While in prison, he was elected Chairman of Kerry County G.A.A. Board and also elected as a member of Kerry County Council. After creating agitation in the prison, Stack and other prisoners were transferred to Portland Prison in Dorset in June 1917. A few weeks later, the House of Commons decided to release all Irish political prisoners. Stack and the others, were released on June 17th 1917. While in prison, he had become a close friend of Thomas Ashe, a school teacher and a native of Lispole, Dingle, Co Kerry, who had taken a prominent part in the 1916 Rising. There was a big welcome home for Stack, Ashe and other Kerry prisoners, when they arrived back in Kerry some days after their release.

Stack addressed a number of public meetings whilst wearing his Volunteer uniform in County Kerry. On August 5th he made a speech at Banna Beach where Casement had been arrested in 1916. On August 28th, he was arrested in connection with his public speeches, whilst wearing a Volunteer uniform. He was convicted and sentenced to two years imprisonment. He was committed to Mountjoy Prison to serve his sentence. On September 20th, a hunger strike commenced at the prison, involving about forty members of Sinn Fein who were seeking political status. Stack and Thomas Ashe were the principle leaders of the hunger strike and the agitation for political status. The prison authorities decided to 'force feed' the hunger strikers. Thomas Ashe died as a result of being forcibly fed. The concessions sought were given to the prisoners. The hunger strike ended on September 25th. Stack's reputation as a Sinn Fein leader, was very much enhanced arising from the outcome of the hunger strike. With other prisoners who participated in the hunger strike, he gave evidence as a witness at the inquest on Thomas Ashe.

On November 8th, he was transferred with other prisoners to Dundalk prison. When political status was refused by the prison authorities there, Stack organised another hunger strike, until their demands were met. On November 17th all the political prisoners at Dundalk prison were released. On his release, he was re-elected to the executive of the Irish Volunteers on November 19th. He was also joint honorary secretary of Sinn Fein, along with Darrell Figgis.

PRISON REVOLT.

By May 1918, Stack was again actively involved in Sinn Fein affairs in Tralee and County Kerry, on May 3rd he was arrested and removed to Cork Prison. Some days later he was transferred to Belfast Prison, to undergo the balance of the two years sentence imposed on him in August 1917. There were about seventy Sinn Fein prisoners in the prison. Conditions there were extremely bad, and the food was very poor. Agitation to have the situation rectified began immediately on their arrival. Following a week of violence and damage to property by the prisoners, their rights were restored on July 7th. Stack acted as leader of the prison revolt while the permanent leader Joe McDonagh, was absent attending court and on 20th July, the Sinn Fein prisoners elected Stack prison commandant. A few weeks later, the prisoners went on hunger strike for political status, it was granted within a few days.

Nevertheless, conditions deteriorated in the prison, representations by Stack to the Prison Governor, on behalf of the prisoners proved fruitless. He made a number of attempts to have representations made on behalf of the prisoners by the Lord Mayor of Dublin, but without success. Things came to a head, when a prisoner admitted to the prison on a charge of shooting a policeman, was not granted political status. A bitter mutiny then took place, involving all the Sinn Fein prisoners.

A major confrontation took place between the Sinn Fein prisoners and the prison authorities. Efforts by the prison chaplain failed to end the hostilities. The police were called in to quell the disturbance. Over the Christmas period, the prisoners went on to the roof and caused serious damage to it. Cell doors were torn off their hinges and internal stairways were pulled out. Stack was the acknowledged leader of the prison revolt, the Catholic Bishops of Dublin and Belfast and the Lord Mayor of Dublin went to the prison to speak to him. They also addressed the prisoners, and on certain undertakings being given to the prisoners, they called off their protest on January 1st. Public meetings were held in several places, all over Ireland, seeking the release of the prisoners from Belfast Prison.

Those involved in the mutiny were kept in solitary confinement, until the end of April 1919, despite representations being made on their behalf by County Councils and other public bodies.

On April 29th, Austin Stack and ten other prisoners were removed to Strangeways Prison near Manchester. They received prisoner-of-war status, from the time of their arrival there. All the other prisoners who had been at Belfast were released by the end of July, only Stack and the other leaders of the prison mutiny remained in prison.

ELECTION TO DAIL EIREANN IN 1918.

When arrangements were made for the holding of a General Election in December 1918, Stack was selected as a candidate for Sinn Fein in West Kerry. He accepted the nomination in November, while still in Belfast Prison. The sitting M. P., Mr Tom O'Donnell of the Irish Party, withdrew as a candidate, resulting in Stack being elected without opposition for West Kerry.

ESCAPE FROM PRISON AND APPOINTED 'MINISTER FOR HOME AFFAIRS'.

Michael Collins organised plans for the escape of Stack and others from Strangeways Prison. This was successfully accomplished on October 25th 1919 by means of a rope ladder being thrown over the prison wall at a pre-arranged time. They stayed around the Liverpool area for some days, before returning to Dublin where they remained in hiding for some weeks. Stack's health was not good at this time. Michael Collins decided that he [Stack] should remain in Dublin. He took up residence at Landsdowne Terrace. He was at this time, the Deputy Chief of Staff at I.R.A. Headquarters and he was also the Honorary Joint Secretary of Sinn Fein. In November 1919, he became Minister for Home Affairs in the new Dail Eireann. His formal appointment was agreed by the Dail Cabinet in January 1920, and ratified by the Dail some time later. He had an office at Henry Street, Dublin, from which he worked.

ORGANISING REPUBLICAN COURTS AND REPUBLICAN POLICE.

Early in 1920, he set about setting up the Republican Courts as a priority. He was also endeavouring to establish 'Arbitration Courts' to deal with land problems. He tried to get finance for these projects, managing to get a number of legal people together, to draw up a suitable framework for the operation of the Courts. He succeeded in having Parish, District and higher Republican Courts established, and in July 1920, they were made the subject of a Suppression Order by the British authorities.

Most of Stack's work as a Minister, was taken up in establishing the Courts and the Republican Police, who were required to enforce orders made and to bring offenders to the Courts. In June 1920, he was allocated £10,400 to run his Department..

The '*Government of Ireland Act*' came into operation on May 3rd 1921, and it was arranged to hold elections in Ireland - North and South. All the Sinn Fein candidates in Southern Ireland were elected without a poll. Sinn Fein decided to contest the election in Northern Ireland, Stack was appointed as Director of Elections for this area.

THE ESTABLISHMENT OF THE PROVISIONAL GOVERNMENT.

Stack vigorously opposed the Treaty. He would not accept it under any circumstances, he maintained this position until his death. He became a bitter enemy with Michael Collins and those who supported the Treaty. He did everything possible to prevent its ratification by Dail Eireann

In accordance with the provisions of the Treaty, the President, Arthur Griffith summoned all elected deputies in the twenty - six counties to attend a meeting at the Mansion House on January 14th 1922, for the purpose of forming a Provisional Government for Southern Ireland. All the anti - Treaty deputies - including Austin Stack - failed to attend that meeting. The parliament met. The Treaty was approved of. Michael Collins was appointed chairman of the Provisional Government and a cabinet was elected. Eamon Duggan became Minister for Home Affairs, resulting in Stack, losing his position as the Minister for that portfolio.

On losing his portfolio with the formation of the Provisional Government in 1922, his obsession with the retention of the Irish Republican Police became even more bitterly pronounced. Austin Stack T.D. became the leader of the opposition to the new police force then being established.

OPERATION OF THE REPUBLICAN COURTS AND REPUBLICAN POLICE.

The Republican Courts, which had been set up by Stack, could not operate without 'police', and the organisation of the Republican Police became his other main priority. In a report to Dail Eireann of August 17th 1921, he reported to the Dail on the development of the Republican Police. –

"The Republican Police ..... have been practically established throughout the whole country. This force is certain to prove an efficient arm of government in the maintenance of order in the execution of court orders. The work of the brigade police officers will be heavy and responsible and I propose to make those men whole-time officials. For this purpose I shall move for a vote."

On the following day, Stack moved for a vote of £5,000 for the police and indicated that the police had already been elected by the army [the I.R.A.] and assigned to his Department.

The establishment and operation of the Republican Courts and police system is well summarised as follows by Conor Brady in his book *"Guardians of the Peace"*.

"In 1918 the R.I.C. had 1,129 stations throughout the thirty-two counties, but by early 1920 that figure had been reduced almost by half. As the police withdrew, other elements of the Castle bureaucracy ceased to function as well. Local authorities made declarations of support for Dail Eireann, health and welfare boards reported to the Dail's departments of state, and

in county after county the Crown courts effectually ceased to operate.

"The withdrawal of the R.I.C. left a massive administrative vacuum in the community. Rates and taxes could not be gathered, court orders could not be enforced and legal debts could not be collected. In a community where deprivation and real hardship were still common, the growth of disorder was widespread and swift. As the area under R.I.C. control diminished, the Dail realised that to be consistent with its own claims of jurisdiction it would have to create alternative police and courts and thus in June 1919 the hitherto largely imaginary machinery of the Dail government was extended to include a system of courts and police.

"County Clare was the first to adopt these new institutions and by the autumn of 1919 the county had a flourishing network of parish and district courts. A police section was drawn from the I.R..A. which, it was hoped, would enforce the orders of Sinn Fein courts as well as performing regular police duties. By early 1920 these courts were functioning in twenty-eight of the thirty-two counties. They were highly successful, operating - with the occasional local variation - on a code drawn up by a number of contemporary legal authorities. Barristers and solicitors pleaded before these courts, whose efficient and impartial operation became a major element in Sinn Fein propaganda to the international press.

"The Republican Police were, unfortunately, less successful. On a purely practical basis, policing in a war - time situation where the enemy would not distinguish between Republican Police and army - if indeed that distinction ever existed - was largely impossible. Moreover, many battalion commanders reasoned that if a good man with a gun was available for active service, he could be put to more productive work than chasing petty criminals and moonshiners.

"The wave of crime and lawlessness which followed the withdrawal of the R.I.C., was a manifestation of long-pent-up resentment and distress among the communities of rural Ireland. Unemployment, low wages and the endemic squabbling over land had all engendered tensions and hostilities, which the firm hand of the R.I.C had long held under control. But by the end of 1919 the smouldering bitterness and hostility had overflowed into a wave of landgrabbing, anarchy and sheer criminal lawlessness. In the south and along the western seaboard, the traditional homes of the poteen industry, there was a massive increase in illicit distillation with all its attendant evils in violence, extortion and drunkenness. Later during

1920 the poteen trade was to expand beyond its traditional geographical confines and covered almost the whole country - even Dublin City".

The individuals who had been seconded from the I.R.A. units to become Republican policemen, gloried in the importance of their role, and in a short while, felt that they were indispensable. They knew that the disbandment of the RIC was inevitable, and that the formation of a new police force to maintain law and order would automatically follow. They were convinced that in a short time they would be the people who would become the natural successors to the RIC [in so far as policing was concerned]. They envisaged secure jobs for themselves, for the rest of their working lives, followed by pensions when they retired.

Early in 1921, Simon Donnelly was appointed as head of the Police. Stack had an extraordinary loyalty to those employed as Republican Police. He could not envisage their disbandment at any time or accept the fact that they would not automatically continue in their 'role' following the RIC ceasing to function. He was passionately committed to ensuring that the I.R.P. would be the police force to replace the RIC, thereby ensuring, permanent and pensionable jobs for the individuals involved, and high rank for the many Captains and Commandants who had emerged from the Volunteer/ I.R.A.

DISBANDMENT OF THE REPUBLICAN POLICE.

From the outset, Michael Collins was adamant, that the Republican Police would not continue on a permanent basis and that they would not automatically take over policing from the RIC. He made no secret of his views at the time, in a letter to W.T. Cosgrave in August 1922, relating to policing, he said :

"It is not necessary for me to illustrate this by pointing to the wretched Irish Republican System and to the awful personnel attracted to its ranks. The lack of construction and control in this force have been responsible for many of the outrageous things which have occurred throughout Ireland".

Staines, who was a pro-Treaty T.D., supported Michael Collins in his view, and early in 1922, Eamon Duggan T.D. Minister for Home Affairs, issued an instruction to all I.R.A. Battalion Commanders, to the effect that all Republican policemen were to return to their I.R.A. Battalions. Those involved were not pleased about this direction. Austin Stack and a number of anti-Treaty T. D.s were furious about the outcome. They were very vocal about the issue at meetings of the Provisional Government in February and March 1922 and they harassed Eamon Duggan, the Minister responsible, at every opportunity.

The grievance held by Stack, and the other anti-Treaty T.Ds, did not go away but 'festered', as the days went by, and continued to loom large in the affairs of the 'fledgling' new police force of the *'Civic Guard'*. This contributed to the despicable mutiny in the new force, which lasted until August 1922. It emerged subsequently, that some prominent members on the anti-Treaty side joined the new force, with a view to disrupting or wrecking it.

As part of their campaign to retain the Republican Police, Austin Stack, with the support of other anti-Treaty T.D.s – Donal O'Callaghan, T.D., David Ceannt, T.D. Professor W.E Stockley, T.D., Sean Etchingham, T.D., Miss MacSwiney, T.D. and to a lesser extent Eamon De Valera, T.D., deliberately set out to discredit the new 'Civic Guard' which was being organised during February and March 1922. Michael Collins and the Provisional Government, obviously expected objections and trouble arising from the issue because the organisation of the new force was kept relatively quiet, during the weeks subsequent to February 9th, while a considerable effort was under way to establish the force, through a number of hard-working sub-committees. There was no advertisement to announce recruiting for the Civic Guards and the media in general were unaware of the arrangements being made until about March 7th.

STACK'S PERSONAL CAMPAIGN AGAINST JOHN A. KEARNEY.

Stack and his fellow anti-Treaty T.D.s had a weak case to make in opposition to the proposed new police force and this is why they targeted District Inspector Kearney, whom they were aware was involved in the organisation of the Civic Guards.

It was understandable that Stack would have his own personal axe to grind with Kearney, as he had arrested Con Collins and himself and charged them with conspiracy to import arms, on the evening of Good

Friday 1916. Kearney would have been in serious dereliction of his duty, if he had not arrested Stack when the latter presented himself at Tralee RIC barracks with several incriminating documents in his possession. It is also understood that a warrant was already in possession of the RIC for Stack's arrest at the time he called to the barracks.

Stack also nursed another grievance. It arose from his failure to take any action to rescue Casement from Tralee RIC station on Good Friday 1916. Up to the time of his death, John A. Kearney always claimed that the rescue of Casement would not have been a problem for Stack or the Volunteers. He maintained that the front door of the building was unlocked during the night and that two men with revolvers walking in to the station could have rescued him.

Kearney had convinced himself from any early stage that Casement would be rescued, he advised his wife on Good Friday night to this effect. Kearney convinced D. I. Britten that Casement should not be handcuffed as he was marched through Tralee to the railway station on Easter Saturday morning. One must wonder if this was another opportunity being given by Kearney, for Casement's rescue. The fact that Sergeant Butler -who was alone - escorted Casement to Dublin certainly presented another opportunity for a rescue attempt. Some Republicans blamed Austin Stack, for not having rescued Casement. While serving imprisonment later in his life, it was alleged that some fellow prisoners had serious misgivings about his failure to take more positive action in Tralee, during the Easter weekend of 1916. This fact must have dominated Stack's mind, and caused him some anxiety as the years went by. It must also have been difficult to live with this suspicion hanging over him and this could also have influenced his attack on Kearney.

There were no reasons and no justification whatsoever for Stack to slander Kearney as he did, making false and malicious allegations about his treatment of Casement.

Stack knew that these allegations were not true. He [Stack] was in custody in Tralee RIC station himself on Good Friday and during that night, while Casement was detained there. He knew that Kearney had not arrested Casement, and he knew that Kearney had not given evidence against him at his trial. He knew Kearney for a number of years in Tralee and was well aware of the good reputation, which he had, for his fairness and impartiality as a policeman. Stack with his allegations very cleverly orchestrated the involvement of the other T. Ds. In supporting him..

They had also cleverly connived to bring up the issue during a debate on the estimates, on February 28th 1922, when they were fairly sure that the Minister for Home Affairs, Mr Eamon Duggan T.D. or other pro-Treaty members of the Provisional Government, were unprepared and would not have been in a position to deny their allegations. Relevant questions were on the Order Paper for the Dail meeting on the following day - March the 1st - and this would have been the more appropriate time to discuss the proposed new police force. Stack used Dail Eireann with its parliamentary privilege, to bring his grievances and false allegations into the public arena.

In the absence of any substantive facts or evidence, which would justifiably oppose the formation of the new police force, or which would make a case for the retention of the I.R.P., he methodically set about making false accusations against the character of District Inspector Kearney. His sole objective in doing that, was to discredit the new force, by taking away the good character of at least one potential high - ranking officer in the person of Kearney.

FALSE ALLEGATIONS MADE AGAINST D. I. KEARNEY DURING DEBATE IN DAIL EIREANN

The following are extracts from the *"Dail Eireann Official Reports"* for February 28th 1922. During the course of the Dail debate on that date relating to the Estimates for the half-year ending 30th June 1922, an estimate was put forward for ratification by Mr E.J.Duggan, Minister for Home Affairs for the sum of £9,000. to cover the cost of police during the half year ended June 1922.

"Dail Eireann - Official Report - Tuesday 28th February 1922."

Mr DONAL O'CALLAGHAN: *I desire to put a question and in doing so I may say I am putting it not with a view to criticising figures here, but to ask for information. Does the Minister propose any change or improvement in the police force? The House is aware that the providing of an efficient police force is one of the prime necessities of the moment. In Cork, for example, we have a Brigade area, which includes the city and embraces two hundred thousand souls. There we have only one police officer. We would wish to find out if it is the intention to extend and make the force more efficient.*

Mr E. J. DUGGAN [Minister for Home Affairs]: *The whole question of the police force is under consideration at the moment. I have received various notices in writing dealing with the matter, which I will answer tomorrow.*

Mr AUSTIN STACK: *This is a matter, which has a lot to do with Dail policy. We who claim that the Dail is the supreme Government of the country would like to know what the policy of the Minister is with regard to the police. For instance I have seen a paragraph in a paper in Roscommon to the effect that a District Inspector of Constabulary named Kearney, a man who was responsible for the arrest of Deputy Con Collins and myself, and the man who was chiefly instrumental in working up a case against Roger Casement has received an appointment from a body set up by the Provisional Government with a view to establishing a police force. Now, if that is done under the Department of Home Affairs and that is done with the knowledge of the Minister, and if that is supposed to be part of the policy under consideration at the moment, we are entitled to know all about it, and it is certainly a matter in connection with which I would move that the Minister be censured.*

The ACTING SPEAKER: *I should like to draw attention to the fact that we are now on the Estimates.*

Mr AUSTIN STACK: *The Minister for Home Affairs has his Estimate included in this, and the question of the police forces come under that. I say that this body and none other has the right to set up a police force to take over charge or control of law and order in the country. We would want to know before we pass the Estimate for the Department of Home Affairs, in respect of police anyhow, what is the policy of the Minister with regard to the police; what kind of police force he intends to set up; and whether he intends to utilise the services of men who have proved themselves to be the enemies of this country by remaining in the police force during the war, and doing their best against the people?. I certainly must be taken as pressing for information with regard to the policy as to the police before I assent to the passing of the Estimate.*

Mr E.J. DUGGAN: *My policy is to continue the policy of my predecessor. The Estimates provide for the payment of the existing Republican police force and that force will be continued as in the past.*

Mr AUSTIN STACK: *Since I was in office the passing of the Royal Irish Constabulary is supposed to have taken place, and the entire maintenance* of law and order has devolved upon Dail Eireann. Many representations are being made in respect of the matter and preparations are being made to set up a new police force. We would like to know the nature of these preparations, and if they are to be subject to the control of the Dail altogether, because we claim that the Government of the Dail is the Government of the country.

President GRIFFITH : *I want to know is it in order to allow all this hectoring to go on ?. There are questions down for tomorrow covering all these points. We have now, when we are on the Estimates, a gentleman trying to introduce obstructive methods. Is this fair; is this right is it in accordance with procedure?.*

Mr EAMON DE VALERA: *I submit if we pass away from this we may not have any other opportunity for discussing it. We have a perfect right to discuss it. I protest against the President saying every question asked for the purpose of seeking information should be regarded as hectoring or as introducing obstructive tactics. We want information. We gave this ourselves formerly, and I do not see any reason why it should not be asked now. If you are going to pass the Estimate for Home Affairs, and the policy as to the extent to which you are going to police the country comes up, it is obvious it has a bearing on the Estimates. It is not fair that every question should be put down as hectoring. As regards the £5,000 loan I suggested, I will give notice of the motion connected with it.*

Mr J.N. DOLAN: *May I say that, as far as I can see, the whole of the present difficulty arises because the opposition will not accept the straightforward answers given by the Ministers. The Minister for Home Affairs has stated definitely that, as a Minister of this Dail, his policy was to continue the police force and the policy of the Home Affairs Office in the same way as under his predecessor. That answer is not accepted; the opposition read something else into it.*

Mr DAVID CEANNT: *Seeing that the answer of the Minister for Home Affairs is not satisfactory, I will now move that the vote on the Estimate be reduced by one thousand pounds. If the allegation made to the effect that the Minister has taken on a man who has engaged with the enemies of Ireland, and who was more or less a "G" man, is true, it is certainly a matter for protest and I protest against such action. It is a scandal, and the people ought to know it in time.*

Mr D. O'ROURKE : *I think it is only fair to the Minister for Home Affairs that he should be asked if the statement is a true one.*

Mr E.J. DUGGAN: *The Estimate is for the payment of eighty-one officers and men who are already members of the Republican Police Force. They are the only paid officers in the police force because recently it was found desirable to disband the rank and file of the force and have the police duty generally done by the Army. The men, who originally came from the Army and who were disbanded, went back to their units, and the Army as a whole was made responsible for the police duty. There is no such man as Kearney in the Republican Police force that I know of.*

Mr AUSTIN STACK: *What I want to know is, is there a Committee dealing with the setting up of a police force, on which this man is serving?*

President GRIFFITH: *In my opinion the member for Kerry is trying to suggest that portion of the money voted here is going to this man. Any money you are voting here is for Dail Eireann forces. The money voted here is for Dail Eireann purposes.*

Following a number of attempts to adjourn the debate and a number of amendments having been made, the debate finally got under way. The following contributions were made by a number of deputies.

Mr DAVID CEANNT; *I would like to move as an amendment: That the vote asked by the Minister for Home Affairs be reduced by one thousand pounds on account of the unsatisfactory answering of the responsible Minister respecting the employment of District Inspector Kearney, late of the R.I.C. to assist in the formation of a new police force.*

THE ACTING SPEAKER: *Who seconds that amendment?*

Professor W.F.P. STOCKLEY: *I beg to second that amendment.*

Mr AUSTIN STACK: *I desire to speak in support of the amendment. I raised this question and it may appear to be a personal matter. I assure the members that, as far as the Ministers or officers are concerned, it is not, neither is it a personal matter with regard to myself and that lovely Inspector Kearney. This man Kearney was, from my experience of him, one of the most vigilant servants the enemy had in this country, and he did his best - by open means and underhand - to beat us. He claimed to have been the means of preventing the Rising in Kerry in 1916, and, I suppose persuaded his superiors that such was the case, because to my knowledge, he was a man who had previously failed in all his examinations for promotion to the position of District Inspector. In consequence of what he did in 1916 he received the promotion. He remained in the R.I.C during the whole period of the war and, in common with other members of the R.I.C. he did not resign when called upon by the country. Instead of recognition, he deserves from the Dail - or any other people's Government in this country - reprobation. I do not wish to say any more about the Department or the head of the police, as the amendment is confined to Kearney, and I simply rise to support it".*

The Debate continued with further distractions, but the employment of District Inspector Kearney in a new police force was raised again.

Mr SEAN ETCHINGHAM: *We have not got an answer to a very simple question. The Minister for Home Affairs can answer the question. Has he employed this man, Kearney, the hunter of Roger Casement, in connection with the new police force?.*

Mr E.J.DUGGAN: *There is a police committee at work but I do not know the names or the records of many of the gentlemen on it; if anyone likes to put down a question I will enquire. I cannot answer the question at this moment.*

Mr AUSTIN STACK: *But you can discuss the policy of the Department.*

Mr FINIAN LYNCH: *Is this the Dail Department or the Department of the Provisional Government? Is the Dail Department empowered to form a police force in substitution for the R.I.C. or the D.M.P.? . I do not believe they have any power to do so.*

Following contributions to this aspect of the Debate, by President Griffith, Mr Eamon de Valera and Miss MacSwiney T.D. [sister of the late Terence MacSwiney, Lord Mayor of Cork who died on hunger strike at Brixton Prison] raised the Kearney issue again.

Miss MacSWINEY: *Will the Minister for Home Affairs give an undertaking that he will not employ in the police force any man, or any body of men, who has or have taken a part against the Irish people, in the recent, or the present war. Can we get an answer definitely that any such man as Kearney is employed by him in any capacity which he holds as an Irishman?*

President GRIFFITH: *Men remained in the R.I.C. during the recent war at our request.*

Miss MacSwiney : *Kearney is not one of them.*

President GRIFFITH: *There were men who offered to resign. I got at least one thousand applications from men who were willing to resign if we could help them out. They were quite willing to help us.*

Miss MacSWINEY: *Is this man Kearney in that category?*

President GRIFFITH: *I do not know who Kearney is. But I know that the question of Kearney is raised only for one purpose.*

Mr FINIAN LYNCH: *In speaking of matters of that sort can we be told who thrust a bayonet through the photograph of Casement in the Volunteer Hall at Cork in Easter Week, 1916 ?.*

Miss MacSWINEY : *He was recently offered a position in the Free State police force.*

The ACTING SPEAKER: *This matter is entirely out of order.*

[N.B. The name of the candidate for the new police force who had thrust a bayonet through Casement's photograph in Cork was not given to the Dail and it had nothing to do with D.I. Kearney.]

Further acrimony followed in the Debate before Mr George Gavan Duffy, T.D. followed with his contribution to the debate. [He had acted as a Junior Counsel at the defence of Roger Casement during his trial in 1916 and by co-incidence wrote the letter to John A Kearney acknowledging the receipt of Casement's watch.].

Mr G.GAVAN DUFFY: *The time has come when we might pass on from this business.*

Mr DAVID CEANNT: *My motion is before the House.*

Mr G. GAVAN DUFFY: *We could easily avoid this unsatisfactory kind of debate if there was a little less of what I will charitably call muddle on the opposite side. Two questions have been raised - the report of Ministers and the case of Mr Kearney. If it is desired to raise at a meeting of the Dail an important matter of policy, it surely would be the obvious course to give a notice to the Minister concerned. In this case it is manifestly unfair to expect Ministers who have been in office something like seven weeks to prepare reports. It would be absurd to ask them to prepare reports on their work during that period. The right way to obtain information is to ask beforehand so that the Minister could prepare an answer. The second thing is a vote of censure about this man Kearney, but the motion that the Minister for Home affairs can deal with that on the minute is perfectly ab-*

surd. The suggestion to reduce a vote upon a question sprung on the Minister like that is one that should not recommend itself to the House. The Standing Orders give you ample means of dealing with an unsatisfactory answer. You have all this now sprung on the House. That is not the best way to deal with public business. After the agreement at the Ard-Fheis, it is rather unfortunate that these matters should develop into a mere party question. That is the effect of bringing up matters without notice. I propose the vote be taken now.

The ACTING SPEAKER: *We have now the amendment proposed by Mr Ceannt*

to the effect that the vote be reduced by one thousand pounds. I will now put this to the House.

The amendment was put.

The ACTING SPEAKER: *I declare the amendment defeated.*

Mr W.T. COSGRAVE: *I want a record of the voting. We will put these gentlemen in their places. Get the names on record.*

A division was then taken on the amendment, when forty [40] voted FOR and fifty-four [54] voted AGAINST. All those who voted for the amendment included Stack and the anti-Treaty members of the Dail. All those who voted against were the members on the Pro-Treaty side.

THE 'SILENCE' OF MR GEORGE GAVAN DUFFY, T.D.

It is difficult to comprehend the omission of one further contribution to the Debate of February 28th. The Minister for Home Affairs and the remainder of the Cabinet were clearly taken unawares by the false allegations made against D. I. Kearney and were not in a position to deny or refute them, there and then.

In attendance at the Dail Eireann meeting of that day was Mr George Gavan Duffy, T. D., who had been a junior counsel on Roger Casement's defence team. He was son of Sir Charles Gavan Duffy, a well-known Irish Nationalist and M. P. who later became Prime Minister of Victoria in Australia. George was a member of the Irish delegation, which negotiated the Treaty in 1921. Later in 1922, he was appointed as Minister of Foreign

Affairs in the Provisional Government. He became a Judge of the High Court in 1936 and President of the Irish High Court in 1946.

He must have known better than anybody else of Kearney's innocence, relating to the manner in which he [Kearney] had dealt with Roger Casement. He knew that Kearney did not arrest him, and he knew that Kearney did not give evidence at the Casement trial. He was the man who received Casement's watch from Kearney, and had signed the receipt sent in acknowledgement to Kearney. As the junior defence Counsel at Casement's trial, he must have - on the balance of probability - been aware of the note which Casement had passed to his senior Defence Counsel, Serjeant Sullivan. In this note, Casement stated how well he was treated by the Head Constable at Tralee. Yet, despite the foregoing knowledge and events, George Gavan Duffy did not make a response to Stack's accusations in the Dail. Had he done so, the affair may very well have been different, and Kearney's good name and reputation may not have suffered as they did. A suitable intervention by George Gavan Duffy in the Dail debate, would at least have diffused the situation to some extent.

Stack had seized the initiative and without a denial from anybody on the Government side, on the day, damaged Kearney's reputation irreversibly to the extent that it could not be repaired. The false allegations had also been made under the protection of Parliamentary privilege.

EFFECT OF THE FALSE ALLEGATIONS ON JOHN A. KEARNEY.

D.I. Kearney appeared to have a very good relationship with Staines and all the other members of the Police Organising Committee, from the time they met and started working together on February 9th. Kearney got on well with everybody, one of his great attributes, was his ability to get on with people and to sort out problems through dialogue. He had no inkling that any move was afoot, by anybody, to single him out for retaliation, with a view to discrediting the new force. All of this changed when national newspapers carried reports of the Proceedings in Dail Eireann of February 28th 1922.

From that time onwards, Kearney became a 'marked man' and a 'hate figure' to those who wanted to believe the allegations made against him. His personal situation became very difficult. It worsened when the first batch of recruits for the Civic Guard arrived from County Kerry. Having been obviously very well primed and counselled in advance, they pointed out Kearney as the man who had arrested and betrayed Roger Casement at Tralee during Easter 1916. This allegation spread amongst the recruits from other counties like wild fire, they all believed it. It led to unrest amongst those in training - an unrest which ultimately manifested itself in the subsequent 'mutiny' of the recruits in Kildare a few months later.

Despite the false and worrying allegations made against him, Kearney kept his head down, working conscientiously over the following weeks at the R.D.S., where he was acting as a staff officer. He was a virtual prisoner in his office, before he departed to London, he was under the protection of an armed guard while he worked in his office. There was concern for his safety, more particularly because there was a supply of firearms available at the R.D.S. training depot.

FURTHER DAIL QUESTIONS RE NEW POLICE FORCE AND JOHN A. KEARNEY.

On March 1st 1922, Eamon Duggan, Minister for Home Affairs replied to questions put down by Austin Stack T.D., relating to Kearney. The extract from the Dail Debates for that day is as follows:-

Mr EAMON DUGGAN, [Minister for Home Affairs.]: addressed the House on the following questions, of which he had received notice from Austin Stack.

> [a] *To ask the Minister for Home Affairs whether there is any truth in the rumour that a police force other than the Republican Police is being set up; and if so, by what authority?*

The Reply is Yes; by the authority of the Provisional Government.

> [b] *To ask the Minister for Home Affairs whether it is a fact that members of the R.I.C. who served against Ireland during the war, and who are at present serving, are engaged in forming a new police force?*

The reply is that certain officers of the R.I.C. have been invited by the Provisional Government to act on a Committee engaged on drawing up a scheme for the organisation of the new police force. The record of each one of them during the recent war was satisfactory. A specific case was raised here yesterday, and in connection with that I have received reports as regards this man, which I will communicate privately to anyone. I would like to say that this man did not arrest Roger Casement; that he did not prosecute him. He happened to be serving in the Barracks to which Roger Casement was brought on his arrival. He came into contact with Roger Casement from the time he was there, and Casement gave him his watch as a souvenir.

Mr AUSTIN STACK: *I want to ask why it was that this man Kearney, who had failed in his examinations, received promotion for his work in connection with the prosecution of Casement?*

The ACTING SPEAKER: *I do not know.*

Stack then went on to question the Minister, as to whether Judges who were serving in Ireland before the Treaty, were going to be retained by the new Government, he did not return to the issue relating to D.I. Kearney's suitability for appointment to the new 'Civic Guard'.

The Dail replies by Eamon Duggan did little to rectify the false allegations of the previous day against Kearney having no influence in reversing the wrong that had been committed. There is no evidence that any of the anti-Treaty T. Ds. perused the documentation or evidence offered by Eamon Duggan for their scrutiny. They had no interest in negating what had been written into the records of the previous day, it suited their purpose to have the false allegations against Kearney perpetuated, for the purpose of destroying the credibility of the new police force.

[For information on Austin Stack's later career, see Appendix 'B']

RECOLLECTIONS OF EX-CHIEF SUPERINTENDENT SEAN LIDDY OF THE GARDA SIOCHANA.

In a feature in *"An Siothadoir"* [a magazine for retired members of the Garda Siochana], of August 1962, titled "Smothered History", retired Chief Superintendent Sean Liddy, wrote about these early days of the new 'Civic Guard'. Having been less than complimentary about the role which the Royal Irish Constabulary had played in the history of Ireland from 1822 to 1922, in the early part of the feature, he then continued:-

"Recruits arriving represented every county in Ireland. Some of the Kerry

lads recognised the newly appointed Deputy Commissioner as the former Head Constable Kearney, who had been stationed in Tralee, and associated him with the arrest at Banna Strand, in April 1916, of Sir Roger Casement, his conviction and subsequent execution by hanging at London. As a reward for the Head Constable's exceptional zeal and energy in connection with the Casement case, he was promptly promoted to the rank of District Inspector, second Class and transferred to Boyle, Co Roscommon, and disbanded from there after the signing of the Anglo-Irish Treaty in July 1921.

"The Kerry lads denounced Kearney as Casement's betrayer and executioner to all and sundry within the camp. This news had an electrifying effect on all the I.R.A. men, producing an explosive force equal to 1,500 lbs of T.N.T., ready to explode with violent eruption at any moment.

"An air of high velocity tension pervaded the camp, in their spare moments groups of men could be seen engaged in earnest discussion: at night-time, meetings were held in the main hall where the men dined and slept. Eventually, a deputation was received by the Assistant Commissioner, Col. Brennan, at which the late Chief Superintendent Martin Lynch and myself were both present.

"The leader of the deputation opened the discussion in a most courteous and dignified manner, putting forward his demands in the form of requests:

No. 1 - The immediate removal of Mr Kearney, whose appointment they regarded as a deliberate insult to all I.R..A. men; his appointment appeared to them as a recognition and a reward by an Irish Government for his zeal and energy in effecting Casement's arrest and subsequent judicial murder.

No 2 - The removal of all disbanded R.I.C. officers presently holding commissioned rank; but there was no objection to their employment in a civil capacity, as instructors, but they favoured the employment of resigned or dismissed members of that Force.

"Mr Brennan made an immediate verbal report to the Commissioner and advised him of the prevailing conditions within the camp, which he, Mr Brennan, regarded as explosive and dangerous, and stressed most forcibly on the Commissioner the urgent need for Government sanction to remove the causes of unrest and discontent which impeded the normal development of the Force.

"I have no idea what action, if any, the Commissioner did take by way of seeking Government intervention, but no changes were effected and the situation was allowed to drift. Recruits and still more recruits kept arriving until all available accommodation was taxed to its full capacity.

"For some weeks camp life appeared normal on the surface. Recruits were formed into companies, numerous appointments to non-commissioned rank appeared on the duty sheets almost daily, men were kept hard at work, at drill and police duty classes throughout the day.

"Mr Kearney was now aware of and fully realised the significance of the situation within the camp, which was fast approaching a crescendo. He confined himself to his office and quarters by day and became a noctambulist after dark, accompanied by two disbanded men. His physical condition began to deteriorate and one evening he quietly disappeared from the camp, driven in a State car to catch the mail boat to England.

"Mr Kearney's sudden disappearance caused a sensational crop of rumours to float around. One suggested that the night before his departure he met Casement's Spirit who taunted him about his pending fate at the hands of the I.R.A. . Another and a more likely one was that some days previously a couple of the boys rigged up an impromptu gallows at a secluded spot within the grounds, captured the poor man at night and led him to the spot where they gave him a practical demonstration of his future fate should he remain on as Deputy Commissioner in the new force.

"With Mr Kearney's departure, tension eased somewhat, but another cloud appeared with the arrival at the camp in a rather surreptitious manner of a contingent of disbanded men, composed of officers and N.C.Os. who became employed as they arrived at administrative work, all earmarked for commissioned rank at a later stage.

"Some I.R.A. men were commissioned. Martin Lynch with the rank of Superintendent and appointed Camp Commandant, and, in passing, this excellent man was some years later promoted Chief Superintendent and throughout his long service with the Force was one of the most efficient, respected and most popular officers in the Service. He was a good disciplinarian, whom he tempered with common sense; he demanded loyalty, and he got it a hundred per cent.

"Patrick Haugh, another I.R.A man was promoted Superintendent and appointed Camp Adjutant. He later acted in the same capacity at Kildare Camp. A few more I.R.A officers were commissioned.

"It was now apparent that Mr Walsh took over the office of Deputy Commissioner and was in complete control to model the force on the only pattern he knew, a replica of the old, the R.I.C., Code [or as some of the boys jocosely referred to it as the 'Devil's prayer book'], was reintroduced and adapted, a railway without a junction over which the new national Police Force was directed to travel.

"Mr Staines, Chief Commissioner, found himself powerless to navigate, he was no longer the skipper. A perfectly honest man, a fine soldier, but as innocent of intrigue as the 'Babes in the Wood', his predominant weakness was his loyalty to Michael Collins, whose pets the disbanded R.I.C. men were. Loyalty is a supreme virtue; blind loyalty to an individual can, in certain circumstances, become a sin against the Holy Ghost. Every individual is given the God-given right of reason, failure to exercise that right is a suppression of the person that is in him.

"Col. Brennan, the Assistant Commissioner, was a strong advocate for the development of the new Force on a broad national basis, completely divorced from the old and here he clashed with Messrs Staines and Walsh, who enjoyed Government support The Colonel, a fearless soldier with a razor edged intellect, blunt and outspoken, was no match in the diplomatic battlefield for the astute Walsh. There was only one road open to him, retreat with honour, which he did at a later stage.

Mr Liddy's feature - with a continuation of the feature in the same magazine of December 1962 - continued with further developments in the early days of the 'Civic Guard', including his account of what happened during the Kildare Mutiny.

It was sad and regrettable to find Mr Liddy, a former high-ranking officer of An Garda Siochana - forty years on from 1922, - still perpetuating the rumours and false allegations levelled against District Inspector Kearney, who was dead for some years at this time. Kearney's son Thomas, became aware of the 'Siothadoir' feature. He subsequently replied to the feature and vehemently denied the false allegations made against his late father. Some of the other detail given in the same feature is also factually incorrect

ALLEGATIONS OF 'BLACK AND TANS' IN THE NEW POLICE FORCE.

Widespread rumours continued, that 'Black and Tans' were employed on the staff of the training depot at the R.D.S. Complaints continued to pour into the Provisional Government about the appointment of Kearney, and other former members of the RIC. There was a Cabinet discussion on the matter on March 21st and Michael Staines, Eamon Duggan and Desmond Fitzgerald, were directed to prepare a statement for the press on the issue. This statement from the Provisional Government was published in the 'Irish Independent' of March 25th 1922, under the heading -

"THE CIVIC GUARD. FALSEHOODS REFUTED.

The Provisional Government announces:-

"False statements are being assiduously circulated through the country with regard to the Civic Guard. It is asserted that the Guard is largely composed of Black and Tans.

"The facts are as follows:-

The present recruited strength of the Civic Guard is 400. Of these, 370 are members of the I.R.A and 30 are resigned R.I.C men. Of these 30, about 25 did war service in the ranks of the I.R.A., in the active service columns and in other capacities.

"The ranks of the Civic Guard include men from the active service units of East Clare, Mid-Limerick, East Limerick, West Cork, Dublin, West Mayo, Sligo and Leitrim, etc.

"All officers of the Civic Guard so far appointed are I.R..A. men. These include - Commandant Patrick Brennan, East Clare A.S.U, I.R.A.; Captain P. Haugh, West Clare I.R.A.; Comdt J. Ring, Commander West Mayo, A.S.U. I.R.A. and Comdt. M Lynch, Brigade Police Officer, Leix I.R.A..

There are no Black and Tans in the Civic Guard".

Ironically, the same issue of the newspaper carried comprehensive reports about the massacre of the McMahon family in Belfast, by men, never identified, but reported to be wearing uniforms, consistent with those of the newly established 'Special Constabulary' of that jurisdiction. Also, about 1,000 officers and men of the RIC who had marched on Dublin

Castle on the previous day, seeking compensation for their disbandment from the Inspector General of the force, and from Mr Andy Cope, the Under Secretary.

At the end of March, Rory O'Connor, who was the officer in charge of the anti-Treaty forces, issued an order to all officers and other ranks – *"presently serving in the Regular Army and members of the Civic Guard to return to their respective units and that recruiting for these forces shall cease forthwith"*.

Issued by Order of the Executive Council of the I.R.A.

10

THE 'KILDARE MUTINY'

REBELLION AND INTRIGUE AMONGST RECRUITS.

On April 25th, the staff and recruits left the R.D.S. premises and moved to the Artillery Military Barracks at Kildare, which had been vacated by the British Army a few days previously. Commissioner Staines led about 900 recruits in a march through Dublin City to Kingsbridge Station, where they entrained for Kildare.

The list of promotions announced on May 1st, further antagonised the rebel committee, amongst the recruits. They were obviously buoyed up by the disappearance of Kearney from the staff, and decided to have other former RIC men removed as well. Thomas P. Daly the leader of the dissident group, kept the momentum going, and on May 15th issued a written ultimatum to Commissioner Staines, to dismiss former District Inspectors Patrick J. Walsh and Bernard O'Connor, and former RIC Sergeants Maher and Prendeville. For some inexplicable reason, Daly did not include the names of former RIC Sergeants Harte, Galligan, McCarthy and McCormack on his list.

Staines, faced the challenge head-on, and ordered a general parade of all staff and recruits at the Kildare barracks on the following day. In total, almost 1,500 men paraded under the command of Superintendent Haugh. The Commissioner read out the ultimatum, which he had received from Daly and his committee and he named the eight signatures to the document. After what appears to be widespread confusion, Staines called on all who favoured his views to fall in behind him. Less than a dozen recruits lined up with him, in disgust he marched off the parade ground. The Depot Commandant, Michael J. Ring, stood by the Commissioner.

On that particular day, Assistant Commissioner Brennan and Inspector Sean Scanlon were absent in County Clare. During Staines' attempt to restore order, there were cat-calls *"We will stand by Paddy Brennan"*. Following the departure of Staines, Depot Commandant M.J. Ring, tried to restore order but only met with abuse and obstruction. He himself had been a prominent Volunteer in West Mayo, during the War of Independence and was a respected figure, but this made no difference on the day. He had to return to his office, with a number of Mayo men, affording protection to him. The events of the day, convinced him that there was no future for him in the Civic Guard. He resigned shortly afterwards and joined the Free State Army. While leading his troops, the anti-Treaty forces at Bonniconlan, near Ballina, County Mayo, ambushed him on September 14th 1922. He was shot and fatally wounded.

The events at Kildare on May 16th, heralded the start of what has become known as the *'Kildare Mutiny'*. On the following day, the military barracks at Newbridge were vacated by the British Military. 350 of the Civic Guard recruits were transferred to it amidst cat-calls and intimidation from Thomas Daly and his followers.

The armoury at the Kildare Barracks was raided and 167 rifles and 240 revolvers stolen from it. These weapons were distributed amongst the dissident recruits. Daly was in complete control, he announced new senior officers for the Civic Guard. These were:- Commissioner, Patrick Brennan; Assistant Commissioner, Patrick Haugh; Depot Commandant, Martin Lynch and Depot Adjutant, Sean Liddy.

Brennan, Haugh and Liddy were from County Clare, while Lynch was from County Laois.

Staines and Deputy Commissioner Patrick J Walsh, tendered their resignations to the Provisional Government. Both officers, with their administration staff, left Kildare and returned to Dublin. Michael Collins was extremely angry about what had occurred, he ordered Michael Staines and his officers to return to Kildare. They did so, but they were locked out and had to return to Dublin.

The Provisional Government was obviously concerned about Daly and his men being in control at the Depot and their access to a large supply of arms there. Arrangements were made for the Free State army in the Curragh, to go to Kildare and collect the arms. This led to a major confrontation between the *'Civic Guard'* rebels, in control of the barracks, and the army detachment from the Curragh. Each side threatened the other with the use of arms, fortunately the army personnel withdrew, a major confrontation between the recruit Guards and the army was miraculously averted.

Several efforts were made to end the Kildare Mutiny, but they all ended in failure. Michael Collins met the ringleaders and he met with Brennan and Liddy. He made it very clear to them, that the RIC men were going to stay in the force and in a towering rage, he told Brennan and Liddy *"By - - - -, if I smashed the country by it, these men will remain in the force"*. Michael Collins visited the Kildare Barracks and spoke to the men personally, but to no avail. At this time, he was involved in very delicate and important discussions about the future of the country, with the British authorities. He was extremely annoyed and disappointed about the happenings in Kildare.

The Provisional Government was in an awkward dilemma over the Kildare affair for another reason, two of the officers caught up in the affair - Brennan and Liddy - were members of Dail Eireann. The Provisional Government, relied on their support in the course of key votes in the Dail.

In early June, Staines and his officers again went to Kildare, their arrival caused a riot in the Barracks and they had to flee the town. The Government decided not to pay the mutineers for the months of May and June.

On June 18th, Thomas Daly convinced Superintendents Lynch and Haugh to travel with him to Dublin, with two official lorries and one motorcar, on the pretext of collecting a party of Civic Guards in Dublin. A few miles outside Kildare town, they were held up by a gang of Irregulars, who were in possession of an armoured car. Superintendents Lynch and Haugh were arrested and held in custody in a roadside cottage. Daly accompanied the Irregulars back to the Kildare Barracks. Three prominent anti-Treaty leaders - Tom Barry, Rory O'Connor and Ernie O'Malley were amongst the Irregulars. At Kildare, Daly used the secret password to gain admission to the barracks, with the Irregulars. They drove straight up to the armoury, tied up the guards on duty and loaded the entire contents of the armoury into the three vehicles.

Having loaded the arms, Daly and the Irregulars drove straight back to Dublin. Ten days later - on 28th June - the stolen firearms were brought into use by the anti-Treaty forces, in the occupation of the Dublin Four Courts, an event which started another sad chapter in Irish history - the Irish Civil War. Daly's act of treachery, confirmed the view that he had at all times been 'planted' within the force, by the anti-Treaty elements, to create dissension and trouble for the new Civic Guard. Weak leadership, at the higher levels of the Civic Guard, had given Daly too much latitude and this contributed to the serious havoc which he caused in the force.

For the duration of the Mutiny, nobody was ever in a position to state with certainty, how many recruits were in the Kildare depot at any one time. The figures given ranged between 910 and 1,500. About 350 men left to pursue training in Newbridge barracks. Up to 300 men became fed-up with the happenings there, left and either returned to their homes or joined the Free State Army. No training took place during the Mutiny but following the publication of the O'Shiel and McAuliffe Report, training resumed there once again.

The Government did not pay the recruits for the months of May or June and considerable bills were run up by the recruits, with traders in Kildare town and in the barracks canteen. The Pay Sheets for all concerned were submitted to Commissioner Staines, when training resumed, and he authorised payment of the outstanding wages to the recruits.

Morale and discipline were at a low ebb amongst the members of the new force, while the mutiny lasted. On June 12th, one recruit, shot another dead, in Newbridge [Co Kildare], following some trivial dispute, and there was a problem in getting some money to pay the funeral expenses of the deceased man. The dead recruit was Farrell Liddy, from Co. Leitrim, and the recruit who shot him, came from the same locality.

The incident occurred around 12 midnight, both men were carrying revolvers, - indicating the serious lack of discipline amongst the recruits at the time. The local Railway Hotel in Kildare was also broken into by some of the recruits and a quantity of cigarettes and drink stolen.

Commissioner Staines, whose resignation was not accepted by the Government, returned to Kildare Barracks on June 28th but failed to regain full control of operations there. This was accomplished only on July 12th, when the remainder of Daly's committee handed over control, before the commencement of an official inquiry into the mutiny. Michael Collins had earlier promised to hold the official Inquiry, with a view to bringing the mutiny to a conclusion. The men appointed to conduct the Inquiry were two senior civil servants, Kevin O'Shiel and Michael McAuliffe

THE INQUIRY INTO THE MUTINY.

O'Shiel and McAuliffe commenced their work on July 13th 1922 at the Kildare Depot. Following the official opening of the Inquiry, Assistant Commissioner Patrick Brennan, adopted disruptive tactics, by asking a lot of questions and making an issue of legal representation for the men. He maintained that all the recruits were under suspension and that they were not being paid, - a fact, which was challenged by Commandant Ring. Staines intervened in the argument saying:-

"Listen Paddy, they are suspended on your recommendation and they are being paid. There is no use in making a complaint like that".

Brennan eventually agreed to co-operate with the Inquiry. The first witness was Commissioner Staines. His evidence, and that of other high-ranking officers, indicated the divisions and bitterness, which existed between the senior officers and a sizeable number of the more junior ranks within the new force.

Staines opened his evidence by stating:

"The Civic Guards came to Kildare on 25th April and after a few weeks it came to my knowledge that intrigues were going on in the Depot, a fact of which the officers should have been aware, and with which I should have been acquainted. This however, was not done, and to a great extent I was in ignorance of what was taking place and which afterwards led to deplorable results.

"Chief amongst the causes for this was the action of the AssistantCommissioner"…. I feel that throughout, I have had insufficient support from officers. I received least support from the officer from whom I had a right to expect the most - the Assistant Commissioner. I am at a loss to understand why, but the facts are incontrovertible.

He said that he was upset about what had happened after what he had done for everybody.

He went on to describe the events which had occurred at the general parade at the Depot on May 15th and about the events which followed. He produced a 'list' to the Inquiry, which gave details of the officers of the force, who were appointed by Daly's militant committee. He blamed the members from Clare for this, as the 'Commissioner' and three high ranking 'officers' appointed were all from County Clare. He also stated that on June 14th and 15th, handbills were posted up in Dublin city, which bore baseless statements about him, intended to harm his prospects of re-election to the Dail.

Staines cited three specific examples, indicating how badly discipline had broken down at the Depot.

1. The loss of the arms and ammunition by the Civic Guard to the Executive of Rory O'Connor on the night of 18th June.
2. The shooting of recruit Farrell Liddy on 25th June, in the public street at Newbridge at 12 midnight when he and other recruits were armed.
3. The recent breaking and entering of the Railway Hotel in Kildare and

the stealing of goods therefrom, by the recruits from the Depot.

Mr Staines was then cross-examined by Mr J.A.O'Connell, [a former solicitor from Derry and a recruit in the new force] who was representing the rank and file members at the Depot.

O'Connell - "You made a statement to the effect that at the start of the Force, you appointed a number of officers who were all experienced in Police business?

Staines - "Yes".

O'Connell - "Was there among these a man named Kearney?

Staines - "No".

O'Connell - "Was there any man named Kearney attached to the Force?

Staines - "There was, but I never appointed him.

O'Connell - "He was appointed to the Civic Guard?

Staines - "He was attached to the organising committee of the Civic Guard. He was not appointed by me. He was appointed by the Provisional Government.

O'Connell - "Have you any information, sir, as to whether this man had been concerned in the arrest of Roger Casement and in the arrest and conviction of Mr Austin Stack?

Staines - "Has this anything to do with the Inquiry ? This man was never an officer in the Civic Guard - this man Kearney he is referring to.

Mr O'Shiel - "What is the question ?

O'Connell - "I wish to ask if this man had been concerned in the arrest of Roger Casement and in the arrest and conviction of Austin Stack?

Mr O'Shiel - "Of course the reasons and the causes for the complaints and the grievances that exist under the present conditions are all within our purview. That being so, there is a very big scope to enquire into all these points and any questions of that sort we will admit, but of course, witnesses can only answer what they know. The ordinary rules of

	evidence prevail in so far as the evidence here - the same as anywhere else.
Staines -	*"I will answer what I believe."*
Mr McAuliffe -	*"What you know. We want no hearsay evidence."*
Staines -	*"Then I don't know anything of my own knowledge. I can answer To what I believe and I am quite willing to answer it. I believe*
	That Kearney had nothing whatever to do with the arrest of Roger Casement. I believe that Austin Stack went in to the barracks in Tralee when Kearney had an order for his arrest in his pocket.
	There were five or six other policemen there when Austin Stack went in to the Barracks and he arrested him. But I would like to make it plain to everybody thatKearney was not an officer in the Civic Guards. He was a member of the organising committee and he was appointed by the Provisional Government, not by me.
	When it came to the question of appointing officers, I sacked Kearney.
O'Connell -	*"Early in March of this year when there were only about 180 men at the Ballsbridge Depot, was there any objection taken to the presence of this man Kearney?*
Staines -	*"There was".*

Before concluding his evidence, Staines gave details of the ultimatum delivered to him at Kildare, demanding the resignations of Deputy Commissioner Walsh, Private Secretary Jeremiah Maher, Superintendents Prendeville, Brennan and O'Connor [all former members of the RIC]. He also produced his letter of resignation to the Provisional Government, in which he gave his reasons for doing so.

Several officers and rank-and-file members gave evidence to the Inquiry. The proceedings went fairly smoothly, except in the case of evidence being given by Sergeant Patrick McNamara, a former active member of the I.R.A., from Co. Limerick. He refused to be cross-examined by Deputy Commissioner Patrick Walsh, on the grounds that the latter had been a District Inspector in the RIC.

Messrs O'Shiel and McAuliffe, submitted their findings to the Provisional Government on August 7th. The report was very detailed and very much to the point. It finalised the blueprint for the new police force. Amongst its findings it made the following observations:-

"The position of the officers who remained on at the camp was to say the least an extraordinary one. It is obvious that either they commanded the "committee" and the men or the "committee" and the men commanded them".

"The whole trouble bears the complexion of a 'Committee' and officers' revolt, with the "Committee" being largely influenced from outside, and certain officers and men from a personal motive in the hope that the result achieved would suit both sections".

"The main cause of this disaffection was undoubtedly the propaganda from outside the force, sided to a small extent from within, with the object of smashing the Civic Guard completely, or at least rendering it helpless".

"We are satisfied that the case made against the ex-R.I.C. men, and has been from the beginning, the principal lever used by the men - by playing on their feelings and sentiments - for other and different objects than the removal of the ex -R.I.C. To understand the real objects we have only to analyse the results:

1. *The "Committee" concentrated on the ex-R.I.C men.*

2. *The ultimatum to the Commissioner calling for the expulsion of the R.I.C.,without any regard being paid to their credentials and officers who were driven from the camp were never in the R.I.C.*

3. *The handing over of arms to the Four Courts forces and the joining of these forces by a small number of the men - about 15. It is significant that amongst the 15 were "Committee" members including the Chairman and others.*

4. *The filling – and in most cases at any rate the acceptance - of the expelled Officers places by other officers of the Civic Guard.*

"The function of the "Committee"; the expulsion of the officers and the consequent disorganisation was essential to the carrying out of the seizure of the arms and the joining of the Four Courts forces by some of the men and this was undoubtedly the main object.

"We do not consider that Commissioner Staines and Commandant Ring handled the serious position thereby created, in as tactful a manner as they may have.

The following, is a summary of other findings and recommendations made in the Report :

1. That the infiltration of the Civic Guard and the seizure of its arms by anti-Treaty forces were planned from the time that the recruits arrived in Ballsbridge.
2. That Thomas Daly and his co-conspirators identified District Inspector John A. Kearney as the most vulnerable amongst the RIC men.
3. That practically all the evidence tendered on behalf of the mutineers, on the question of former RIC men's influence in the Civic Guard and the extensive utilisation of the RIC men, may have been unwise, considering that the rank and file were ex-I.R.A. men.
4. That Commissioner Staines had appointed policemen, who were naturally specially qualified and more especially, where their credentials were satisfactory to the Provisional Government.
5. It was decided that Commissioner Staines, who was a member of Dail Eireann and a politician, should resign as Commissioner, on the obvious grounds that, with his role as a politician, he was compromised in his role as Commissioner of police.
6. That all members then in the Civic Guard, should be disbanded but not dispersed, and immediately thereafter, the force should be re-constituted by a process of selective enrolment of temporary officers and men, all of whom should be placed on probation.
7. That the new police force should be disarmed, even to the point where no member should have a privately owned weapon.

The latter recommendation had the effect of making the new *'Civic Guard'* an unarmed police force, rather than the original concept, which was that it should be 'lightly armed'.

In the course of evidence, given by officers to the Inquiry, two rather unusual facts emerged. The first was that all their appointments - including that of Commissioner Staines - were 'Temporary' appointments. The other was that the officers had never been 'attested' to the *'Civic Guard'* force nor sworn in. These facts should have made appointments or other official functions carried out by them of very questionable legality.

Apart from District Inspector Kearney, none of the other RIC men were forced to resign. D.I. Walsh's resignation, as Deputy Commissioner, was accepted in May, but he was retained as an adviser to Commissioner Staines. When General Eoin O'Duffy was appointed Commissioner in September 1922, he appointed former D. I. Walsh, as an Assistant Commissioner.

The Government had obviously taken a decision, that it was not going to accede to the ultimatum, and demands of Daly's committee, in relation to the other RIC men.

Jeremiah Maher resigned in September 1922, to become Intelligence Officer in the Free State Army. All the other RIC men retained the ranks, which they were given, some went on to get further promotion in the Civic Guard, which was re-named *"An Garda Siochana"* [Guardians of the Peace] a year later.

Of the former I.R.A. officers, Lynch and Liddy attained the rank of Chief Superintendent; Superintendent Haugh resigned shortly afterwards and Patrick McNamara rose to the rank of Superintendent. Patrick Sellars who was Daly's right-hand man left the force shortly afterwards joining the National Army.

When Michael Staines submitted his resignation, at the start of the Kildare Mutiny, it was not accepted by the Government. Michael Collins ordered him back to Kildare, when he failed to gain admission there he returned to Dublin and made arrangements for the training of recruits, at two temporary locations there. The first of these was in a warehouse at Denmark Street, Dublin, where about 200 recruits were accommodated and trained. The other centre was at Clonskeagh Castle where 75 recruits were billeted.

Following the publication of the Shiel and McAuliffe Report, on the Mutiny, in August 1922, he submitted his resignation straight away. A few days later, - on August 22nd - General Michael Collins was shot dead at Beal na Blath, Co Cork. The Government directed Staines, to resume his duty as Commissioner, until a replacement for him was appointed later. General Eoin O'Duffy took over from him as Commissioner early in September 1922.

Staines lost his seat in Dail Eireann at the General Election of 1923. He served in the Irish Senate for a period before going into private business. He died in 1955.

Gregory Allen makes the following observations on Staines in "*The Garda Siochana*":

"*On 17th August [1922] Staines led a contingent of the new police into the Lower Castle Yard. Under the command of Chief Superintendent McCarthy, the policemen dressed in the unfamiliar new uniform, paraded for inspection under the gaping windows of the Revenue building - a proud experience for the young men taking part. For Staines personally in his last weeks in office, his own role in the highly symbolic occupation of Dublin Castle by unarmed servants of the new state compensated in no small measure for the disappointments of previous months. He was again a candidate in the August 1923 elections, losing his seat in the re-drawn constituency of Dublin North, he was appointed to the Senate of the Irish Free State and later established himself in business as a manufacturer's agent.*

"*The revolutionary years had called for 'ruthless leadership', the secretary of the Joint Representative Body, Sergeant P.J. Gallagher, recalled on the death in 1955 of the first Garda Commissioner - 'Michael Staines was the gentlest of men, and his whole life was characterised by a complete absence of bitterness'. His one act of ruthlessness, the unjust 'sacking' of District Inspector Kearney in the highly charged atmosphere in the Ballsbridge Depot, was out of character. The idealist of non-violent Sinn Fein, friend of Arthur Griffith, the organising genius identified by Collins and confirmed by Mulcahy as the 'obvious choice' for the top job in the new police, by a single misjudged decision gave himself as a hostage to history. The assistant commissioner, Patrick Brennan, made greater mistakes; with Staines, he left the force to take up a job as 'officer in charge of communications' in the Dail*".

11

THE DEPARTURE OF JOHN A. KEARNEY TO LONDON

HIS FINAL WEEKS WITH THE *'CIVIC GUARD'*.

The final paragraph in D. I. Kearney's personal RIC service record sheet reads :

"Paid up to and for 5th April 1922, and discharged on pension on disbandment of the R.I.C. Awarded a compensation allowance of £433. 6s 8d per annum with effect from 6th April 1922".

The foregoing confirms that he was a member of the RIC up to his disbandment on April 5th. In reality, he could not have been appointed as an officer in another police force, until his disbandment from the RIC had been completed. He was invited personally by Michael Collins, to assist in setting up the new police force, which replaced the RIC. He had the full support of the Provisional Government, in the considerable amount of work, which he continued to do, in the organisation of the new force. He had the goodwill and support of Michael Staines. The fact that he was elected as Vice President of the Mess Committee, indicated the good standing in which he was held. In view of the very firm line taken by the Provisional Government, that the organisation of the new force would be under the control of 'Professional' police officers, it was accepted that the RIC officers, who remained on, after submission of the initial report of the organising committee, would be appointed to at least the rank of Superintendent, following their disbandment on April 5th. Their participation in the future management of the *'Civic Guard'* was seen as a foregone conclusion.

The false allegations made in Dail Eireann by Austin Stack and others, created major problems for Kearney. His character was maligned and he had no redress. The allegations were made under cover of Dail Privilege and widely publicised.

These were followed by the arrival of the recruits at the Ballsbridge depot from Kerry, announcing to all and sundry that Kearney was *"the betrayer and executioner of Casement"*.

Within the organisation itself, he had major opposition. This came principally from the members of the 'Daly committee', who targeted him from the very outset, for dismissal. He was the number one on their list. There was clearly little sympathy for his plight from Assistant Commissioner Brennan, or the other former I.R.A. officers who were initially involved with the new force. They also perceived Kearney as a man who was likely to get one of the higher ranks in the force, thereby depriving them of their control of the force, as they wished from the outset. They also perceived District Inspector Walsh as a threat to them and this was later manifest when he was actually promoted and they demanded his dismissal.

The entire internal organisation became riddled with intrigue and suspicion.

Kearney was in the weakest situation, due to the wild allegations made against him. The campaign against him, through the use of leaflets, by the anti-Treaty elements grew in intensity.

His work situation became untenable. While in his office each day, he had to have armed protection. He became a figure of hate and suspicion to those who chose to believe the false and malicious allegations made against him, relating to his treatment of Casement.

Commissioner Staines, was amongst those who distanced themselves from him.

His loyalty and support for Staines from the outset could not be questioned. As time went by, Staines obviously aligned himself with the views and demands made by those seeking Kearney's dismissal. From the evidence given by Staines at the Inquiry into the Kildare Mutiny, it was quite clear that he [Staines] had been let down by the officers whose promotion he had recommended and most particularly by Assistant Commissioner Brennan.

When the list of newly promoted officers was announced, Kearney knew that he was being ostracised by those around him, particularly by Commissioner Staines. There was no way, that any man could have continued to work in the environment in which he found himself, at that particular time. He knew that it was time to get out of the organisation, and this he did. He was an intelligent man and he recognised that he was in an intolerable situation and in effect was *'being sent to Coventry'*. Seeing that there was no likelihood of a future for him in the new force, and fearing for his own personal safety, he left the Ballsbridge Depot, taking the mail boat to England and travelling on to London.

Even though, Michael Staines gave evidence on Oath that, "*I sacked*

Kearney" this would not appear to be accurate. What Staines did, was that he failed to recommend him for promotion and obviously took deliberate steps, not to have him promoted. It was most unlikely that Michael Collins would allow Kearney to be 'sacked', as he thought too highly of him. Collins fought a hard battle, to keep on every member and former member of the RIC and DMP, that he had selected. He would not have made an exception of Kearney. Kearney's contribution to the setting up of the force, was probably greater than that of anybody else, as he chaired the sub-Committee on Organisation.

He, was the only victim of the allegations and intrigue in the first months of the 'Civic Guard. His departure, was of course hailed as a great victory for Thomas Daly and his Committee, the *'Clare clique'* and the former I.R.A. men within the force.

Kearney chose not to speak on the precise circumstances, surrounding his departure, but everybody who knew him, and his family, realised how grievously hurt he was by the whole affair, which affected him for the remainder of his life. He had effectively been squeezed out of the new *'Civic Guard'* force, and deprived of an opportunity to serve in it for at least another ten years. Against this, Kearney knew that he had a valuable contribution to make to the new force if he had been given an adequate opportunity to do so.

ARRIVAL IN LONDON.

On arrival in London, John A. Kearney was practically penniless, as his salary from the RIC had ceased with his disbandment from the force on April 5th. He had to wait for some time before payment of his pension commenced. As far as can be ascertained, he did not receive any salary or remuneration whatsoever - other than accommodation during his stay in Dublin, - whilst he was assisting with the organisation of the new Civic Guard. Most of the rank and file members of the RIC on disbandment, received a cash lump-sum, to enable them to pay for their passage to foreign lands. Due to the huge logistical problem of the situation, there were delays in making payments in many cases - particularly in the case of officers. It was at least two months before pensions were paid out. After some days in London, he obtained a temporary post at Whitehall, assisting in sorting out personal files and entitlements etc relating to the disbanded

RIC personnel.

THE CAMPAIGN OF JASPER TULLY EDITOR OF THE "ROSCOMMON HERALD".

John A. Kearney's wife and children, who were extremely worried and anxious about his safety, continued to live on at 'Abbey Villa' near Boyle. Initially they had no problems following his departure, but then their situation changed for the worse, and life was made very difficult for them. The family have remained adamant, that this was brought about by systematic criticism and 'sniping' at John A. Kearney, by Mr Jasper Tully, editor and proprietor of the local *'Roscommon Herald'* - a provincial newspaper, - after John A. Kearney had left for London. The newspaper had been founded in 1857, and in time became one of the best established rural newspapers in the country.

In the issue of the paper dated February 11th 1922, the following account is given of the departure of the RIC from Boyle :

"BOYLE R.I.C. DEPART".

"Yesterday, Friday, - crowds watched - Brigade Commandant Martin Fallon of the North Roscommon Brigade, accompanied by local I.R.A. officers were in consultation with Head Constable Gilleece and the procedure for handing over of the Barracks to the Irish Republican Police was gone through. Later Mr Joseph Finlay, Liaison Officer for Co. Roscommon attended at the Barracks.

"All the police arms and property except for some tables and chairs, were removed in motor lorries. A number of motorcars conveyed the men and some went in the lorries. Prior to their departure, a group of the R.I.C. were photographed. Their destination was Roscommon town.

"Immediately following their departure, Police Officer Sheehan of the I.R.P. appeared at the window of the Barracks and proceeded to remove the R.I.C. badge from over the door - the harp surrounded by the Crown.

"The emblem fell to the street amid cheers from the crowd and a large tricolour was thrust out a window.

"The next incident was the arrival of a group of 50 I.R.A men in charge of Commandant S. Brennan. They marched in military formation from Boyle

Workhouse, some of them carrying rifles and all very smart in appearance. They filed in the Barrack door to the accompaniment of cheering from the crowd. It was observed that many of the young men had been prisoners in the building in the possession of which they now are.

"Brigade Commandant Fallon and Commandant S. Brennan and other officers also interviewed the military authorities in Boyle Barracks, which are to be handed over next Monday to the I.R.A.

"The English soldiers there are leaving for Ballykinlar between 4 a.m. and 5 a.m. on next Sunday morning.

District Inspector John A. Kearney had left Boyle some days prior to this, to attend the meeting at the Gresham Hotel, relating to the formation of a new police force. He had remained on in Dublin.

Based solely on the false accusations made against Kearney by Austin Stack T.D. in Dail Eireann on February 28th and March 1st 1922, Tully went out of his way to mount a campaign of vilification against Kearney, through the first half of 1922.

The first report on the matter appeared in the '*Roscommon Herald*' of March 4th 1922. The report in the Editorial read:-

"The meetings of the Dail resounded with loud outcries about the engagement of District Inspector Kearney, late of Boyle for some police work for the new Government. Mr Austin Stack T.D. and Mr Con Collins T.D. - both fierce followers of De Valera - attacked the appointment bitterly and associated Mr Kearney's name, it appears wrongly, with the arrest of Sir Roger Casement in Tralee. It was always understood amongst North Roscommon Sinn Feiners that Mr Kearney had nothing to do with these arrests and that it was another man of the same name who was involved.

"Austin Stack and Con Collins however asserted the contrary. They declared that he had worked up the case against Casement and had got his promotion to District Inspector for his efforts in Tralee. The Rebellion records show that a Head Constable Kearney had got Stack and Collins sentenced to penal servitude for life and that their arrests were mixed up in the case put before the Courts."

"If a different man was involved and after six years it is a petty case, but this is just the kind of transaction that makes splendid electioneering fodder. If Mr De Valera's party can tar the new Police Force of the Provisional Government with anyone figuring in these trials and arrests, it becomes a

serious matter when vote - catching is the business of the hour".

Another report in the same issue of the newspaper carried the headline:

"MR J. KEARNEY, D .I. BOYLE, HIS CASE IN DAIL EIREANN".

and it was followed by the report :

"Somewhat of a sensation was created in North Roscommon by the attack made by Mr Austin Stack, T.D. of Tralee at the Dail Eireann meeting of Tuesday, on Mr John Kearney, District Inspector of the R.I.C. in Boyle. He accused Mr Kearney of working up the case which led to the execution of Sir Roger Casement and declared that he was not a person to organise a Republican police for the Provisional Government.

"All this comes as a surprise in North Roscommon as Mr Kearney while in Boyle was on most friendly terms with Sinn Feiners and helpful to them in numerous ways, and it was always stated amongst Sinn Feiners that he had nothing to do with the arrests of Stack and Casement and that it was another man of the same name who was involved. Mr Austin Stack however made the accusation that Mr Kearney was the man".

The feature continued with a detailed account [taken from the '*Freeman's Journal*'] of the debates in Dail Eireann of February 28th and March 1st, relating to the Kearney affair.

From then onwards, Tully carried out his campaign against Kearney. He obviously felt that it made good post-Treaty reading, in a strong Republican circulation area, thus helping to sell his newspaper. He was also confident that Kearney was in no position to take an action against him for libel. Kearney was not the only victim of Jasper Tully's acerbic writings. He demonised people in other professions as well, from time to time and was involved in notorious Court proceedings for libel etc. In a bye- election held for parliamentary representation of North Roscommon on February 5th 1917, to fill a vacancy created by the death of Mr J.J. O'Kelly, Tully stood for election. The result was that Count George Plunkett, got 3,022 votes; T.J Devine [Official Nationalist] obtained 1,708 votes and Jasper Tully [Independent] received 687 votes.

He was an extremely eccentric and controversial individual. He was editor of the newspaper for approximately 60 years. He spent his early years in the United States, before coming back to Ireland and taking over as editor of the paper. He was married, but had a strained relationship with his wife. When she died, it was alleged that he re-addressed letters received for her 'To Hell'.

He was also an exceptionally mean man, who refused to pay any overtime to his reporters or staff. He often sat up all night doing the manual typesetting for his paper, while he sipped coffee from a pot, which was kept hot on the stove. He judged the performance of his reporters by the weight of the paper on which they had written their material. He was difficult to get on with, and there was always friction between himself and his staff. He died in 1938.

During the War of Independence and the Irish Civil War, printed leaflets or hand – bills, were a favoured means of spreading propaganda amongst the general population by the Republicans. They were printed in hundreds of thousands and distributed throughout Ireland, the U.S.A. and elsewhere, through a network of Republican contacts. The leaflets played a vital role in the very efficient 'Republican publicity machine'.

When the false allegations against D. I. Kearney came into the public arena, several leaflets were printed and distributed, with a view to denigrating him, and by implication, the new police force, which was being established. The anti-Treaty Republicans and Irregulars carried out this campaign. These leaflets provided fodder, for Mr Tully's views in the *'Roscommon Herald'*.

The issue of the paper dated Saturday April 1st 1922 carried the following feature in a prominent centre of page location:-

"A REPUBLICAN LEAFLET. THE CASE OF MR. KEARNEY D. I.

"The Republican Party have not been slow to seize the advantage given them from a political point of view by the connection of Mr J. Kearney D. I. late of Boyle, with the Provisional Government and the 'Civic Guards'. In the 'Heads Up' series of leaflets, there is one devoted to his relationship to the arrest of Casement at Tralee in Easter Week, 1916. The following leaflet is extensively circulated in Sligo and is published prominently in the Republican organ **'THE COMMENTS'**:-

"Are you a party to re-instating the Murder Gang?

"If not, read this :-
"I know who it was arrested me in 1916, it was Head Constable Kearney, then of Tralee, now engaged in setting up the Provisional Government's police force in Ballsbridge.

"I know who had charge of the prosecution of Con Collins and myself when we were sentenced to Penal Servitude for life. It was the same policeman.

"This man received special promotion for his work in 1916. He is now a District Inspector of the R.I.C

"Signed : Austin Stack.

"Mr Eamon Duggan of the Provisional Government says -

'This man's record was satisfactory.'

One week later - on April 8th - the contents of another leaflet again got a prominent location in the centre of a page and in bold type:

"The connection of Mr John Kearney, District Inspector of the R.I.C. in Boyle with the police force sought to be established by the Provisional Government is being made the subject of active propaganda by the Republican Party and apparently with deadly effect against the Treaty.

"The New York 'Irish World' displays in big type a leaflet in circulation in the United States about the incident. This is technically inaccurate. He was an old R.I.C. man but he commanded "Black and Tan" constables. The following is the leaflet appearing in the "Irish World":

"BLACK AND TAN REWARDED"

"Collins' Provisional Government promotes former Head Constable Kearney. He is made Chairman of a Provisional Government Commission. His anti-Irish record is preferred to loyal Irishmen who fought for the Republic.

"Head Constable Kearney represented the Imperial Government in Tralee in 1916.

"He was the gaoler of Roger Casement. He arrested Austin Stack and Con Collins and afterwards obtained their convictions. He was made a District Inspector after Easter Week.

"He was on active service as a 'Black and Tan Officer during the whole period of the war.

"He is now the Chairman of the Provisional Government's Commission for the foundation of a Free State Police Force.

"In the meantime, the Irish Republican Police are dismissed and those who fought for the Republic are replaced by Truce recruits.

On April 15th, another centre of page feature referred to D. I. Kearney.
"A Soldier of Easter Week" - What he said about D. I. Kearney".

"At a public demonstration in Ballina, Mr Sean Etchingham, T. D., who was described as a soldier of Easter Week said that they should be proud of the part that Countess Marchkivec and Mr Ruttledge were playing in the Dail for their great defence of the Republic. They could bear him out that at the last Session, a quarter of a million pounds was voted away and they would not be given one word of explanation of what was meant by 'special work'. The greater portion of it had been used to wean away young men from the I.R.A. to create the Free State Army.

"They had heard of the Civic Guard. One of the organisers of which was Kearney, the man who arrested poor Casement.

In the issue of April 29th, there was a headline on the front page titled :

"CASEMENT'S ARREST IN TRALEE"

This was over a report arising from a meeting held by Michael Collins in Tralee, when the question of the arrest of Casement arose. The report continued:

"Fr Brennan, C.C., Castleisland, addressed the meeting and said that he had the honour that day of meeting Sir Roger Casement's brother and he thought of the day when Sir Roger Casement was brought through the streets of Tralee by 3 or 4 'peelers'. He said that if Michael Collins had been in charge of the Volunteers that day in Tralee, Roger Casement would not have been taken away as he was.

"Those who were harried during the war he said - amidst interruptions - were warriors today".

The same issue had three full-length columns of features titled:
"How they fought in Easter Week - The Republican Story" and
"The Great Chance of Easter Week - Austin Stack's Fateful Orders".
On May 6th, another feature again located in the centre of a page read:

"THE KEARNEY MYSTERY"
and quoted a short report from the *'Irish Independent'* :
"Mr Andrew Lavin, T.D, questioned Mr Duggan in Dail Eireann about

District Inspector Kearney.

"Replying to Mr Lavin, Mr Duggan stated that District Inspector Kearney had never held any position in the new force. He was one of a number of officers of the R.I.C. who in conjunction with officers of the I.R.A. and D.M.P. and resigned members of the R.I.C. acted on a Committee preparing a scheme of organisation for the new police force. That committee had received no remuneration".

The same issue of the newspaper, carried six full-length columns of a report on a public meeting held at Longford, which had been addressed by Eamon De Valera, T.D., Harry Boland, T.D., Sean Etchingham, T.D. and County Councillors Killane and McCarthy.

At every opportunity that presented itself - even in completely un-related matters - Mr Tully commented on the Kearney affair, never in a complimentary manner.

Considering that his newspaper was purchased by every household in Boyle and throughout North Roscommon, it is quite understandable, how life was made so difficult and intolerable for Mrs Kearney and her family, who continued to live on at 'Abbey Villa'.

Jasper Tully's name and ill - repute, has lived on through all generations of the Kearney family, since 1922 and the feelings of injustice and wrong which he caused to John A. Kearney, will never be erased from their minds and will continue to live on in their memory and family folklore. When commenting on Tully, John A. Kearney described him as :-

"A man who licked the boots of the English, when they were in power [in Ireland] and bravely screamed invective about them, when they were gone".

Another leaflet/hand-bill was widely circulated over the same period about John A. Kearney. It was headed **"UP THE R.I.C."** and then continued:

"George Plunkett [Brother of Joseph Plunkett, Executed in 1916, Writes:

"At Arigna, Co Roscommon, in 1918, **I was present when District Inspector Kearney ordered a Baton charge by armed R.I.C. men on a crowd of unarmed Irish people.**

"He also threatened to shoot them. Some of his constables captured a Republican flag. Six of us had our heads broken by the policemen's

batons.

"At the instigation of D. I. Kearney, I was subsequently arrested and jailed for four months.

"This District Inspector Kearney is now on a committee advising the Provisional Government on the formation of a new police.

"Mr Eamon Duggan, T.D., Provisional Government Minister says that this man's record was satisfactory."

A CAMPAIGN OF HATE AGAINST THE KEARNEY FAMILY AT BOYLE.

The Kearney family became victims of a 'hate campaign' at Boyle, while John A. Kearney lived an anonymous life in London, for his own safety. Threatening letters to kill them, and to burn them out of their home, were received through the post.

Shortly before Mrs Kearney passed away, she burned a threatening notice, which had been tied to their gate at '*Abbey Villa*'. It bore the stark heading:

"DEATH TO JOHN KEARNEY'.

This was followed by false allegations against John A. Kearney. Underneath the writing at the foot of the document there was a very good sketch of a coffin.

The motorcar belonging to the Kearney family was stolen. They were convinced that it was taken by somebody, who knew the family well as their very alert dog never raised the alarm when it was taken away.

A violent attack was made on the home, when masked and armed men, who were members of the local anti-Treaty element, raided the house and terrorised the family.

The house was systematically searched and ransacked by the raiders, who made no secret of the fact that they believed that John A. Kearney was hiding there, and they had come to shoot him. This was the 'last straw' in so far as Mrs Kearney was concerned, she became convinced that either herself or her children, would become victims of the antagonism which had been engendered.

Carrying Dympna - a baby of less than six months old - in her arms, and accompanied by her nine other children, she fled from the family home at

'Abbey Villa' at night. They made their way by train and boat to England. Mrs Kearney and the children took whatever essential clothing and provisions they could carry with them on the journey. Most of the family possessions had to be left behind - including some items of valuable furniture. Through loyal family friends, they later succeeded in retrieving some items of furniture and had them forwarded to London. The priority of the family, was to get away safely from Boyle, and join John A. Kearney in London. This they succeeded in doing.

Kearney was deeply upset and traumatised, at the ordeal and suffering, which his wife and children had been through. The ordeal was all the more bitter to him, as it was based on malice and vindictiveness, arising from the blatant untruths and false accusations made against him. Some of those involved may have been individuals, whose lives he had saved just a few years before, when he became aware that they could be victims of assassination by the Auxiliaries.

TAKING UP RESIDENCE IN LETCHWORTH.

Houses were extremely difficult to obtain, in and around London at the time. Through the goodwill of an English Police Authority, who became aware of the family's plight, the Kearneys eventually obtained an official 'Police House' in the village of Letchworth, located about thirty - five miles north of London. It was a semi-detached house with a small garden. The accommodation was very small, but comfortable, it enabled the family to make a fresh start in life. Suitable schools were obtained for the children, and despite the bitter memories of the past, a normal family life was resumed once more.

The same village of Letchworth, was also home to a number of other former RIC families and to the widows and children of deceased members of the force, who had lost their lives in the course of duty in Ireland. Many of the former members of the RIC, had to flee from Ireland with their wives and children following disbandment, as they had been singled out by the Irish Republican Army, to be shot or maimed. This was in retaliation for those members of the Force being seen, to perform their duties conscientiously, while in the RIC.

Members, who were single when the RIC was disbanded, had greater options. While it was not possible for the great majority of them to remain on in Ireland, they were able to emigrate to the United Kingdom, Australia, New Zealand, North America and a number joined the Palestine Police Force at the time. Married members did not have the same options.

The different families at Letchworth, supported each other in a very understanding and neighbourly way, they all had very much in common with each other. They later spoke of each other with love and affection. They became a very closely - knit Irish community. The Kearney family never forgot the loyalty and spirit of good neighbourliness, which they received from their neighbours. The friendships that were forged between the families at that, time carried on to the next generation. Amongst those who lived in the police houses at that time were families named McNamara, Golden, Scully, Fitzgerald, Scotland, Cahill and Davis. Other families of former RIC men, lived there for relatively short periods, before moving to live elsewhere.

LIFE FOR JOHN A. KEARNEY IN THE U.K.

The temporary employment of John A. Kearney at Whitehall, lasted for a few years. He was employed there, at work connected with the disbandment of the RIC. This involved the examination and updating of personnel files before they were finally filed away. Some of his work related to the establishment of the Royal Ulster Constabulary, due to the transfer of a big number of former RIC men to that force.

The British authorities, obviously realised and appreciated the personal disaster which had befallen him, and being aware of his exceptional flair and ability, he was offered a post as a senior police officer with the Royal Canadian Mounted Police in Canada.

He gave the offer very serious thought and consideration, and while he would personally have liked to take up the appointment, he decided to turn it down. He felt that it would not be fair to his wife and large family, to move them again, so far away from home. He felt that they had already been through enough trauma. When he turned down the offer of the R. C. M. P. post, he was offered another position as a senior commander with the Seychelles Police. After much thought and deliberation as to what it might have involved for his family, he also turned down this offer.

On his arrival in London in 1922, he was only 51 years of age. After leaving the temporary employment in Whitehall, he entertained hopes of finding suitable employment, but did not succeed in doing so. Two more children were born into the family, while they resided in Letchworth - making a total of twelve children to be provided for. Having left his employment at Whitehall, he continued to live solely on his RIC pension, which amounted to about £9. 0s 0d per week. Some of his family were gradually taking up employment as time went by, this resulted in an increase in the family income.

He maintained his deep interest in British and world affairs. He closely monitored events in Ireland, from his departure in 1922, watching with interest the development of the Irish Free State through the 1920s and '30s. He was very upset about the death of Michael Collins, in August 1922. He had a very high regard for Collins and his ability, he frequently spoke about him, and mourned his loss for the remainder of his life. Civil strife in Northern Ireland also upset him greatly, and he frequently expressed his sympathy for the Nationalists, who were living there. While he would have been a great supporter of Michael Collins, and those who voted for the Treaty, he appeared to hold reservations about the fact that Ireland ever had to be partitioned in two to appease the Northern Ireland Unionists.

He naturally had a keen interest in the progress of the *'Garda Siochana'* [police force], which he had played an important role in establishing, and must have often wondered what the future could have been for him, in that force, were it not for the disaster which had befallen him. In this regard he must have monitored the career of former D. I. Patrick Walsh, who was a fellow RIC officer and who had also been invited by Michael Collins, to assist with setting up the 'Civic Guard'

District Inspector Patrick Walsh, was one of the RIC officers, who remained on in the 'Civic Guard' organisation. Walsh was born in 1871 near Castleblayney, Co Monaghan. He was the son of a small farmer and a Roman Catholic. He joined the Royal Irish Constabulary in 1890 and was appointed to the County Kerry RIC Division. His first allocation was to Lyreacrompane Station in North Kerry. Over a period of twenty years, he made remarkable progress through the ranks of constable, acting sergeant, sergeant and head constable until he was promoted to District Inspector in 1911. He was a very intelligent individual and a conscientious officer who maintained high standards of performance and integrity. He had served in a variety of RIC stations during his career, including Fermoy, Swanlinbar, Castlepollard, Carrick-on-Shannon and Killarney. In 1906, he married Miss Mary Francis Courtney whose parents were proprietors of Courtney's Hotel, Killarney.

In 1919, he was appointed District Inspector in charge of Letterkenny District in Co. Donegal. During the War of Independence, he prevented Black-and-Tans running riot in the town and carrying out reprisals on the civilian population after a young constable had been shot dead by the I.R.A.. D.I Walsh was known to have nationalist sympathies and was a very close personal friend of Dr McGinley who carried on a medical practice in the town. When it was announced that the Provisional Government intended to recruit a new police force to replace the RIC, Dr McGinley recommended to Mr Kevin O'Higgins, a Minister in the Provisional Government, that D. I. Walsh should be considered for selection.

In early February 1922, he received an invitation in the same format as that received by D. I. Kearney. Michael Collins, Chairman of the Provisional Government, personally signed it.

D. I. Walsh, accompanied by his office sergeant - Michael McCormack - attended the meeting as requested by Collins. Sergeant McCormack was appointed to the committee dealing with 'organisation' and which was under the chairmanship of D. I. Kearney. He was later appointed 'Accounting Officer' for the new force and went on to become a Chief Superintendent in the Garda Siochana.

The new Commissioner of the *'Civic Guard'*, Mr Michael Staines, took on D. I. Walsh as his special adviser. They monitored and co-related the reports and recommendations of the different sub- committees. They submitted the preliminary report to the Provisional Government on February 17th outlining the blueprint for a *'People's Guard'*. By virtue of his wide experience in the RIC, Michael Staines depended on Walsh's wide experience to assist him [Staines] in his new role.

Along with D. I. Kearney, Walsh continued to have a big role in the arrangements for the formation of the new force. While carrying out this preparatory work he too was still an officer of the RIC until he was disbanded on April 5th 1922. Michael Staines was appointed Commissioner of the new Civic Guards on March 10th and on D.I Walsh's disbandment from the RIC, he was appointed Deputy Commissioner with the unequivocal support of Michael Staines, Michael Collins and Kevin O'Higgins. D/Commissioner Walsh put in a considerable amount of work in getting the new force off the ground and he with D. I. Kearney, were unquestionably the most dominant figures involved in the early organisation.

The members drawn from the Volunteers/I.R.A. - as it was to the other former RIC members took objection to his appointment. Even though he was named in all the objections and ultimatums issued by the objectors to the high rank he had obtained, he was never subjected to, the same malicious allegations, innuendo or vicious personal attack, such as those made against D. I. Kearney. He survived the calls made for his resignation. During the Kildare Mutiny he resigned his position as Deputy Commissioner but was retained as an adviser to the Commissioner. When General Eoin Duffy took over as Commissioner of the Civic Guard, in September 1922, he appointed Walsh as Assistant Commissioner.

It is widely acknowledged that no member made a grater contribution to the establishment of the Garda Siochana and to its success as an unarmed police force during the 1920s and 1930s than Patrick Walsh. His professionalism as a police officer and his commitment to his duties, allied to his considerable experience in the RIC made his contribution to the new fledgling police force invaluable.

As the years went by John A. Kearney became very withdrawn, spending all his time with his growing family. He was an excellent father, who did everything possible for his children. He and his wife gave them every encouragement and opportunity in life, which they could afford.

There were many times and many events, to which he would have liked to return to Ireland, but he never did so. There was always the fear of retaliation being taken against him if he did so, and at times, it would have been difficult for him to financially justify it. As a good Christian and Catholic he would dearly have loved to visit the grave of his first wife Bridget [interred at Glin, Co Limerick] and his daughter Ethna who was interred at Boyle.

It was during those years at Letchworth, that he became very involved in tracing the origins of the Kearney clan. This took up a considerable amount of time, involving research from books, maps, family - trees and all kinds of genealogical, religious and civil records. He managed to trace the clan back to the fourth century A. D. and established that they are descended from Maine, the son of Niall of the Nine Hostages [379 A.D.] a noted warrior in Irish history. The clan held territory in County Meath until the Norman invasion of 1169 when they were supplanted by the Norman Nugent dynasty. In the centuries that followed, members of the clan were scattered all over Ireland. Many emigrated and joined foreign armies in France, Spain and Austria. Members also fought with distinction in the American Civil War. Some of those who remained on in Ireland, fought with the Jacobite army, while others played a key role in the 1798 Rebellion. He also discovered that there were towns in Nebraska, U.S.A and in Canada, which bore the name Kearney, in memory of famous army officers who bore the surname. In Western Australia, a relay station bore the name, perpetuating the memory of a great engineer with the Kearney surname.

He concluded, that his immediate paternal ancestors bearing his surname had lived at Walsh Island, Co Offaly, for ten generations. He regretted the fact that nobody named Kearney now lived there, since his father Thomas and his brother William, left the ancestral home. Considering the difficulty in carrying out research in the 1920s and 1930s - at a time far removed from the facilities now available, - the amount of information which he collected and collated about the Kearney clan was truly remarkable, and must have taken a considerable amount of time.

The preamble, which he wrote as an introduction to the history of the Kearneys, which he researched and recorded for the benefit of his family and descendants, is most revealing in relation to what he held dear in life. It gives an in-depth view into his character, and of the main value, which he treasured most in life – *'integrity'*. On this he wrote -

"Whether it is a human failing or not, the vast majority of humanity are always conscious to learn something about their ancestors. What were they like? What manner of life they led? Were they handsome or otherwise? Were they of sterling character and the women above reproach? What was their physique and health? Were they strong men or weaklings? To my descendants, I rather think that it is essential to give a clear account of my ancestors and for this reason that I have left Ireland probably forever with my family and adopted England as our country henceforward, I give these details for another good reason. I would that all my descendants, no matter where they find themselves, will have the "Pride of Race" that in their integrity, they can look every man - prince or peasant - in the face, full of confidence in themselves and in their honesty of purpose.

"That word "integrity" means a great deal - more than honesty and more than truth. It is a trait in an honourable man's character, that prevents him from doing any mean action or omitting to do that which is his duty to do. To a man it is more than a gold-mine. Riches are a poor thing without integrity. And where riches are, it is seldom found. But in going through life, I found it in many men, more particularly in two members of the Royal Irish Constabulary. In my own relatives I have found it as a particularly

strong trait in their character and I am proud to write that I have seen this trait growing in my own boys and girls.

"*Integrity, that's the word - without it, man is but a poor 'specimen'. Hence I may mention that that trait of character was one well-developed in our race.*"

It will be noted from his introduction to the subject, that he appeared to be reconciled to the fact, that he had left Ireland for ever, and that England was going to be the future home, for himself and for his family.

CHANGE OF RESIDENCE TO BARNET.

In 1937, the Kearney family moved from their home at Letchworth to Barnet in Hertfordshire. This was nearer to central London, where a number of the family had obtained employment, and it was more convenient for them to commute to work.

The house in Barnet had five bedrooms, and was much bigger than that at Letchworth. It was a rented house, but when John A. Kearney died, his three daughters arranged a mortgage for the purchase of the house, for the financial security of their mother and sister Eithne, who was suffering from an intellectual disability.

By a rather extraordinary co-incidence, one of John A. Kearney's daughters, met and married a young man named Butler. His father was the former Sergeant Butler, attached to the RIC in Tralee, who was the lone escort for Sir Roger Casement when he was being transferred in custody from Tralee to Dublin on Easter Saturday 1916.

Sometime after leaving Letchworth in 1937, John A. Kearney commenced to write his memoirs, but abandoned the project with the outbreak of the War. When the War ended, he appeared to have no enthusiasm for completing the project and did not pursue it further. This was understandable, due to the heart - break he had suffered, as a result of losing his two sons in the conflict.

When World War 11 broke out in 1939, John A. Kearney and his family acknowledged, that they had an obligation to make a contribution to the war effort. John A. Kearney himself founded a branch of the St Vincent de Paul Society at Barnet. For six years he worked full time in that organisation, giving tremendous service to the poorer sections of society. He devoted his entire time to the work involved, to the exclusion of every other interest, which he had in life. He had a total commitment to it. The work was purely of a voluntary nature.

THE TRAGIC DEATHS OF TWO KEARNEY BROTHERS IN WORLD WAR 11.

John A. Kearney had five sons in all - Dermot Thomas; Matthew Manning; Brendan Shane; Thomas Moran and Shane Brendan. All five sons joined the armed forces during the War.

Matthew joined the United States Army in 1943 and completed his military service.

Dermot, who was married to the daughter of a former RIC man and had three children, joined the Royal Army Service Corps in 1941 and served throughout the War.

Thomas joined the British Army in 1939 and served with the *'Irish Guards Regiment'* through the hostilities. He volunteered for service with the 'commandos' and was engaged for a lengthy period of distinguished service with the 'Chindits' in Burma. He died in 2000.

Brendan who was married, joined the *'Irish Guards Regiment'* in 1939. He saw service at various locations in Europe, with the armoured brigade of his Regiment. He was back in England with his unit in February 1943. While in service there, with his Regiment, he was tragically killed, when a military tank exploded. Once again, the Kearney family was hit with another tragedy. John, and all members of the family were grief stricken at Brendan's death.

Brendan at this time had a little daughter aged six months. He was buried with full military honours. Fully-kilted pipers from his Regiment, playing laments on the bagpipes, appropriate to the occasion preceded the funeral cortege. Brendan was interred in the family home - town of Barnet.

Shane Brendan joined the *'London Irish Rifles'* in 1939 at the outbreak of the War. He volunteered for duty, first, with the First Paratroop Regiment and then with the *'Sixth Airborne Division'*. Just after the successful crossing of the Rhine, he was killed in action, on 28th March 1945. Due to the circumstances pertaining at the time, his body could not be brought back to England for burial. He was buried with other British military casualties, at Reichenwald in Germany. Shane was unmarried. His intention was to join the priesthood as soon as his war service ended.

Following the tragic death of Brendan, two years earlier, the death of Shane really devastated the Kearney family. It was worsened by the fact that his remains could not be returned home for burial beside Brendan. The absence of a funeral, or the return of Shane's remains resulted in the grieving process being made all the more difficult for the family.

THE FINAL YEARS.

John A. Kearney, who had been hit with so many family and personal tragedies in his lifetime, failed to come to terms with the deaths of his two brave sons. He was extremely proud of all of his sons, and closely followed their careers and military exploits on a daily basis. His family were unanimous in their view that from the time of Shane's death, John A. Kearney simply *'lost the will to live'*, his health and general disposition deteriorated rapidly. He became but a shadow of the man whom they had known, when he was full of enthusiasm; passionately interested in world affairs; interested in everything taking place around him and supporting and encouraging his family in everything that they did.

Less than twelve months later, and some months after the War had ended, he died on January 28th 1946. He was interred in Barnet - in the same burial plot where his son Brendan had been interred three years before.

His widow, Mrs Mary Catherine Kearney, continued to reside at Barnet after his death with her daughter Rosaleen and her family. Until her death, she never failed to recall the traumatic time , which she, her husband and children underwent during those awful months in 1922. She was a highly intelligent woman, who shared many of her husband's interests, and was a great support to him through all the tragedies and trauma in their lifetime. She was devoted to her big family, and maintained very close contact with them right up to her death. She died on Christmas Day 1967 and was interred with her husband John, her son Brendan and daughter Eithne at Barnet Cemetery.

APPENDIX 'A'

District Inspector Frederick Ambrose Britten was born in Leicestershire in the U.K. in 1875. He attended College in Oxford and graduated with a B.A. Degree. In 1899 he joined the RIC as a Cadet and was promoted to District Inspector - 3rd Class - in September of the same year. He was promoted to District Inspector - First Class -while serving as a District Inspector in Tralee on February 20th 1912.

While still serving in Tralee, he was promoted to the rank of County Inspector on October 1st 1920 and transferred to Lurgan where he took charge of the County Antrim Division. On the formation of the Royal Ulster Constabulary, he retained his position as County Inspector for Antrim. He later took up position as Commissioner of Police in Belfast. On his retirement from the Force in 1938, he moved with his wife and daughter to reside at Down Road, Tavistock, in the U.K. He was awarded the O.B.E. for his outstanding contribution to policing. He died at his home in Tavistock in May 1974 and he was aged 99 years.

The written statement taken by D. I. Britten from Daniel Bailey on Easter Saturday 1916 had an extraordinary sequence. Bailey passed on a considerable amount of critical information to D. I. Britten relating to the plans made for the Easter Rebellion and the landing of the arms by the '*Aud*' etc. Britten realised the significance of the information and sent details by way of a coded telegram to Dublin Castle. On receipt of the telegram at Dublin Castle it was decoded and taken to the Chief Secretary's office at the Castle. The Chief Secretary was not in and the vital message was left on his desk. A window in the office was open and the document was blown into a waste paper basket in the office. The Easter Rebellion took place the next day and it was not until the following Wednesday that D.I. Britten's warning telegram was located. Had D. I. Britten's telegram been dealt with and treated with the urgency, which it deserved, it may have to some extent changed the course of Irish history

APPENDIX 'B'

After the establishment of the 'Provisional Government' in 1922, Austin Stack was again re-elected as a Sinn Fein T.D. for the Kerry/West Limerick constituency. With the other Sinn Fein T. Ds. he refused to enter Dail Eireann and continued to do so, even though Eamon De Valera and his Fianna Fail party decided to take their place in Dail Eireann in August 1927. He was a very close friend of Eamon Dr Valera and was extremely disappointed when De Valera left Sinn Fein and formed the Fianna Fail party. There was a General Election on September 15th 1927 but due to a lack of Sinn Fein funds, the Sinn Fein party did not contest the election. This was effectively the end of Austin Stack's political career. He continued to pursue a campaign to obtain pensions for members of the Royal Irish Constabulary who out of sympathy for the Republican cause had resigned from the Force. His efforts met with no success. He maintained his involvement with Sinn Fein. From the time he became Secretary of Sinn Fein he never once waivered from his Sinn Fein ideals and principles. He began to study law and passed his first examinations.

He was engaged to be married to a Miss Frances O'Dolan but to everybody's surprise he married Mrs Una Gordon at Booterstown Church, Co Dublin. She was widow of the late District Inspector Patrick Gordon of the RIC. She was born in County Fermanagh in 1881. Her husband died in 1910 and in 1912 she went to live in Paris. She worked with the ambulance service in France during the early years of World War 1 . She returned to Ireland in 1916 and became involved with the Republican movement and was a member of Cumann na mBan. Members of the I.R.A. who were 'on the run' frequented her home.

She was a very wealthy woman and after their marriage, Austin Stack moved in to live with her at Number 167, Strand Road, Merrion, Dublin. He continued to be in very poor health and this has always been attributed to the hunger strikes, which he underwent in the different prisons.

Austin Stack's last public appearance was at an Easter commemoration ceremony at Cahirciveen on Easter Sunday 1929. On April 25th he became very ill and was removed to the Mater Hospital. He underwent an operation for appendicitis but some complications arose and he died there on April 27th. His remains were removed to St Joseph's Church at Berkeley Road where they lay in state surrounded by an I.R.A guard of honour. Sinn Fein took charge of his funeral arrangements. Huge crowds turned out for his funeral and the funeral cortege passed through the centre of Dublin en route to Glasnevin for interment there. He was buried adjacent to the Republican Plot and Brian O'Higgins delivered a moving oration at the graveside.

The well-appointed 'Austin Stack' G.A.A. Park, the Austin Stacks's G.A.A Club and a terrace of houses named 'Stack's Villas' commemorate him in Tralee.

BIBLIOGRAPHY.

Books.

Abbott, Richard, *Police Casualties in Ireland, 1919 - 1922*, Dublin and Cork, Mercier Press, 2000.

Allen, Gregory, *The Garda Siochana Policing Independent Ireland 1922 - 1982* Dublin, Gill and MacMillan, 1999.

Barrett, J.J., *In the Name of the Game*, Dublin, Private, 1997.

Beckett, J.C., *The Making of Modern Ireland 1603 - 1923*, Revised Edition, London, Faber and Faber, 1973.

Beaslai, Piaras, *Michael Collins and the Making of a New Ireland*, 2 Vols, Dublin, Phoenix Publishing Co., 1926.

Bennett, Richard, *The Black and Tans*, New York, Barnes and Noble, 1975.

Brady, Conor, *Guardians of the Peace*, Dublin, Gill and MacMillan, 1974.

Breathnach, Seamus, *The Irish Police – from the earliest Times to the Present Day*, Dublin, Anvil Books, 1974.

Brewer, John D., *The Royal Irish Constabulary, an Oral History*, Belfast, Queen's University, 1990.

Buckland, Patrick, *Ulster Unionism and the Origin of Northern Ireland 1886 – 1922*, Dublin, Gill and MacMillan, 1973.

Comerford, Maire, *The First Dail*, Dublin, Joe Clarke, 1969.

Coogan, Tim Pat, *Michael Collins, a Biography*, London, Hutchinson, 1990.

Conroy, John C., *Report of the Conroy Commission on the Garda Siochana*, Dublin, 1977.

Curtis, Robert, *The History of the Royal Irish Constabulary*, London, 1869.

Dail Eireann, *Tuairisg Oifigiuil [Official Report] For Periods 16th August, 1921, To 28th August 1921, and 28th February, 1922, to 8th June 1922*. Dublin, The Stationery Office, date not stated.

Desmond, Liam, *With The Constabulary in Roscommon*, Midle-

De Vere White,   ton, Co Cork, Litho Press, 1993.
Kevin O'Higgins, 2nd Edn., Tralee, Co Kerry, Anvil Books, 1966.

Dwyer, T. Ryle,   *Tans, Terror and Troubles*, Cork, Mercier Press, 2001

Gaughan, J. Anthony,   *Austin Stack Portrait of a Separatist*, Dublin, Kingdom Books, 1977.

Gaughan, J. Anthony,   *Memoirs of Constable Jeremiah Mee, R.I.C.*, Dublin, Kingdom Books, 1975.

Green, George Garrow,   *In the Royal Irish Constabulary*, Dublin, 1905.

Harrington, Nial C.,   *Kerry Landing*, Dublin, Anvil Books, 1992.

Herlihy, Jim,   *The Royal Irish Constabulary, a Short History and Genealogical Guide*, Dublin, Four Courts Press, 1997.

Hyde, H Montgomery,   *Famous Trials 9 : Roger Casement*, London, Penguin Books, 1964.

Inglis, Brian,   *Roger Casement*, London, Hodder and Stoughton, 1973.

Kelly, Denis,   *Salute to the Gardai*, Dublin, Parkside Press, 1958.

Kerryman,   *Kerry's Fighting Story, 1916 - 1921*, Tralee, Co Kerry, The Kerryman, 1947.

Kerryman.   *With the I.R.A in the Fight for Freedom, 1919 to the Truce* Tralee, the Kerryman, 1946.

Kiberd, Declan,   *1916 Rebellion Handbook*, Dublin, Mourne River Press, 1998.

Lieberson, Goddard,   *The Irish Uprising*, Dublin, MacMillan

Litton, Helen,   *The Irish Civil War*, Dublin, Wolfhound Press, 1995.

Macardle, Dorothy,   *The Irish Republic*, London, Corgi, 1968.

MacColl, Rene,   *Roger Casement, a New Judgement*, London, Hannah Hamilton, 1956.

Mac Giolla Choille, Breandan,   *Intelligence Notes 1913 –16*, Dublin, Oifig an tSolathair,1966.

McDowell, R.B.,   *The Irish Administration 1801 - 1914*, University of Toronto Press, 1964.

McNiffe, Liam,   *A History of the Garda Siochana*, Dublin, Wolf-

Mitchel, Angus,	hound Press, 1997. *The Amazon Journal of Roger Casement*, Dublin, Lilliput Press, 1997.
Moyvoughley Historical Committee	*Moyvoughley and its Hinterland*, Ireland, Topical Newspapers Ltd.,1999.
Mullins, William [Billy]	*Memoirs of Billy Mullins, Kenno Tralee. 1983.*
Murphy, John A.,	*Ireland in the Twentieth Century*, Dublin, Gill and Macmillan, 1975.
Neeson, Eoin,	*The Civil War in Ireland, 1922-23*, Cork, Mercier Press, 1966.
Neligan, David,	*The Spy in the Castle*, London, MacGibbon and Kee, 1968.
O'Broin, Leon,	*Dublin Castle and the 1916 Rising*, Dublin, Helicon Ltd.,, 1966.
O'Connor, Seamus,	*Tomorrow was Another Day*, Tralee, Anvil Books, 1970.
O'Donoghue, Florence,	*No Other Law.* Dublin, Anvil Books, 1986.
O'Malley, Ernie,	*The Singing Flame*, Dublin, Anvil Books, 1978.
O'Sullivan, Donal J.,	*The Irish Constabularies,1822 - 1922, A Century of Policing in Ireland*, Dingle, Brandon Books, 1999.
Philips, W. Alison,	*The Revolution in Ireland,1906 – 1923*, London, Longmans & Green & Co., 1923.
Reith, Charles,	*The Blind Eye of History*, London, 1952
Ryder, Chris,	*The R.U.C 1922 - 1997 a Force under Fire*, [Revised Edn.] London, Mandarin Paperbacks, 1997.
Sawyer, Roger,	*Casement, the Flawed Hero.* Ruttledge, Keegan, Paul. London 1983
Shea, Patrick,	*Voices and Sound of Drums – an Irish Autobiography*, Belfast, Blackstaff Press, 1981.
Sinclair, R.J.K. and Kelly F.J.M,	*Arresting Memories – Captured Moments In Constabulary Life,* Belfast, R.U.C. Diamond Jubilee Committee, 1982.
Spindler, Captain Karl,	*The Mystery of the Casement Ship*, Tralee, Anvil Books, 1965.
Sullivan, A.M,	Serjeant, *Old Ireland – Reminiscences of an Irish K.C.* Thornton, Butterworth London 1927.

	Tales of the R.I.C. London, Blackwood and Sons, 1922.
Younger, Carlton,	*Ireland's Civil War*, London, Frederick Muller, 1968.
Younger, Carlton,	*Arthur Griffith*, Dublin, Gill and MacMillan, 1981.

Newspapers.

"Irish Press", January 9th 1989 and January 7th 1936.
"Kerry Weekly Reporter", 26th August 1916.
"Irish Times", April 23rd 1949.
"Roscommon Herald", January 1st to July 1st 1922.
"Irish Independent", October 5th 1914; March 7th and 25th 1922; April 8th and 9th 1966;
"The Evening Herald", 8thMarch 1965.
"The Kerryman" - miscellaneous issues.
"Kerry's Eye" - miscellaneous issues.
"Kerry Champion", May 4th 1929.

Journals/Periodicals.

An Siothadoir [Journal of the Garda Pensioners Association] 1962 to 1971.
Siochain, [Journal of Garda Pensioners Association] 1972 - 2002.
Garda Review, 1925 - 1935
Guth an Garda, 1924.
Irishleabhar an Garda 1922 - 1924 and 1935 - 1969.
Royal Irish Constabulary Magazine, 1912 to 1922.
The Kerry Magazine [Kerry Archaeological and Historical Society] No 9 [1998].
Royal Irish Constabulary List Directories 1912 - 1921.

Other Sources.

Private Papers of the late District Inspector John A. Kearney.
Miscellaneous documents, photographs and memorabilia in possession of family members of the late D. I. John A. Kearney.
Interviews with relatives of the late D. I. John A. Kearney.
National Archives, Bishop Street, Dublin, File NA. H235/329, and mis-

cellaneous files of Department of Justice [incorporating the Department of Home Affairs] from 1922.
Garda Siochana Archives, Record Tower, Dublin Castle, miscellaneous papers and publications relating to Garda Siochana and RIC.
National Library of Ireland, Kildare Street, Dublin, newspaper collection, collection of Anti-Treaty leaflets and Official Dail Reports.
Kerry County Library Archives, Tralee, collection of Kerry newspapers.
Official Programme – Unveiling of Casement Memorial at Banna strand, 1968
Memoirs of RIC Constable John Feeley - not published.

ACKNOWLEDGEMENTS.

I gratefully acknowledge the assistance, which I received from the following persons in the course of research for this book.

Mrs Rosaleen Stevens, Maidstone, Kent; Mr Stephen A. Clements, Maryland U.S.A.;

Mr Sean Cleary, Cardiff, Wales; Mrs Dympna Burkhart, St. Pete Beach, Florida, U.S.A.; Mrs Lorna P. Lincke, Pensacola, Florida, U.S.A.; Mr Gerry Kerrigan and Mrs Mary Ann Kerrigan, Moyvoughley, Co Westmeath; Mr John Feeley, Christchurch, New Zealand.

Mr Finbarr Keane and Mrs Jacinta Keane, Woodlea, Tralee; Ms Dearbhla O'Sullivan, Auckland, New Zealand; Mrs Olivia McGowan, Navan, Co Meath;

Mr Donie Kelly, Strand Street, Tralee; Mr John Pierse, Listowel, Co Kerry;

Mr James J. Groarke, An Garda Siochana, Anglesea Street, Cork; Mr Pat J.O'Sullivan, Upton, Innishannon, Co Cork; the late Mr Miceal O'Rourke, Tralee. Mrs Olive O'Sullivan, Tralee.

Sergeant Pat McGee and Staff Members at the Garda Siochana Museum and Archives, Dublin Castle; the late Mr Gregory Allen, former Curator of the Garda Siochana Museum and Archives; Mr John Reynolds, Curator, Garda College Museum, Templemore, Co Tipperary; Mr John Duffy, former Curator of Garda Museum, Dublin Castle; The Director and Staff members of the National Archives, Bishop Street, Dublin; The Director and Staff members of the National Library, Kildare Street, Dublin; Mrs Kathleen Browne, County Librarian and Staff at Kerry County Library, Tralee; The staff of Copy Write Print, Rathass, Tralee; the late Mr Daniel Crowley, Fenit, Co Kerry, Seamus Breathnach, Tralee, Colm O' Sullivan, Virginia, Co Cavan, The Management and Staff members of Trafford Publishing, Victoria, Canada.

ISBN 1-41206403-1